Convergent Forces

Immediate Causes of the Revolution of 1688 in England

Convergent Forces

Immediate Causes of
the Revolution of 1688 in England

GEORGE HILTON JONES

Iowa State University Press / Ames

George Hilton Jones, now retired, was most recently a professor of history at Eastern Illinois University, Charleston, Illinois. His scholarly work has concentrated on English foreign relations in the late seventeenth and early eighteenth centuries.

© 1990 Iowa State University Press, Ames, Iowa 50010

Manufactured in the United States of America
∞ This book is printed on acid-free paper.

First edition, 1990

Library of Congress Cataloging-in-Publication Data

Jones, George Hilton.
    Convergent forces : immediate causes of the Revolution of 1688 in England / George Hilton Jones. — 1st ed.
      p.   cm.
    Includes bibliographical references and index.
    ISBN 0–8138–0629–1 (acid-free paper)
    1. Great Britain — History — Revolution of 1688 — Causes. 2. William III, King of England, 1650–1702. 3. James II, King of England, 1633–1701. I. Title.
DA450.J63   1990
941.06′7 — dc20   90–40079

Contents

Preface

SINCE I FIRST ENVISIONED THIS STUDY, intended to fill a gap that I had discovered during work on another subject, several authors have given us books on the English revolution of 1688, notably J. R. Jones and the late J. R. Western. As I have progressed, however, I have found much that these authors did not do: The history of the revolution and its immediate causes needed further study because writers had been preoccupied with more distant causes and consequences, and they had neglected many details, to the detriment of general conclusions.

In this book, only a portion of what I hope to lay before the public in time, I have chosen to recount the story of the revolution's precipitating causes, in England and the Netherlands, from the latter part of 1687 to the autumn of 1688, and King James's attempt to delay or avert the expedition of William of Orange and deprive William of support in England. This I have tried to do as thoroughly as the availability of contemporary sources permits, wishing to say what happened, who did it, and their immediate reasons for doing as they did. (The bibliography and notes will show to the discerning how seriously I took my task.)

As many of these people were not prominent, I also undertook to learn about as many of them as possible and to convey to the reader the most relevant of what I had learned. Compiling identification files has been one of the most burdensome, but most enlightening, preparations for the work. I hope that the knowledge they give will add to the reader's perception of what I call the texture of the history of that time.

The construction of a single chronological narrative in the detail here given would be, though barely possible, exceedingly difficult and would confuse the reader and (worse) the writer. I have therefore placed after my Introduction, in what seems a reasonable order, several parallel narratives, to show how not one but several sequences of royal actions and resistant reactions led to the readiness of subjects for revolt and the willingness of a foreign power to intervene in English affairs. Two chapters then describe the king's efforts to reach reconciliation with discontented groups at home and to keep the Dutch republic at peace. The arrangement is not perfect, but if the reader objects to it, I assure him or her that the alternative would make inconceivable demands on memory and patience.

Sources I have used were written in four languages other than English — French, Italian, Dutch, and German. I have translated almost all the quotations into English. I give dates for events in England in the older Julian style, then in use there; for those in countries that had adopted the newer Gregorian style, I give dates in that style. (The same day is ten days later in the New Style [N.S.] in 1688 than in the Old Style [O.S.] Where use of one style alone might mislead, I sometimes give both; for example, March 11/21.

My debts and acknowledgments must be many. I have used manuscripts and printed materials of all kinds in large quantities in the British Library, Reference Division, formerly the Library of the British Museum. I found the archival resources of the Public Record Office, and those of the Algemeen Rijksarchief in The Hague essential. Her Majesty the Queen of the Netherlands gave her gracious permission to use the Koninklijk Huisarchief, also in The Hague. I have made especially heavy use of the Widener Library at Harvard University, the Bodleian Library at Oxford, and the University Library at Cambridge. Dr. Williams's Library, London, and the libraries of All Souls College, Oxford, and the University of Nottingham have allowed me to use papers in their possession. I hereby extend thanks to all for access, for help, and for courtesy. The former Ministère des Affaires Étrangères (now des Relations Extérieures) in Paris and the Archivio di Stato in Modena supplied microfilms of diplomatic correspondence of the period, and the History of Parliament Trust allowed me to consult biographical files of members of parliament from 1660 to 1690 and thus to verify my identifications of M.P.'s. I wrote a large part of the first draft of this book in the England Room of the Institute of Historical Research in London. To those bodies I also render thanks.

It is incumbent on me to state that the trustees of Dr. Williams's Library are not responsible for my selection of extracts from the Morrice Entring Book and that I waive any copyright I may have in extracts that might debar other scholars from using or publishing the same material or from working for that purpose in the same manuscript.

Among individuals, I especially single out for tribute the late Neville John Williams, a friend from Oxford, for many years a member of the staff of the Public Record Office, and later secretary of the British Academy. My debts to him are many and great, not least for help in the early stage of the work that has made this book. I also wish to thank other friends whose society has sustained me during many years: Donald and Luisa Derx, Betty Williams, John S. and Maureen Street, John Best, Robert H. Clarke, Ralph Smith, Richard and Lawrence Reichard, Gloria Carrig, Frances Burian, Frank and Marion Miller, Herbert and Jane Lasky, Leonard Wood, Stewart Easton, Roy Johnston, Andrew Smart, and Walter Lazenby. Bless them all.

Introduction

IN THE BEGINNING of James II's reign was its end. When he succeeded to the crowns of England, Scotland, and Ireland on February 6, 1685, the international affairs of Europe were approaching a general crisis. Louis XIV of France had become a threat to neighboring princes and states during the preceding twenty-five years by making his armed forces powerful and feared, and by extending his boundaries. Almost as bad, his example and incitement encouraged others — the king of Denmark and the sultan of Turkey — to disturb the peace of their neighbors, who were or might be enemies of King Louis. The sultan was actually at war with Holy Roman Emperor Leopold in Hungary, forcing Leopold to neglect the western states of his ramshackle empire, while Christian V of Denmark's aggressions distracted Sweden and the north German states from plans for common defense against France.

Opponents of France were disunited, some of them pathetically feeble. Spain's King Charles II was mentally incompetent, his advisers corrupt and unwise. The United Provinces of the Netherlands — the Dutch republic — was hindered from effective action by its loose, decentralized constitution and by division between the prince of Orange's party, hostile to Louis XIV, and anti-Orangists, too fearful of France to oppose it. Pope Innocent XI was on bad terms with Louis, yet preferred to direct Christian attention to the war against Moslem Turkey in the East. Frederick William, elector of Brandenburg, might help to rally other potentially strong German princes of the empire, but he had not yet clearly decided to do so. Emperor Leopold himself was indecisive and not overintelligent.[1] A number of lesser potentates hoped to stand neutral in a future general war, and some, such as the elector of Cologne, accepted the influence of King Louis. The policy and power of the Stuart ruler of the British Isles might make a great difference to the hesitant and thus determine the result of the conflict.

Charles II of England had appreciated this danger since 1677 and had attempted to organize alliances to withstand it, but he had not had the money to fight for allies and could not have obtained it from his last parliament; from 1681 to 1685, indeed, he held no parliament at all. The new king might be more effectual if he would; his brother had prepared the way for election of parliaments that would follow the royal lead. Moreover, observers knew that James had a strong will and a great interest in military and naval affairs. He might, of course, suffer a handicap as a Catholic king in a Protestant country.

Nevertheless, in 1685, James's subjects accepted him and seemed relieved by his gracious initial utterances and the convening of an early parliament, the first in four years. The political classes helped him by electing a friendly House of Commons, which gave him supplies of money, and by suppressing the duke of Monmouth's rebellion. His relations with the Church of England and the Anglican-dominated Tory party deteriorated, however, when James began open extension of favor to Catholics, who were not eligible for it under the law, particularly by appointing some of them to commissioned ranks in the army. When, in November 1685, even many of his supporters in the two houses of Parliament objected, the king prorogued them, eventually dissolving that parliament and reigning alone.

His later actions did not dispel English fears. He enlarged his army and thus increased his power to carry through illegal or unpopular measures by force (though he in fact did not so use the power). He founded the Commission for Ecclesiastical Causes to govern the Church of England for him, and it acted oppressively against Anglican churchmen who displeased him. He also encroached on the Anglican privileges in the two universities, intruding Catholic fellows into the colleges there, protecting converts to Catholicism against loss of their positions, and imposing a Catholic president on Magdalen College, Oxford. He challenged all Protestant opinion when he reopened diplomatic relations with the pope and welcomed Catholic prelates at his court and allowed them territorial jurisdiction over their coreligionists in England. He dispensed with or suspended the enforcement of anti-Catholic penal laws and seemed to remove the protection of Protestantism, which such laws were held to afford.

James had about him a mixed group of advisers—Protestants, Catholics, and opportunists. He did not recognize or accept the best advice when he heard it because his judgment on the political effects of his religious actions was poor. He made enemies, and many of his new enemies would more naturally have been his friends.

James believed that he had a right to the loyalty and obedience of his subjects, even those of sharply different political and religious opinions. He regarded obedience to his royal commands as a religious duty, and Anglicans and many other Christians agreed. No one knew how far he could press this agreement without destroying it, but religious (as against philosophical) authority was clear on the subject. The king therefore expected everyone in his kingdoms except criminals or the perverse to submit and follow where he led, though the way was stony underfoot and he did not slow for the weak or hesitant. God was on his side, and he believed that Anglicans knew that he ruled by God's choice and with godlike authority. Certainly, he was correct in his assumption that most of his contemporaries believed in his right to power, but many of them also believed that he should rely on broad public acceptance of his right. Others remembered Charles I, who had outraged too many to be permitted to live.

James lost that acceptance not only by offending his Protestant subjects but also by acting contrary to laws that his predecessors had made in parliaments, laws that he set aside by his sole will and without approval by Parliament. Many thought he had no right to do so.

The king's foreign policy did not in any case please governments opposed to France, though he disapproved of Danish encroachments in the North and some French ones in Germany and the Spanish Netherlands, and he took unfeigned pleasure in Emperor Leopold's victories over the Turks in Hungary. He disliked his son-in-law (and nephew), William of Orange, Stadhouder in the United Netherlands, and when several rulers combined in the League of Augsburg against France in 1686, he held aloof. He openly resented various actions of the Dutch Republic as well as William's. Some anti-French foreigners believed James to be secretly allied with France. William, believing that or not, was concerned for the safety of his country.

That country admitted British fugitives to its protection and allowed them to attack their king publicly; its East India Company used its ascendancy to stifle British commerce in the East Indies. William of Orange courted the opposition to James as a Protestant rival for English affections.[2] By the end of 1687, James was seriously irritated by his relations with the Dutch and suspected all their actions.

At that time the king's domestic enemies had not yet united with the Continental opponents of Louis. James, on his side of the English Channel, helped to effect that union in 1688 when he drove more of his subjects into resistance and most of the resisters into reliance on

William of Orange, who on his side welcomed English and Scottish adherents who could make him one of the most powerful monarchs in Europe. At the same time, Louis XIV helped to create agreement by his support of King James, his increasingly menacing foreign policy and use of force, his military preparations, and his persecution of French and foreign Protestants.

Historians and biographers have often described James in strong contrasts — lecherous and penitent, generous and thrifty, arrogant and forgiving, assured in public and full of private doubts. In a sense, this book is a depiction at length of his personality as it was in 1688 and of its contemporary consequences for Great Britain and other parts of Europe.

His great antagonist, Prince William, was at least as complex as the king. Very likely homosexual, possibly not powerfully driven toward either sex, and childless, he had made a mere political marriage and later kept a mistress so that everybody knew about her. (His wife showed some of the symptoms, especially anxiety, commonly attributed to unsatisfied wives.) From the age of twenty-two, he had been asserting his masculinity in politics and on the field of war, even fighting an unnecessary battle in 1678 after the conclusion of the peace at Nijmegen. When he could not fight, he liked to hunt. In his native country he demanded and received power, which he used as we shall see. His vision of world affairs was unusually broad for the time, helped no doubt by his fluent use of foreign languages. He presented on the stage of Europe a figure of heroic stature, especially for victims of Louis XIV, but he was physically small and frail.

The "great Louis" was the third principal actor. Then well past the folly and carelessness of youth, he had assumed his full proportions, also marked by contrasts: Catholic and Gallican, ex-satyr and portly figure of piety, sun to the submissive and thunder to those who resisted him, he emanated power from Versailles and Marly in every direction, and he relished the use of force. He had already added Roussillon, the Franche-Comté, and Alsace to France and annexed or occupied portions of the Spanish Netherlands. He had surprised Strasbourg and forced it to make terms, and he had garrisoned German strongholds from which he could launch attacks on the Holy Roman Empire. The duke of Savoy seemed his puppet, and he attracted German states of the empire to his side by use of subsidy, cajolery, and threats. He detested the newly risen prince of Orange, his cousin; he spread lures for a nearer cousin, the king of England. If his enemies needed England — that is, its armed forces, manpower, and wealth—Louis was determined to keep these assets neutral or in hands of a king allied with him.

France maintained at the English court an insinuating and usually perceptive ambassador, Paul de Barrillon d'Amoncourt, marquis de Branges. Generally known as Barrillon, the ambassador represented in the eyes of the English opposition a mysterious and hostile force, frequently aligned with James's political and religious views, which King Louis used for his own benefit.

The Dutch ambassador in England, Aernout van Citters, was the appointee of the supreme executive of his government, the States General, and was therefore not Prince William's man. All the same, he was no friend of James, and his long dispatches in 1688 almost always show the king in an unfavorable light.

James employed two secretaries of state, the earls of Sunderland and Middleton, to conduct his foreign and English correspondence. (Both secretaries shared in both kinds.) Sunderland had earned James's displeasure during the Exclusion crisis, when the enemies of the duke of York had attempted to keep him from the throne. By 1688, Sunderland would do anything for royal favor, even change his religion. A compulsive gambler who suffered great losses, he compensated himself with the rewards of high office. (He was lord president of the council as well.) Middleton, who remained a Protestant for many years after these events, had a more pleasing reputation and a good deal of common sense, but he does not appear to have influenced his master's more important decisions. There were also at court certain Catholics, who did not hold high English offices of state but had some influence as privy councillors. Among these were Father Edward Petre, S.J., and John Drummond, earl of Melfort, a Scottish secretary of state, both bold men, tactless and obnoxious, neither aware of the underlying conformation of the political landscape. They advised James as he liked and did him great harm.

Only insecurely in royal favor were unchanging Anglicans who still hoped that the king would moderate his measures. Such were the brothers Hyde, earls of Clarendon and Rochester, and a number of the Anglican bishops (some still submissive and others less so). I shall have more to say of these in the next chapter. Such Anglicans were Tories.

The other political "party" was also ill at ease at court. The Whigs had originally attempted to exclude James from the succession. In 1687, he began courting many of them, giving additional disgust to his more natural Tory friends. He had not conquered the hearts of the old opposition, however, because many of its members did not trust him. Some did harken to the king's promise of kindness to Protestant Dissenters (non-Anglicans) in return for support of his policies, but they recalled the bitterness and vexation of the middle 1680s, when the same man had been their greatest enemy. Some were almost forced into serving him (as Sir William Williams was) by use of the royal powers of clemency. Others sought obscurity in inaction. Very disgruntled Tories, like the earl of Danby, former lord treasurer and party organizer, were out of office and favor, and they could not understand James's actions. The great "Trimmer," the marquis of Halifax, was a man of great talent and no party who (as K. D. H. Haley has pointed out) "was not temperamentally suited to be anyone's lieutenant."[3] Halifax, one of the most intelligent of English politicians, had no great reverence for the legitimist political theory of the day. He had a personal following, and he believed that he knew with certainty everyone else's motives, but it is possible that he did not yet clearly perceive his own.

At the beginning of 1688, very few, English or foreigners, could have foreseen what they would be called upon to do and how they would respond to calls, and no one could have known that the resultant of their responses would be the establishment of a new regime, even a new dispensation, an order of government less influenced by the conception of the supernatural, in which "Nature" would be human nature. It was the fortune (or misfortune) of these men to go on as before in vastly changed circumstances—veiled by the familiar aspect of almost all governmental, social, and economic institutions— to survive as mere men, without the support or the bar of divine right or its derivative notions—except in the minds of an inspired or stubborn few. Let us see how it all happened, or how they did all this to themselves.

Convergent Forces

Immediate Causes of the Revolution of 1688 in England

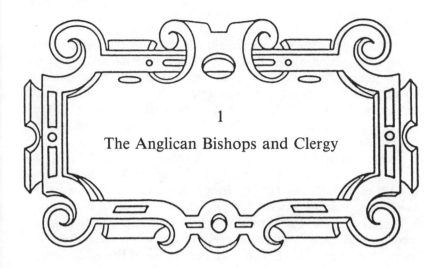

1
The Anglican Bishops and Clergy

SO FAR, the Church of England had not declared itself. Though a Catholic, James was by Anglican doctrine and the law of the land the supreme governor of that church. He had attempted to avoid that fact by a pretense of delegating authority over churchmen and church institutions to the Ecclesiastical Commission, which he had established (probably illegally). The tradition of the church was monarchical and legitimist, recently more so than before; since the Restoration and the reestablishment of episcopal church government, the restored Anglican hierarchy had relied for its own support on royal power and had reciprocated support for that power in full measure. The doctrine of nonresistance to a legal king had become a central one for the clergy and its most constant adherents in the laity; it was frequently preached from Anglican pulpits in the most unlimited form, and with no qualifications but that a wicked command might be only passively obeyed. The king was now, however, imperiling the position of the church itself.

Next below him were the two archbishops—in early 1688 only one, for the see of York had been vacant since Archbishop John Dolben's death in 1686. A double responsibility thus devolved upon William Sancroft, archbishop of Canterbury and a devout believer in nonresistance. Below him were the bishops, whose attitude toward recent changes was not agreed.

That some of the bishops were predisposed by the sordid motive of self-interest and by the doctrine of nonresistance to support the king is not puzzling. What was unexpected was that there would be any important resistance in the episcopal ranks. James did not doubt that he could command almost all of the bishops and be obeyed. They had often told him so, as before his accession they had told his brother. And the lower clergy would follow them, as duty bound it to do. When things did not fall out so, the king was baffled.

The bishops had all been promoted to their rank by the authority of Charles II or James II. The former had made more diverse appointments than the latter; however, Charles had always considered the loyalty of his nominees to be very important. For James, absolute obedience mattered more than other considerations. (Jonathan Trelawny, when only thirty-five, had earned the see of Bristol by helping the king against the duke of Monmouth.) After installation, ambitious bishops of poorer sees demonstrated full loyalty in order to obtain promotion to richer ones. Those who wished only to keep what they had got might fear the king's power to suspend or deprive them. (Bishop Compton of London was under suspension during most of 1688.) The potent influence of what Trollope calls "the loaves and fishes" was there, as it had always been.

The Anglican episcopate consisted chiefly of men who had passed through the Interregnum and (if old enough) the Civil Wars. They knew what deprivation meant, some having suffered it and most having seen it: to have weathered such a period and survived was much. The Restoration had ushered the loyal into favor, influence, and power: to have attained episcopal rank, authority, and income was almost incredibly good fortune. Never again to take a chance seemed the best course to Bishops Thomas Barlow of Lincoln, William Beaw of Llandaff, Herbert Croft of Hereford, Humphrey Lloyd of Bangor, and Thomas Wood of Lichfield. The average age of these bishops was well over seventy-five years. (Another elderly bishop, Seth Ward of Salisbury, was thought to be senile and incapable, whatever his motives.) Perhaps Thomas Lamplugh of Exeter and Thomas Smith of Carlisle should also be grouped with them — neither was a heroic figure.

James had found active assistance from Bishops Thomas Cartwright of Chester, Nathaniel Crew of Durham, Thomas Watson of St. David's, and Thomas Sprat of Rochester. Among these only Sprat had much ability or learning. Watson and Cartwright were thought such sneaks that their colleagues would not talk freely before them.

What distinguished these two groups from bishops who took another course? They had attended the same universities, Oxford and Cambridge (Oxonians outnumbered Cantabrigians), but no university influence appears in their choices of action or inaction. Neither does college membership within the universities make any clear connection with these choices. Apart from the preference of the very old for doing nothing, age seems not to have mattered. As to birth, the four undoubted members of the landed upper class—Compton, Crew, Croft, and Trelawny—were divided, as were the six sons of Anglican clergymen—Cartwright, Humphrey Lloyd, Sprat, the two William Lloyds (of Norwich and St. Asaph), and Francis Turner (of Ely). They read the same books and held many of the same opinions.

Perhaps it is no more than coincidence that Robert Frampton, Thomas Ken, the two William Lloyds, Peter Mew, and Sancroft among the "concerned" bishops, had spent periods ranging from a few months (Ken) to twelve years (Frampton) abroad, while of the others only Beaw had done so.

There is nothing obvious here, but rather something intangible, a thing that turned the opinion of the mass of the clergy and the more religious laymen against the fainéants and collaborators with King James. Those who could be driven into resistance were on the whole better men, in some sense, for their posts. Long before a breach was made, Sancroft, Ken (of Bath and Wells), and Frampton (of Gloucester) had earned reputations for piety, learning, and self-denial. Others had won notice as active administrators in their sees—scrupulous about admission of candidates to holy orders or punctilious in avoidance of pluralism and nonresidence. Henry Compton, unpopular for other reasons, was popular in resistance to James's Ecclesiastical Commission. Thus, in different ways and with widely differing personalities, a certain set of bishops forming a bare majority had shown their concern for the welfare of their church and its members. Concern might become alarm if the existence of the church seemed to them to be threatened. Concern, and later alarm, drew them together in the spring of 1688.

James, if he had continued in power, might have forced a schism in the Church of England; schism was not the aim of the bishops, who rather dreaded it. Bishop Ken, on December 28, 1687, consulted his friend William Wake to learn "what others doe" about the barring of

deprived fellows of Magdalen College, Oxford, from church preferments.[1] To form an opinion common to other good churchmen and
take a common course of action was Ken's intention, and Ken was not
alone. But argument over opinion might have continued for a long
time: there were legal technicalities, fears to be surmounted, and
above all the doctrine of nonresistance, in which Ken had been as
resolute as any. Union was achieved more quickly as a reaction to
James's consistent arrogance.

There was also the pressure of time. One of the fears of the
"concerned" bishops, and of other concerned churchmen, was that
episcopal ranks would be thinned and gaps refilled with unworthy and
subservient nonentities, even Catholics. In April 1688, there were
twenty-four Anglican bishops and two vacant sees (York and Oxford).
York had been kept vacant beyond the usual interval, some thought to
be filled by the Jesuit Father Edward Petre, in fact to provide revenue
for James's Catholic bishops, as the king was the custodian of vacant
sees and entitled to use their profits.[2] Other vacancies might occur at
any time (four of the bishops of 1688 were to die in 1689). Either
persuasion or a stand against some obvious encroachment upon the
church's rights must induce the king to change his policy. Sancroft
and his troubled colleagues hoped and prayed that God's providence
would do the work for them; they knew the king's fury at any crossing
of his designs.

The lower clergy, especially better-educated university graduates
and eminent preachers and writers, were also afraid for their church.
At Oxford and Cambridge there had been royal attacks on Anglicanism at Magdalen and Sidney Sussex Colleges, respectively, and
Catholics held positions for which they could not legally qualify. Per-
formances of masses in the universities and in the capital, against law
and the expectations of men of sense, provoked a common reaction
from the three greatest centers of Anglican clerical abilities in the
country. The disturbance of the London clergy, intellectually strength-
ened in the period by Sancroft's and Compton's use of their numerous
advowsons (rights of nomination) in the City and its environs, made
urgent a decision by the bishops to resist, and it also motivated much
of the support for the decision when it was made.[3]

Particularly shocking to clergymen of this stripe was the installation of a rival Catholic episcopate in England: four bishops *in parti-
bus* with territorial jurisdictions. This (to Anglicans) plainly invaded
the jurisdictions of Anglican bishops; it violated, moreover, the law of
praemunire, which condemned acknowledgment of a foreign power

(the pope) within the country. The law had been made by earlier monarchs in Parliament; James was deliberately setting it aside without the consent of Parliament. The bishops were not subject to Parliament, but they were subject to acts made by the monarch in that body, and they were members of the House of Lords. The king claimed the power of suspending the force of acts of Parliament and dispensing with their provisions in individual cases. The last expression of parliamentary opinion on this power, a resolution of the House of Commons adopted in 1673, firmly rejected as illegal a claim made to it by Charles II.[4]

King James was sure that he was exactly right in the policy he had adopted and the measures he was taking to carry it out. Toleration was desirable. The laws that stood in the way, punishing Catholics and Dissenters for religious offenses and excluding them from office by imposing a religious test, were relics of an uglier age and must sooner or later be repealed. Parliament had not gone so far in 1685 as to consider repeal; it was obvious (and not only to the king) that the two houses would have refused if they had been asked. James would make sure of repeal in time by remodeling municipal corporations and assuring seats for supporters of toleration in a parliament that in April 1688 he proposed to hold in the following November. In the meantime he found it ridiculous to threaten priests with execution for converting Anglicans to Catholicism or to fine Catholics for being absent from Anglican services. He had, he believed, this overriding power to set aside certain kinds of laws: "such Laws only as prohibited things not evil in themselves, 2dly . . . such as vest no propertie in the subject, and thirdly that the King's intent was chiefly to have a libertie of makeing use of his Subjects as he thought good [which] My Lord Cooke sayd was a power so inseparably annexed to his Royal person, that no Act of Parliament could restrain it."[5] As a Catholic, James did not see the conversion of an Anglican to Protestantism as evil in itself, nor the stripping of Magdalen College's fellows of their incomes as interference with their "property," nor the use of Catholics in offices of power or influence as dangerous to Anglicanism; he also did not see that many Anglicans, having long regarded Catholics with dread, must necessarily disagree with him and would fall back on Parliament and parliamentary law for support, though their preference would have been to place reliance in him.

He had acted according to his lights in April 1687 when he had issued a Declaration of Indulgence suspending the test and penal laws. The result was a visible decline in the number of cases in the courts involving failure to attend Anglican services and alleged immorality.[6]

James's stated object was laudable—to treat all Christians as equals and to share among them the good things at his disposal. He used traditional means to prevent expression of opposed opinions; that is, he attempted to control speech and the press. He was very sensitive about attacks on his religion and his fellow Catholics by Anglican ministers, and he forbade the preaching of anti-Catholic sermons. According to the earl of Ailesbury, spies posted themselves in churches to detect and report ministers who spoke against Catholicism or otherwise disobeyed the king.[7] Though control of speech and press were traditional and accepted, this seemed to be going too far. Control was traditionally for the suppression of the wicked or erroneous opinion of non-Anglicans, not for that of the general opinion of Protestants that Catholicism was a bad religion. Had James been evenhanded and restrained his Catholic priests as he restrained Anglican parsons, he might but probably would not have secured more acceptance of his position. Either way, he was not trusted, for he had promised at the beginning of his reign both to favor the Church of England and to observe the laws. As an anonymous writing left in the anteroom of his bedchamber put it, "Caesar to keep the law did pledge his troth [;] / He made his will the Law, soo saved his oath."[8]

In April 1688, James was dissatisfied with the effects of the 1687 Declaration of Indulgence. Its exact contents, though he believed them to be well judged and wholesome, were not widely known, and its motive and meaning were slandered. He therefore announced to his Privy Council, on April 27, that he had resolved to reissue it.

In the new issue James expressed the hope that the next parliament, which he promised to call, would show the effects of satisfaction with his policy of toleration. "We must conclude that not only good Christians will join in this, but whoever is Concern'd for the increase of the wealth and power of the nation; It would perhaps prejudice Some of our Neighbors [the Dutch] who might loos part of those vast advantages they now enjoy if Liberty of Conscience were Setled in these Kingdoms, which are above all others most Capable of Improvements and of Commanding the Trade of the world." He adjured his readers "to lay aside all private animosities . . . and to choose Such Members of Parliament as may do their part to finish what we have begun for the advantage of the Monarchy over which Almighty God hath placed us"; a parliament was to meet in November at the latest.[9]

A week later, on May 4, the king decided to add to the publicity of the declaration by requiring parish ministers to read it aloud from their pulpits at the usual time of divine service on May 20 and 27 in the churches and chapels of London, Westminster, and within ten miles of them, and on June 3 and 10 at other churches and chapels throughout the land. (All those days were Sundays.) "And it is further Ordered, that the Right Reverend the Bishops, cause the said Declaration to be sent and distributed throughout their several and respective Diocesses, to be read accordingly."[10]

The bishops were thus required to assist the king in a policy that a number of them believed to be wrong and destructive to their church. As Charles Hornby, a Tory journalist who lived through the time, remarked many years later, "This was trying the utmost stretch of Obedience."[11]

Whether discussion of resistance began among the bishops or among the lower clergy is now impossible to tell. In any case, it soon began; the chief scene was London, and the clergy met in three places there: Sancroft's palace at Lambeth, Turner's Ely House, and William Sherlock's house in the Temple. James had allowed little time for delay; there was no time at all to consult the clergy outside the metropolis. Some London clerics met at Ely House, probably on May 7, the day when notice of the required reading appeared in the *London Gazette*. The majority at first inclined to obey the command and read the declaration in their churches, but John Tillotson (dean of Canterbury), Edward Stillingfleet (dean of St. Paul's Cathedral), Symon Patrick (rector of St. Paul's, Covent Garden), and Sherlock (master of the Temple) argued successfully that the clergy should not read it. All of these opponents were eminent and marked for future promotion, as was Bishop Turner, their host.[12]

Sir John Lowther, later Viscount Lonsdale, was then in London; he heard and described the arguments on the two sides. In favor of reading the declaration was only to be said that the king would be angry if disobeyed; against, that reading would at least imply that the Anglican religion was not superior to others. Moreover, the declaration was illegal, being founded on the suspending power, which might overturn all laws. Then the clergy, if it obeyed James's command, would lose its reputation among noblemen and gentlemen, many of whom had "lost offices of honour and profitt ffor the sake of religion and the laws." Many Anglican ministers had written and preached in favor of their church, and obedience would seem a failure to stand to their words. Further, Lowther reported, "If they should complie in this, something wors would certainly be imposed upon them to ruin

them, and having lost their reputation, they should fall unpitied; that
they could never take an opportunity of refusing, upon a point more
popular or more justifiable; that their consenting to this, made their
condition as precarious as that of anie other Dissenters, who having
no legal establishment, were fforced to flie to the declaration for
protection."[13]

After a second meeting at Ely House, the London clergy met
again on May 11 at Sherlock's house; wròte Patrick, "we came to this
resolution, that the Bishops should be desired to address to the King,
but not upon any address of ours to them. For we judged it best that
they should lead the way, and we follow them."[14] Lowther learned
from a leading minister that the bishops would apply to the king, but,
if they did not, "the clergie of London were readie to doe it in a bodie;
and that some of them would make a speech, setting forth their reasons, and that they could not doe it [read the declaration in their
churches] in conscience."[15] No doubt Hornby was right in saying that
the bishops undertook to lead, at least partly because they foresaw
"the general Calamity likely to follow on the refusal of their Clergy" if
the declaration was distributed according to the king's command.
Revolters from the lower ranks of the clergy would be much more
vulnerable than the bishops, who therefore decided to run the risk of
not distributing copies of the document.[16]

On May 12, Sancroft entertained a few other bishops and the earl
of Clarendon at Lambeth. Cartwright and Watson were present at
first, and the others could not speak freely until the suspects had left
after dinner. Those remaining decided to prepare a petition to the
king, to which as many bishops as possible were to be invited to put
their signatures. Sancroft insisted on solidarity among the clergy of
London as a condition of his own signing; it was therefore necessary
to test clerical opinion about the city.[17] The bishops were also allowed
a little time to respond to the invitation.

The next day Bishops Turner and Thomas White (Peterborough)
met with fifteen clergymen at Dean Tillotson's house. Except for the
two bishops, all were London clergymen, though six were also deans
and at least one an archdeacon. The general opinion was at first for
obeying the king and reading the declaration: to do otherwise might
cause a schism and offend Dissenters, who expected relief. Those
present reported no firmness among temporal lords. Dr. Edward
Fowler, vicar of St. Giles Cripplegate, son of an ejected Nonconformist and himself friendly toward Dissenters, denied that the case was
complex and asked all to answer "Yes or No . . . he in conscience

could not read it; to read it was to desire his people to obey it, which he thought unlawful." Deans Tillotson and Patrick supported him and won over the moderates present.[18]

Two participants, perhaps more, had brought papers to the meeting as bases for a petition. Those that survive are Fowler's and Stillingfleet's; both dwell on the illegality of the dispensing power; neither gives attention to opinions of Dissenters. The meeting turned its thought toward that subject.

Fowler and Tillotson were known to and respected by leading Dissenting ministers. Tillotson had favored reunion of Dissenters with the Church of England since 1674. The two would have known that moderate Anglicans had conferred with some of the Dissenters as early as May 7 and that Nonconformists also objected to the reading of the declaration.[19] A second consultation would probably only confirm the first, but it might strengthen the hands of those who wished to petition the king against his order. On May 15, "everyone resolving, for one reason or other not to read the Declaration," some twenty Anglican ministers were asked to learn the intentions of the other ministers of the capital.

For use in consultation with Anglican ministers, a statement of intention was drafted, "The Comprehensive Sense of the Clergy," which local beneficed clergymen were asked to sign. It raised an objection to the king's dispensing power, but not to toleration of other Protestants: "We are not averse to publishing the Declaration for any want of the tenderness towards the Dissenters, in relation to whom we shall be thought willing to come to such a temper as shall be thought fit when that matter comes to be considered and settled in Parliament and Convocation."[20] The statement neatly avoided a possible misinterpretation of what the drafters clearly intended to be only protest against an illegal and repugnant command.

James may have issued the command to read the declaration with the consideration that the Anglicans would either obey or alienate their fellow Protestants. Indeed, some Anglicans did object to "a direct promoteing the use of that unlawfull [religious] Liberty," as Jonas Proast of All Souls College did.[21] If James hoped to keep Anglicans divided from other Protestants, he was circumvented.

The pollers brought the results together on May 17 at a house in St. Paul's churchyard. It was reckoned that seventy (a substantial majority) would not read the declaration; "some could not be found, and a few spoke dubiously." Patrick delivered a fair copy of the list of refusers to Bishop White, who took it to Archbishop Sancroft, then fixed at Lambeth. Assured of support in London, Sancroft invited the bishops in or near town to come to him the next morning, a Friday. It was fitting, he said to Patrick and Thomas Tenison, minister of St. James's Piccadilly, that the Friday should be a day of prayer and fasting.[22]

More bishops had been arriving in London — Lloyd of St. Asaph on May 16, Ken and Trelawny on the next day. Five bishops met with Patrick, Stillingfleet, Tenison, and Dr. Robert Grove, rector of St. Andrew Undershaft. They decided that a petition should be presented and (according to Patrick) drafted one then and there.[23] As seven bishops signed it, and one more was present but not signing, the decision and the drafting must have given time enough for only three to join the meeting. Such was the haste of the moment. Finally present and signing were Sancroft, Turner, Lake (of Chichester), White (of Peterborough), Ken, Trelawny, and Lloyd (of St. Asaph).

The basis of the petition, to be offered by the bishops in the name of other bishops and of the clergy in their dioceses, was the "Comprehensive Sense of the Clergy," with perhaps some reliance on a memorandum by Sancroft entitled "Reasons for Not Publishing the Declaration." Its final form shows the effects of hours of discussion in several important changes.[24]

> The great averseness they find in themselves to the distributing and publishing in all their churches your majesty's late Declaration for Liberty of Conscience, proceedeth neither from any want of duty and obedience to your majesty, (our holy Mother the Church of England being both in her principles and in her constant practice, unquestionably loyal; and having, to her great honour, been more than once publickly acknowledged to be so by your gracious majesty), nor yet from any want of due Tenderness to Dissenters, in relation to whom they are willing to come to such a temper, as shall be thought fit, when that matter shall be considered, and settled in Parliament and Convocation; but amongst many other considerations, from this especially, because that Declaration is founded upon such a Dispensing power, as hath been often declared illegal in parliament, and particularly in the years 1662, and 1672, and the beginning of your majesty's reign; and it is a matter of so great moment and consequence to the whole nation, both in Church and State, that your Petitioners cannot in prudence, honour, or conscience, so far make themselves parties to it, as the distribution of it all over the nation, and the solemn publication of it once and again, even in God's house, and in the time of his divine service, must amount to, in common and reasonable construction.

Your Petitioners therefore most humbly and earnestly beseech
your Majesty that you will be graciously pleased not to insist upon
their distributing and reading your Majesty's said Declaration.
And your Petitioners (as in duty bound) shall ever pray, &c.
Signed

W. Cant.	*Tho. Bath & Wells*
S. Asaph.	*Tho. Petriburgens.*
Fran Ely.	*Joh. Bristol.*
Jo. Cicestr.	

Bishop Henry Compton did not sign the petition, although he
was present at the meeting, as James had suspended him from his
functions. Bishop Frampton (of Gloucester) was chagrined to arrive
after the petition was carried off to the king. Mew (of Winchester)
was delayed by illness, and the invitation to William Lloyd of
Norwich was delayed in the mails. The signers could take no time to
accommodate them, for they completed the petition at about six
o'clock Friday evening. At divine service on Sunday, May 20, the
king's command required the first reading of the declaration in and
about London.

Sancroft had been forbidden King James's presence earlier in the
reign. Therefore, only six bishops set out by water from Lambeth for
Whitehall bearing the petition. They were sure of the support of the
mass of parochial clergymen and others who feared for the Church of
England as they did. They could also count on the sympathy of unknown numbers of Dissenters. Protestants of most sorts would stand
by the prelates of the Church of England on this occasion, for the
exclusion of Catholics from the government and the services, and for
preservation of legality from the powers claimed by the king. The
barge carrying the bishops rode on another, greater river, with tributa-
ries everywhere in the country.

James's *Life* later described as insincere the refusal of the bishops
to distribute copies of the declaration to the clergy. They had not
protested against the declaration before (its first issue was a year old),
and they had not allowed time between the submission of the petition
and the scheduled first readings in the capital for James to consult.
Certainly there was no time; but James had allowed the bishops very
little between the gazetting of the declaration and the first readings.
That was his fault. Also, it looked "as if they had been numbering the
people: to see if they would stick by them, and finding it in their
power to whistle up the winds were resolued to rais a storme, tho they
seemingly pretended to lay it."[25] Except for the interpretation put

upon the hurried consultations from May 7 to May 18, the description fits them very well. James could not see that because this course was the only one the bishops could conscientiously take, it was the one they would take. In his opinion, their proper course was to obey him.

Arrived at Whitehall, Bishop Lloyd of St. Asaph thought it best for the group to be brought into the king's presence by one of the two secretaries of state. The earl of Middleton was a Protestant and more popular, but Lloyd found him ill and confined to his bedroom. The earl of Sunderland had recently become a Catholic and was otherwise of battered reputation; besides, he was unsympathetic to Anglicans. Lloyd nevertheless left his five colleagues at Lord Dartmouth's house and went to seek an introduction from Sunderland. The earl would not read the petition, but he did go at once to the king to tell him that several bishops had requested an audience.[26]

As Sunderland did not know what was in the petition, and the petitioners had excluded Bishops Cartwright and Watson from their deliberations, James had no inkling of the contents. Indeed, Cartwright had guessed wrongly that the bishops objected to distributing the declaration as work more fit for the chancellors of their dioceses than for themselves, and he had told James so.[27] The king could easily and graciously deal with that objection.

He allowed the bishops to come at once into the "closet within his Bed-chamber," in which he was probably preparing to go to bed. (It was perhaps ten in the evening.) The bishops knelt, and Lloyd presented the petition. The king recognized Sancroft's writing before he understood the gist of the paper; when he had read it all and folded it up, he "said thus, or to this effect . . . This is a great surprize to me: here are strange words. I did not expect this from you. This is a standard of Rebellion." He was right, of course, though none of the bishops would admit it. He had issued an order to men sworn to obey him and overcome with the importance of obedience, and they had refused.

All six bishops present protested that they had not intended rebellion. Lake and Trelawny reminded the king that they had indeed assisted in quelling rebellion. Turner said that the petitioners were willing to die at James's feet (a standard profession of loyalty, never acted upon). Ken and White were to the purpose: if James offered liberty of conscience to all mankind, surely he would allow it to Anglican bishops; and reading the declaration would be against their consciences.

James attacked them for questioning the dispensing power after some of them had preached and written in favor of it. White and Lloyd answered that the petition referred only to resolutions of Parliament against it. (Sancroft's "Reasons for Not Publishing the Declaration" had contained a statement that he believed the dispensing power illegal, but it had not been retained in the petition.)

The king still held the petition to be rebellion and stated his will to have the declaration published. Ken defined the conflict of loyalties in members of his order. "We are bound to fear God, and honour the king. We desire to do both: we will honour you; we must fear God." James asked rhetorically whether he deserved such treatment and said, "I will remember you that have signed this paper. I will keep this paper; I will not part with it. I did not expect this from you; especially from some of you. I will be obeyed in publishing my Declaration." To which Ken replied, "God's will be done." James asked, "What's that?" and Ken repeated his submission to God, this time joined by White. The king was not appeased: "If I think fit to alter my mind, I will send to you. God hath given me this dispensing power, and I will maintain it. I tell you, there are seven thousand men, and of the Church of *England* too, that have not bowed the knee to *Baal*."[28]

There was nothing more to be said. James forthwith dismissed the bishops.

That night, a paper purporting to be the petition was printed and sold in the streets. Actually, it appears to have been "A True Copy of a Paper Presented to the King's Majesty," which J. R. Western has reproduced. The "True Copy" was the "Comprehensive Sense," which had been shown to all the accessible clergy of London before the drafting of the petition, with the following emphatic "Kings Answer": "I have heard of this before, but could not believe it; you look like Trumpeters of Rebellion; You Aim at my Prerogative; But I will not lose One Branch of it. Take Your Course, and I will take mine, my Commands shall be Obeyed, do it at your Peril." If Mr. Roger Thomas is correct in his identification of this paper (I believe he is), its publisher had no copy of the petition — only one of the "Comprehensive Sense" and a brief report of the king's reaction. He was not therefore necessarily one of the bishops. That is possible, but not likely; any petitioning bishop would have known more of the petition's contents than was included in the "Comprehensive Sense." He may have been some London clergyman who had been polled with the latter document or some knowing courtier.[29]

On Sunday, May 20, according to various accounts, four, five, or seven Anglican clergymen read the declaration as the king commanded. Four can be precisely identified: Richard Martin (or Martyn), rector of St. Michael, Wood Street; Dr. Francis Thompson, rector of St. Matthew, Friday Street; Adam Elliott, perpetual curate of St. James's, Duke's Place, and chaplain to the Whiggish Lord Grey of Werk; and Timothy Hall, rector of All Hallows Staining, who had apparently earlier been a Dissenter.[30] Thompson and Martin were pluralists. Elliott, Martin, and Thompson were Cambridge men. (Hall had been at Oxford.) Elliott, Hall, and Martin had not proceeded beyond the degree of B.A. They were an undistinguished lot, as university biographical registers show.

Deans Stillingfleet and Tillotson absented themselves from their churches and went to the country. A minor canon read the declaration at Westminster Abbey on the order of Bishop Sprat, who was also dean there, but Sprat himself went out of town; as Lord Clarendon wrote, Sprat was a "poor-spirited man." Ministers who read it were stigmatized by their colleagues.[31]

King James was receiving addresses of thanks from several quarters for the reissue of the declaration: from the mayors and others of Devizes, Cambridge, and so on. These were produced on demand, as were many such addresses; they did not express the feelings of most of the political classes, or there would have been no revolution. Sir John Reresby recorded that, at quarter sessions in Yorkshire on April 25, a few Catholic justices of the peace and two other gentlemen sent up an address as though it were approved by all present. Reresby thought that the king was sometimes deceived by such means.[32] If so, the failure of the command to the bishops and the collapse of the declaration's first reading could have been useful correctives, but the king could not accept correction. He set out at once to find a punishment for the seven bishops without awaiting the reading; in the morning after the presentation of the petition, "all the Judges were sent for to Whitehall; the report was, yt 'twas about the B$\overline{pp}$s Petition."[33]

The next few days were active ones for the resisters of the king's command. Other bishops added their signatures (not of course on the original) to the first seven, on May 21 (Frampton), on May 23 (Compton and Lloyd of Norwich), and on May 25 (Seth Ward of Salisbury). Curiously, on May 29, the timid Thomas Lamplugh, bishop of Exeter, signed a copy of the petition. These signatories were not included in the subsequent legal proceedings, however. Frampton, according to one account, had missed signing the original by half an hour, though Clarendon reports his arrival in town with Lloyd of Norwich on May

21.[34] By a day at the most, he had escaped the reward of heroes and the persecution of martyrs.

William Sherlock, it seems, was the author of an anonymous *Letter from a Clergy-man in the City, to his Friend in the Country,* dated May 22, 1688, giving reasons for not reading the declaration. Thousands of copies were distributed with the intent of reaching every parish clergyman in England before any further reading of the declaration took place. Some attributed the letter to Humphrey Prideaux, though Prideaux attributed it to Lord Halifax.

Sherlock, if he was the author, began by stating that the order to read the declaration was intended to ruin those who complied — by opening "our Church-doors" to popery and drawing the hate of good Protestants — and to ruin those who did not comply through punishment for disobedience. To read something aloud in church was to teach it; to teach the contents of the declaration would contradict the proper teachings of the Church of England; in future, Catholic homilies might come to be read in the same way: "whether I consent to the Doctrine or no, it is certain I consent to teach my People this Doctrine; and it is to be considered, whether an honest man can do this." The king would wish the reading in the churches to be taken for approbation, as he would the addresses of thanks for the issue of the declaration. Perhaps the people would understand the business as being performed under duress, but though "some may excuse it, others, and those it may be the most, the best, and the wisest men, will condemn us for it, and then how shall we justifie ourselves against their Censures? . . . the plain way is certainly the best."

The author of the letter had a good deal more to say on the error of reading the declaration, much already touched upon here in quotations from other sources. One of the last considerations was that it was not good to alienate Dissenters by showing a "Persecuting Spirit." The author thought it more important not "to disoblige all the Nobility and Gentry by Reading it . . . than to anger the Dissenters." As for the latter,

> The Dissenters who are Wise and considering, are sensible of the snare themselves, and though they desire Ease and Liberty, they are not willing to have it with such apparent hazard of Church and State: I am sure that thô we were never so desirous that they might have their Liberty (and when there is opportunity of shewing our inclinations without danger, they may find that we are not such

Persecutors as we are represented) yet we cannot consent that they
should have it this way, which they will find the dearest Liberty that
ever was granted.

A postscript rejoices in the ill success of the reading of the declaration
in London on Sunday, May 20.[35]
    The distribution of copies of this letter was a dangerous task and
was kept very private. Edmund Prideaux, son of Humphrey Prideaux
(then a canon of Norwich), preserved his father's story of the work
Humphrey did in the diocese of Norwich, receiving two thousand
copies of the *Letter* and dealing them out so well that "every clergy-
man was furnished with one of these letters . . . which had so good
an effect, that out of one thousand two hundred parishes in the
diocese . . . there were not above four or five, in which it was read on
[June 3], and in those the Ministers were obliged to read it out of the
[London] Gazette." To conceal that the pamphlets were sent from
Norwich, he arranged that some be posted at Yarmouth, leaving the
impression that they had been sent from Holland. Others bore no
marks of origin and went by the hands of the weekly carriers from
Norwich to other parts.[36] Perhaps the diocese of Norwich was particularly well managed, for the bishop and dean were also whole-
heartedly opposed to James's religious policy and in sympathy with
the seven petitioners. All the same, the king had support there: Dr.
Nathaniel Vincent—rector of Blo Norton, Norfolk; fellow of Clare
Hall, Cambridge; and a royal favorite—preached at Norwich on May
29 on the text "Rebellion is as the sin of witchcraft."[37]
    The king was little obeyed in this matter elsewhere: in the county
of Durham, part of the diocese of the compliant Bishop Crew, the
declaration was read in only twenty-one churches. We hear of most of
the congregation of the one compliant minister in Chester leaving the
church and of few reading the declaration in Cheshire in spite of
Bishop Cartwright's menaces.[38] Anthony Wood knew of only six
ministers of Oxfordshire (who received notes from the bishop's regis-
trar, the see being vacant) who complied on June 3.[39] All had parishes
in one small part of the county; it would seem that they reinforced
one another's principles or fears. The gentry and nobility in many
places supported the petitioning bishops. Some discouraged clergymen from reading the declaration: Theophilus Brooks, rector of Horton, Leicestershire, wrote on June 2: "our Bishop [Thomas Barlow of
Lincoln] has sent it to our several churches and our gentry very much
oppose the reading of it. My Lord Ferrars, as Mr. Burdett told me,

swore it would not be read in his church."⁴⁰ That church was presumably that of Staunton Harold, Leicestershire, where Lord Ferrers's seat was. At least one bishop who had no part in the petitioning (Thomas of Worcester) detained copies sent to him for distribution. He explained his action:

> I could not transmitt [it] to the Clergy of my Diocese committed to my pastoral charge (salva conscientia, salvo honore ecclesiae *Anglicanae.*) It is a piercing wounding affliction to me to incurre his Majesty's displeasure . . . whose special Mandate I have receaved in the concerne of the Indulgence imparted to me by the Lord Bishop of *St. David's* [Watson, who supported the king]; wherein nothing could divert or slacken my intire submission . . . but my dread of the indignation of the King of Kings, to whom being neare . . . the grave I must shortly give an account . . . I apprehend it a duty . . . to be a skreene to my Clergy, to endeavor to secure them from sinnes and perills, not to lay traines for either, by recommending the publication of that to their parishioners, wherein my own judgement is abundantly dissatisfyed, and theirs also.⁴¹

Anthony Wood believed that only four hundred ministers among those of England's nine thousand churches read the declaration.⁴² As in London, those who complied were despised.

The author of James's *Life* blames the decision to punish the petitioning bishops on givers of pernicious advice; but there, at least, some of James's most unpopular advisers, Lords Sunderland and Jeffreys, were innocent. As F. C. Turner points out, the king's own "prepossession against the yielding temper," which had as he thought ruined his father and endangered his brother, was really responsible.⁴³ For a king to yield under pressure made him seem weak both to his subjects and to other rulers such as Louis XIV or the States General of the United Provinces. He was aware that reports on the matter were being sent home by foreign ministers at his court;⁴⁴ what other governments thought of him mattered much.

Of course, the king heard advice. Barrillon, who was informed, told of it in his dispatch of May 24/June 3. Some officials and leading Catholics thought the king ought to suspend the petitioners, perhaps through action by the Ecclesiastical Commission. Others thought suspension would exaggerate the importance of the bishops' action; their fault was grave, but according to the laws, it did not clearly warrant suspension; the legal proceedings would be long and would stir up the country. The suspension would not keep the bishops from their seats in the House of Lords, and they might attend and oppose the king's measures. James would be prudent if he simply let them know their error and that he would pass over it because of the past fidelity of Anglicans to his father and brother. He should give them time to return to their usual principles and repair in Parliament the damage they had done. His indulgence toward them would be a consequence and an effect of his declaration. Sunderland and Father Petre gave this advice, Barrillon said, and the king would apparently follow it.[45]

A week later, the ambassador reported a change: the soft party (*"party de la douceur"*) was obliged to give way to the arguments of its opponents because a rumor was spreading "that the court did not dare proceed against the bishops by law and the seditious were deriving a great benefit from it."[46] James could not bear either the imputation of fear or the opposition's gain of prestige.

There was a proposal to issue the declaration a third time, order that it be read in the churches, and add a clause depriving disobedient clergymen of their positions. James felt strong enough in law to reject this tedious repetition, as well as a suggested "Proclamation for reading the Declaration & Dispersing it by the Sheriffs." The latter proposal was perhaps frustrated by belief that the temporal peers would petition against it. Barrillon reported that the marquis of Halifax and the earls of Shrewsbury, Devonshire, Nottingham, Clare, and "Dance" were willing to sign a petition of some kind, perhaps against that proposal.[47]

The party of douceur was apparently (besides obvious moderates) Sunderland, Jeffreys, and most of the Catholic English lords, who were nervous of making more enemies than they already had.[48] The party of punishment was led by Father Petre, though Barrillon wrote otherwise on May 24/June 3. The rumor that the king would not dare to attack the bishops, alluded to above, which helped him to make up his mind to attack them as he certainly wished to do, might have been put about by anyone. The bishops, by the way, knew better than to believe it.

James must have observed this growth of the opposition as lines were drawn. To be sure, the opposition had no hope of gaining Watson, Sprat, Crew, or Cartwright, but seven or eight bishops, including Frampton and Lloyd of Norwich, expressed sympathy with the petitioners. Yet Lord Clarendon, a knowing layman, listed Barlow of Lincoln and Wood of Lichfield as unpredictable, "old and very odd men."[49] At least thirteen bishops were definitely in opposition, with a few hedging, while James counted on only five—Crew, Sprat, Cartwright, Watson, and Wood.

One of James's objects in what he now did was to reduce opponents to impotence and (if necessary) poverty; another was to bring hedgers to rest on his side.

Expected dissenting support did not materialize. The king requested a small group of leading Dissenters—William Penn, Sir John Baber, Alderman Daniel Williams, Samuel Slater, Richard Mayo, Stephen Lobb, and Vincent Alsop—for an address of thanks for the issue of the declaration and waited in his closet to receive one. Williams, who had recently been in Ireland and feared Catholic persecution of Protestants, dissuaded the others from approving such an address.[50] As Penn, Lobb, and Alsop had earlier availed themselves of James's liberty of conscience and gone to court, this was ominous.

On May 27, St. John Taylor, one of the court messengers, took to Archbishop Sancroft an order to attend a meeting of the Privy Council on June 8 and answer to "matters of misdemeanour." Similar summonses were sent to other petitioners, either in London or in the country.[51] There was, it seems, no secret about it, for at about this time Samuel Hill, a Somersetshire rector, wrote to Bishop Turner, asking for Turner's prayers. "The prayers of those that are bearing the Cross have more than an ordinary virtue and reception with our blessed Saviour."[52] Hill's view of the bishops' position soon became common.

The petitioners had already sought legal counsel because they expected questions that they might wish not to answer. Sir Robert Sawyer supplied them with information about procedure in the Privy Council: not being a court of record, it never required recognizances or committed for misdemeanors. Members of the House of Lords did not give recognizances for misdemeanor, he reminded them. He also gave formulae useful to avoid giving testimony against themselves. They were to ask what misdemeanors were alleged against them and request time to consider their answers.[53] Some temporal peers supported his advice on entering recognizances because it would "injure theyre Peerage."[54]

At five in the afternoon of June 8, the Privy Council met with the king in the council chamber at Whitehall. The petitioning bishops, already waiting in an anteroom, were called into the council chamber about half an hour later, when James had explained to the councillors the reason for the meeting.[55] Asked whether a paper then on the table was the petition written and signed by him and signed and presented by the bishops, Sancroft said he hoped that as he was unhappily called before the council as a criminal, he would not offend the king by caution in answering. "No man is obliged to answer questions, that may tend to the accusing of himself."

King James was apparently surprised that a bishop should take advantage of the law for his own protection; he "called this chicanery, and hoped, he [Sancroft] would not deny his hand." Nevertheless, Sancroft and Lloyd of St. Asaph insisted on their right to avoid self-incrimination, though the king pressed them impatiently. Sancroft offered to answer, if the king commanded him to do so, relying on "your Majesty's justice and generosity, that we shall not suffer for our obedience, as we must, if our answer should be brought in evidence against us." The king was baffled: he wished to get an answer from the petitioners without giving a promise not to use the answer in court. Jeffreys ordered the bishops to withdraw.

A few minutes later they were summoned again into the council chamber and commanded to answer the question "Whether these be your hands that are set to this Petition?" Then each owned his part in the writing and signing of the paper. Attempts made to get them to go beyond the words of the petition and incriminate themselves further, failed, however. Asked whether they had dispersed a "printed Letter in the Country," the bishops replied, "If this be one of the articles of misdemeanor against us, we desire to answer it with the rest"; that is to say, in court. Again they were ordered to withdraw.

When they were called in for a third time, Lord Chancellor Jeffreys informed them that the king would proceed against them for the petition and required them to enter into recognizances. The archbishop replied that they would be ready to appear and answer whenever called, without recognizances. Jeffreys represented the recognizance procedure as a favor; Bishop Lloyd said that a favor might be declined, and as the giving of recognizances might be prejudicial to the bishops, they hoped that the king would not be offended at their declining it. The bishops held that there was no precedent for binding peers in recognizance for misdemeanor. Jeffreys said that there was but could name none.

After a third withdrawal, the bishops again rejected the recognizance procedure. The king took offense at the bishops' reliance on their legal counsel rather than on him. During a fourth withdrawal the earl of Berkeley tried to change the bishops' minds.

At last, a sergeant at arms came out of the council chamber with warrants to take the petitioners to the Tower and there keep them in custody. Father Petre, the earl of Berkeley, and Sir John Ernle, chancellor of the exchequer, were said to have refused to subscribe the warrant for committing the bishops to the Tower; according to one source, Ernle was alone.[56] The king ordered the attorney general and solicitor general to prepare an information against them for "making and publishing a seditious libel."[57]

James had got answers to his questions, but under such circumstances and by such methods that if he prosecuted the bishops and used their answers, no one who knew would ever believe in his justice or generosity again, and the trial would be public and so well attended that everyone interested would know. This much Sir Robert Sawyer had already achieved by his legal advice.

The bishops did not seem displeased at being confined, according to Barrillon, because they believed that it would make them more popular as "supports [soustiens] of the Protestant religion." They had refused to enter into recognizances to drag out the proceedings until the Michaelmas court term, when Parliament was expected to meet: "That is what his Britannic Majesty wished to avoid . . . to be able before that time to make an example for it [Parliament] in the person of these bishops." Some advised the king that the petitioners deserved suspension, loss of their revenues, and heavy fines, even deprivation of their sees.[58]

They went under guard, by water, from Whitehall to the Tower, waited for and watched by a great crowd. "Wonderful was the concerne of the people for them, infinite crowdes of people on their knees, beging [sic] their blessing & praying for them as they passed out of the Barge."[59]

Many visited them during their stay in the Tower, among others (on June 12) the earl of Clarendon. The marquis of Halifax had been there before him and had advised the bishops each to ask three peers in writing to give bail at the Court of King's Bench. The prisoners were not inclined to follow this advice. Halifax puzzled Clarendon: "I am sure when the reading the Declaration was under Consideration, and the Petition . . . he was soe cautious, yt he would give no advice at all."[60] Ten Nonconformist ministers also went to visit them, and the king was vexed, sending "for four of them to repremand them. They answered that they could not but adhear to them [the bishops] as men constant for the Protestant faith." Sir Edward Hales, lieutenant governor of the Tower, heard that soldiers of the Royal Regiment of Fusiliers in his garrison had drunk to the confined bishops' health, and he sent to forbid it. The captain of the guard "returnd answer that it was doing at that time, and that they would drinke it and noe other health whilst the bishops stayd ther."[61] The suspended Bishop Compton visited Sancroft and the others regularly and arranged to have noblemen ready to give bail for them if required.[62]

Advisers were working out legal strategy. Sir Thomas Clarges wrote Sancroft on June 14 that the earl of Nottingham thought the bishops ought to "plead the general issue," that is, question the legality of the dispensing power, in order to be able to "say more" and "give more in evidence." Heneage Finch, a former solicitor general and one of the bishops' counsel, was not sure that that would be wise. Mr. Grange, an attorney, believed that the "general issue" should be pleaded if "the matter was fully mention'd in the Information" lodged against the petitioners. They were scheduled to appear before the King's Bench on June 15. Twenty peers would be there to give bail, but Clarges doubted that the prosecution would be ready.[63]

While they were in the Tower, the bishops had the liberty of the place. Their visitors, "many of the nobility and innumerable crouds of others of all ranks begging their blessing," must have made great demands on their time, and the prisoners were no doubt anxious about the outcome. On Sunday, they received the sacrament together.[64] The lieutenant governor bothered them with a demand for fees said to be due to him from his prisoners by antique and deplorable custom — £250 from the archbishop and £150 from each of the other six. "My Ld Archb. told him hee would give him what was his due, ye Bp of Bath & Wells, yt hee could not pay it, & Peterb. yt hee would not." Sancroft actually paid £200 to Hales and £60 to other Tower officers.[65] At the last minute, Lord Dartmouth, admiral, master of the ordnance, and a good Anglican, attempted to persuade Bishop Turner to submit to the king.[66] He did not succeed.

The king had a last chance to withdraw gracefully. His son was born on June 10; on such joyous occasions kings commonly pardoned offenders or eased their penalties. The very day after the bishops were taken into custody (which was also the day before the young prince was born), the earl of Huntingdon, a privy councillor who had signed the warrant for it, confided to Sir John Reresby, "If the king had known how farr this matter would have gone, he would not have enjoined the reading of the declaration in churches." The king had already said that he would be clement to the bishops when he had them at his mercy; when his son was born, both Sunderland and Jeffreys urged the dropping of the bishops' case, but James refused.[67]

On the other side, William Sherlock, who had been so active, expected the bishops to lose their case and other clergymen to lose their places.[68] The offer of James's good graces amid the celebration of the royal birth might have divided the Protestant opposition, but James's refusal to yield made it impossible to pardon an opponent until James's foot was on the other's neck.

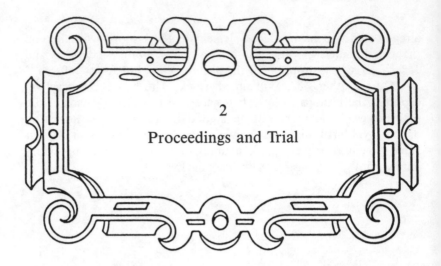

2
Proceedings and Trial

JUNE 15 was the first day of the legal term, and the prosecution began proceedings that day by moving for a writ of habeas corpus, on which the accused came escorted from the Tower to the Court of King's Bench at Westminster. A careful notetaker observed that eighteen English peers attended the court; among them were such political figures as the marquis of Halifax and the earls of Danby, Shrewsbury, and Nottingham. Another names eight of those listed in the former source and reports that "at least 12 or 13 more" were present.[1]

The bishops were brought in to be charged. The prosecution also expected them to plead. Attorney General Sir Thomas Powys and Solicitor General Sir William Williams led; they feigned belief that the proceedings should be quick and easy. Powys was self-confident at this stage, although his only courtroom gift seems to have been sarcasm. Williams was abler, but his Whig past hampered his rendering forced service to the king, to whom he owed a heavy fine. The defense had far more talent on its side: Sir Robert Sawyer had preceded Powys as attorney general; Sir Francis Pemberton had once been chief justice of King's Bench, the court in which he now defended his clients; Sir Creswell Levinz had been a *puisne* (junior) justice of King's Bench; Heneage Finch had served as solicitor general. These were all Tories, and all had lost their places as James moved away from the Tories and courted Whigs and Dissenters. They were also eminent lawyers. It was ominous for James that three Whigs were their colleagues in the defense: Sir Henry Pollexfen, Pollexfen's cousin Sir George Treby, and a comparative unknown, John Somers.[2] The judges were not the best. Sir Robert Wright, the chief justice, had been raised up to render decisions supporting the king against opposition. Sir John Powell seems a luminary by comparison, though thought very loyal. Sir Richard Allibone was a Catholic, unlearned in the law and absolutely subservient. Sir Robert Holloway, another supporter of the king, was more knowledgeable than Allibone.[3]

The defense at once raised the technicality that the bishops had been irregularly committed. The court overruled it and postponed the question of commitment of peers for misdemeanor. Powys and Williams did their best to silence defense counsel by complaints of repetition and ill-chosen time for objections, but Chief Justice Wright gave at least lip service to fair play, saying to Finch, "[W]e are very willing to deliver these Noble Lords, if we can by Law, and if the Exceptions you make be legal."[4] Williams already showed personal animus against Anglican bishops, no doubt arising from his previous Whiggishness. After some shuffling about whether a misdemeanor such as libel was a breach of the peace, the information against the bishops was read in Latin, though Bishop White (who knew Latin very well) alleged that he did not know the Latin of the courts. The drafters had included texts of both Declarations of Indulgence in this charge. In short, they also said in it that the bishops had made and published a seditious libel.

Finch, for the defense, asked the court to consider whether the bishops should plead immediately, as the prosecution expected. The judges did not agree on the subject. Pollexfen argued for allowing time to deliberate before requiring the accused to plead. Compulsion to plead immediately was a recent thing: "We have indeed seen strange [new] things of this kind done before, but I hope to God they are now at an end."[5] The judges again did not agree, and the prosecution responded bitterly to the defense. The safe course was to go by the old precedents, the older the better, for such was law. Sir Samuel Astrey, clerk of the Crown in the Court of King's Bench, testified from his own memory and from what a much older clerk named Waterhouse had told him that the court had always required immediate pleading in such cases as the bishops' (that is, when the defendants had only just heard the information read). Solicitor Williams stood absolutely on past practice and against an "imparlance" (postponement) for six months until Michaelmas term. Defense counsel, he said, when acting as prosecutors in the past, had required immediate pleading.

Justice Powell tried to persuade the court to allow such a delay, but the prosecution answered with precedents, whether good or bad, and the other judges were too much concerned with safety in precedent to yield to his arguments, which seem to a modern reader quite fair. Pollexfen cited the case of Sir John Eliot and asserted that Waterhouse had always been incompetent and had at last lost his memory. John Ince (the bishops' attorney, probably not a barrister) volunteered that Waterhouse had told him that the practice of the court had been quite different from what the prosecution said, but the chief justice crushed him at once with the command "Pray be quiet Mr. Ince."[6]

More precedents were given and clerks questioned, but when the defense asked for a single day's postponement for production of affidavits and certificates, Chief Justice Wright said that he could not do it and ruled that the bishops must plead. Sancroft tendered a plea in writing, and the other defendants said that they would stand by it. The plea was in effect that they would hold to their privilege as peers—not to plead without time to "imparl" upon the information against them.

Delay was entirely unacceptable to the king. Powys and Williams asked the court to reject such a plea. Williams was amazed that the court had already spent three hours "by my Watch" in this proceeding. Defense counsel desired a ruling that would settle the whole question of imparlance. The two sides referred to more cases, with reciprocal personal slurs. At last the judges gave their opinions: Wright thought the plea frivolous, as did Allibone, although Powell believed that the precedents having been "only obiter" treatment, there might be a judicial determination at that time. Holloway was for rejection of the plea. Wright ruled that the defendants must plead more regularly.[7]

They all pleaded not guilty. Attorney General Powys moved for trial "this day fortnight"; Sawyer, for the defense, agreed and asked for release of the bishops on their own recognizance (which they were willing to give in the Court of King's Bench as according with custom). Sawyer asked for a panel of forty-eight jurors, to be chosen by Astrey, the clerk of the Crown. Wright ruled that it should be so; the jurors would be selected from the "Freeholders Book," with each side to strike out twelve names. Archbishop Sancroft gave £200 as a recognizance, the other bishops £100 each. The court rose.[8]

The peers who had come to give bail for the bishops were not needed for that purpose, but their presence in court showed their sympathy to all observers. On the other hand, three of the judges were unfavorable to the defendants. The legal defense had distinguished itself under the circumstances, and the prosecution had caused laughter by calling the case "an almost treason." The crowds were on the bishops' side: "As they went to ye Waterside & so to Lambeth, there was ye greatest throng of people yt ever I saw (10 deep on each side on their knees begging their blessing) & ye hugest hollow & huzza, ecchoing from one shore to ye other as ever I heard." People made bonfires of celebration, but the archbishop would allow none near his house.[9]

A period of busy preparation on both sides and suspense among the people followed. It was evident that fear for the bishops went far beyond those directly concerned. The universities were almost in mourning. The clergy was so nearly unanimous in support of the accused and reacted so strongly against the clergymen who had read the declaration that one of the latter, Sidrach Simpson, rector of Stoke Newington (Middlesex) wrote to a bishop, probably Compton, that he had not been able to find proper direction and had been intimidated into reading the declaration on the first Sunday but not on the second.[10] The Dissenter John Howe, speaking for himself, would not contemplate profiting from replacement of Anglican ministers by Nonconformists, much to the delight of William Sherlock. (Sherlock had had much controversy with Dissenters and held valuable preferments.) The group of London Dissenters that had denied James the expected address of thanks had declared, "We are utterly against letting Papists into the government."[11]

The Anglican nobility and gentry stood appalled by the prosecution and for the most part held firm by the defendants. Lawyers, it was said, brought pressure to bear on Sir Creswell Levinz, forcing him (against his first inclination) to defend the bishops in court, threatening to bring him no more briefs. Sir John Maynard and other barristers, asked to be counsel for the prosecution, replied that "they would act according to their consciences and so spoiled the King's business."[12] The bishops themselves were staunch. Bishop White wrote on June 24 to excuse himself for not visiting Lord Hatton, "having very little time allowed me to dispose of my affaires here, so as to preserve my selfe from Utter Ruine, But tis no matter what becomes of Seven men, if their suffering may prevent that Comon Calamity which we feare."[13]

The king mustered what support he could get. The aged Bishop Croft of Hereford agreed to write a paper supporting with citations of

Scripture the authority of the crown to order the reading of the declaration.[14] A report ran, however, that part of what Croft wrote was
omitted from the printed version. Several other papers were published
against the bishops or their petition.[15]

Bishop Sprat of Rochester seems to have tried to argue Sancroft
into submission, for the archbishop, a man of simple life, had cause
to remark dryly to Sprat, who was extravagant, "I know how to live
on sixty pounds a year as well as I formerly did."[16] Such support as
Croft's and Sprat's probably misled James as much as any one else. It
is remarked in his *Life* that he "saw . . . that other Bisshops made not
the same difficulty, and since many complyd, it seem'd natural to
think those punishable, who did it not."[17]

The selection of the jury was important to both sides. Four
bishops met with a sheriff and representatives of the prosecution at Sir
Samuel Astrey's house. The sheriff returned a panel of forty-eight,
and each side seems to have chosen twelve for the final panel.[18] A
newswriter said of the resulting twenty-four, "[M]ost . . . are known
to be Church-of-England-men: several are employed by the King in
his navy and revenue; and some are, or once were, of the Dissenters'
party."[19] The prosecutors challenged Thomas Cooke (apparently the
goldsmith of London bearing that name) and Sir Thomas Clarges of
Westminster and kept them, among others, off the panel. Some
grumbled that "there was not fair dealing in the naming of the Jury."[20]

Twelve of the first thirteen names in the panel were chosen for the
actual jury (one of the first twelve was absent). The list was headed by
Sir Roger Langley, Bart., who was elected foreman. Langley was the
widower of the sister of Thomas Keighley (husband of James II's first
wife's sister, Frances Hyde) and had been sheriff of Yorkshire.
Langley was certainly interested in the navy, to the extent of getting a
commissionership of prizes later.[21] Sir William Hill, knight, of Ted-
dington, Middlesex, was second in rank. Roger Jenyns, of Hayes,
Middlesex, was related to Princess Anne's faithful servant, Sarah,
Lady Churchill.[22] Thomas Harriott of Islington was a Middlesex justice of the peace who had consented to the repeal of the penal laws
and test.[23] William Withers of Cripplegate, a linendraper of London,
had been a commissioner of the London lieutenancy in James's reign
and was later a knight, lord mayor, and member for the City in
several parliaments.[24] Michael Arnold, M.P. for Westminster in 1685
and the king's brewer, had the clearest connection with James, who
also made him a deputy lieutenant of Southwark in January 1688.[25]
Nicholas Grice of Haston was a son of a "London gent.," an Oxford

man and former student of Gray's Inn, and had married into a family of Hayes, Middlesex.[26] Thomas Done of Lincoln's Inn was auditor of the imprests (a revenue official) under Charles II and James. His post was later said to be worth "upwards of 1000 *l*. per ann[um]."[27] Richard Shoreditch of Twickenham was a sergeant at arms in the royal household.[28] Geoffrey Nightingale of Cripplegate had been sheriff of Suffolk in 1686, appointed by the king despite lack of residence there; He was to be one of the London lieutenancy in 1690.[29] Thomas Austin of South Mimms was said to have an income of £3,000 a year; William Avery, though a younger son, was a gentleman of Enfield.[30]

All, except Langley and Hill, were designated as esquires, the mark of property ownership and standing. Almost all were justices of the peace at one time or another. Several held posts or did business then or later requiring large amounts of ready money. Just such a jury, carefully picked from among property holders, was considered the best from the point of view of the time, for property and standing were thought to make for independence of mind. But several had connections with the court or administrative offices, and none can be identified as then an opponent of royal policy. The chief corrective force in the mind of any juror needing one was the sense of scorn, disgust, even danger that he would suffer if the trial was not fair.

On June 28, the day before the trial, a newswriter observed, "The officers of the Court [of King's Bench] will get well by the trial for places and conveniences to hear the same, which are sold excessively dear. Most of the nobility are also come up and will be present."[31] Accounts of the trial do not agree on the number of temporal lords present, but it seems that there were thirty or so. Halifax, Shrewsbury, Nottingham, and Danby appear again among those whose names are given, with the earl of Clarendon and the magnate earls of Pembroke and Chesterfield.[32] A fierce Whig, Viscount Newport, also appeared to support the bishops for the first time. "This Splendid Appearance was chiefly owing to the indefatigable Care and Solicitation of the Clergy, and especially of the Reverend Dr. [Thomas] Tennison."[33] The absence of several important Whigs, so far as we know (the earls of Devonshire and Macclesfield, and Lords Wharton, Delamer, Colepepper, and Montagu of Boughton), may be attributed either to special fears in that party or to the clergy's natural first appeal to Tories.

Present and supporting the prosecution were Bishops Cartwright and Sprat, whom the other peers ignored.[34]

The only report of the time consumed by the trial is that the proceedings lasted some five hours before commitment to the jury.[35]

The long manuscript account on which I rely (with due parallel reference to the standard printed one) may not be quite complete; it suggests that so many hours were passed in "debate or rather wrangling."[36]

After the usual formalities, the information was read that the accused bishops

> ye sd. 18th day of May . . . with force & armes &c. [a routine, meaningless phrase] at Westminster aforesd. in ye County of Middx aforesd. falcely & unlawfully maliciously seditiously & scandalusly a certain falce feighned malicious pernicious and Seditious Libell by them ye sd.aforesd. [list of Bishops' names] wth their own proper hands . . . subscribed the day yeare and place last menc̄oned in the presence of our sd. Ld. ye King . . . did publish & cause to be published . . . in manifest contempt of our sd. Ld. ye King & ye laws of the Kingdome of England . . . agt. ye peace of our sd. Ld. ye King his Crown & dignity.[37]

(It will be noticed that the authors of the information followed the usual practice of magnifying a simple offense, if offense it was, into something quite dreadful.)

Seventeenth-century trials were not modern: The judges could form the proceedings more freely than they could do today, and rules of evidence were ill defined. Readers acquainted with modern standards will probably find much of what follows strange.

The first task of the prosecution was to authenticate the signatures on the petition, a proceeding which met with unexpected difficulties. The witnesses were Sir Thomas Exton, dean of the Court of Arches; Sir Thomas Pinfold, chancellor of the diocese of Peterborough; William Middleton, collector of money for the rebuilding of St. Paul's Cathedral; a bookseller named Clavell; and others who were supposed to know the bishops' signatures very well.[38] Yet Exton was not willing to say that the text of the petition was certainly in Sancroft's hand, and Middleton, though he identified Sancroft's writing, could swear to no one else's. Clavell believed, but would not swear, that Bishop White's signature was authentic. There was much vagueness and some contradiction. Perhaps the witnesses were merely punctilious about oaths; there were no true experts. Be that as it may, Chief Justice Wright remarked to Solicitor Williams that the prosecution was "very Lame in this matter." Of course, Williams blamed the unwillingness of witnesses. Justice Powell raised what seems now the voice of reason: "Truly to me for a man to sware his beliefe in such a matter is an extraordinary thing."[39]

The question arose whether the case could proceed without better proof of the handwriting, especially, said Pemberton for the defense, as proof by comparison of hands would not pass in a cause worth forty shillings. The chief justice was in doubt; the opposing counsel fought a skirmish of precedents. Levinz interjected a question whether the petition had been written in Middlesex, as was stated in the information. (He must have known very well that it had been written at Lambeth, in Surrey.) A little later, Finch supported Levinz. Wright ruled that it was too early to consider the place of writing.

Justice Powell remarked that the proof of authorship was inadequate, but Chief Justice Wright and Justice Allibone thought it good enough. Justice Holloway advocated greater strictness as to proof in criminal cases than in civil ones. Finding the court divided, Wright demanded production of more proof. Attorney General Powys called on William Blathwayt, a clerk of the council and secretary at war. He testified that the bishops had acknowledged their signatures at the Privy Council meeting on June 8. Asked Justice Holloway, who was not perceptive, "Could not this have bin done at first & so saved al this trouble?"[40]

The prosecution counsel had wished to avoid using this acknowledgment to avoid revelation of the circumstances, although willing to have Blathwayt testify to it if necessary. They now attempted to prevent questions by defense counsel. Pemberton, knowing the whole story, tried to lay it before the jury by questioning Blathwayt. Though secretary at war, Blathwayt was no hero: He had instructions to say little, and when pressed by the bishops' defenders, he appealed to Wright for guidance. By law, the chief justice could only tell him to answer. A partial reply did not satisfy Sir Robert Sawyer; he demanded the whole. When the prosecution tardily went to Blathwayt's rescue, the defense insisted that the witness must tell all.

Proper sentiments came out as neatly as pocket handkerchiefs. Pemberton: "God forbidd that they should skreen ye King's evidence from telling ye truth." Sawyer: "And forbid yt half evidence should condemn any man." And Wright: "God forbid the truth should be concealed any way."

Under pressure from the chief justice, the unfortunate Blathwayt admitted that on June 8 the bishops at first did not admit their signatures and that before answering they had said that they hoped their answer would not be used against them. Alarmed at the odium about to be cast upon the king, Powys objected that the defense questions might be "onely to inflame & so possesse people with foolish notions and strang conceits," but the court let the testimony run on.[41] Blathwayt, under oath, had to speak frankly, and the bishops' ordeal in the council chamber gradually unfolded. Powys asked what this line was leading to. Pemberton confessed that he hoped to elicit testimony that the king had promised not to use the bishops' acknowledgment of their authorship to incriminate them. Solicitor Williams affected to be shocked: "[I]t is to put somthing upon ye King wch I dare hardly name." Justice Wright was, as often, not sure. Counsel clashed with personal remarks, but the questioning went on. When forced to say whether King James had made such a promise, Blathwayt replied that he had not. This seems to have been the truth, but counsel for the defense could make it appear that the bishops had assumed that James had accepted their request for one when he had pressed his own questions upon them two weeks before the trial. Or the jury was free to believe that James's extreme ungenerosity was as bad as a broken promise. Blathwayt, made to go over the matter again, pleaded failure of memory as to the exact words of acknowledgment used by the bishops. Powys, for his part, accused defense counsel of making the world believe that the king had broken a promise to their clients.[42]

The chief justice then proposed the reading of the petition in the court. The defense (after the irrepressible Finch had again raised the question of the writing of the petition in Middlesex) saved its objections and waived its opposition to the proposal. When the petition had been read, the prosecution rested its case "for the Present." Finch was then allowed to say, "[H]itherto they have totally failed for they have not proved any fact done by us in Middx nor have they proved any Publicacōn at all." Wright held that acknowledgment of authorship to the king had been made in Middlesex, and Levinz asked him whether confession in Middlesex to a crime in Yorkshire would make a man guilty in Middlesex.

Williams tried to make light of the matter, but it was serious: The bishops were defending themselves against a charge of a seditious libel in Middlesex; if the prosecution could not prove them to have offended there, the proceedings must fail, and Levinz promised to prove that Archbishop Sancroft had "not been in Middx for three or four months before." The information was harshly criticized as omitting the second paragraph of the petition, in which the bishops humbly requested that the king not insist on "their distributing and reading" the Declaration of Indulgence. Counsel then resumed argument on the site of the supposed offense. Williams, whose shoulders bore most of the work of the prosecution, asserted that the owning having been made in Middlesex, the place of the writing did not matter. Powys unwisely challenged the defense to prove that it was done elsewhere.

Pemberton and Levinz accepted the challenge. But first Francis Nichols, a servant of Sancroft's bedchamber, took the oath and testified that his master had not left Lambeth since the previous Michaelmas (September 29). A long argument followed whether the prosecution was required to prove anything beyond acknowledgment of signatures to have occurred in Middlesex. Finch said truly that that act had never been heard to be the publication of a libel. Serjeant Henry Trinder, a lesser light of the prosecution, said that publication could be assumed to have occurred in Middlesex. Neither Chief Justice Wright nor Justice Powell would swallow this presumption.[43]

Wright, Powell, and Holloway finally agreed that there was no proof that the bishops had done anything in Middlesex. Sir Bartholomew Shower, recorder of London and another lesser prosecutor, declared that delivery of the petition to the king was publication. Holloway and Powell would not agree with him. Shower asked whether persons could affront the king and the king have no way of punishing them. Wright said there was a way, but not without proof.

Solicitor General Williams offered proof of delivery to the king and recalled Blathwayt for testimony, but Blathwayt remembered no mention when the signatures had been acknowledged of how the petition had reached the hands of the king, "att which there was a great Laughter" in the court. The witness then said that he had heard the king say several times that the bishops had given him the petition, but when he could not remember, when pressed, that the bishops had admitted delivering the petition to the king, his admission caused "a great shout, which the Court rebuked."[44] The spectators were clearly happy for the bishops' sake.

William Bridgeman, another clerk of the council who was in the court, testified that he did not remember whether the bishops had been asked about delivery of the petition. Solicitor Williams suffered a rebuke from the bench for trying to elicit Bridgeman's personal opinion. Sir John Nicholas, another clerk of the council, also could not remember, and the people in court shouted again. Samuel Pepys, the diarist and secretary of the admiralty, only remembered that the bishops were generally understood to have delivered the petition; he recalled no discourse on the subject. Philip Musgrave, the fourth clerk of the council to testify, remembered that the bishops had all denied publishing the petition but not that they had been asked about its delivery. The archbishop had admitted writing the whole petition himself, without his secretary's help.[45]

Attorney General Powys and Solicitor General Williams then submitted the case to the jury. Chief Justice Wright began his summing up of the evidence. It has been the general opinion ever since that had there been no interruption, acquittal of the bishops for lack of evidence would have been overwhelmingly probable.[46]

Heneage Finch alarmed his colleagues in the defense by interrupting the summing up, to ask whether what the prosecution had offered was evidence, for if so, the defense had evidence to offer. Wright was irritated at the interruption. Pemberton, Pollexfen, and Levinz were aghast and begged Wright to continue, but the chief justice refused and made Finch go on with what he had to say, which was this: "[T]here being no Evidence agt us, wee must of Course be acquitted." We have been told that Finch's motive was to force the court to allow discussion of the legality of the dispensing power, but the record contains no mention of that at the time, only babble of further evidence or of the failure of the prosecution to offer evidence. My impression is that Finch made a stupid blunder which was retrieved, luckily for him, by the success of the defense counsel (not of Finch alone) in the subsequent arguments. At first, while the bishops' case seemed imperiled, "all men condemned Mr. Finch."[47]

Wright returned to his summary but was interrupted a second time, by Solicitor General Williams, who informed the court that a person "of very great quality" was coming to testify that the bishops had approached him in order to present the petition to the king. The chief justice wryly observed that this was the result of Finch's interruption: "[N]ow wee must stay." The proceedings then halted for a long time. After half an hour the prosecution tried to persuade the judges that proof of making the petition in Middlesex was unnecessary. Wright was unmoved. The defense begged the court to proceed with the case, but the pause continued, with feeble exchanges between the two sides.

The delay of the witness's appearance was explained under oath by the court crier; a messenger had gone for the earl of Sunderland, who had started for the court but returned when told the summing up had begun, and was now again on his way. At last the earl came into the court, in a sedan chair. He was already unpopular and had been blamed for the king's most arbitrary actions; furthermore, he had recently become a Catholic. He heard a cry: "Popish Dog; which it is like disordered him; for when he came in Court he trembled; changed colour, and looked down." An overpolite courtier named John Hodges bowed to the earl and was kicked hard from behind.[48]

Sunderland could say only that Bishops Lloyd of St. Asaph and Lake of Chichester had come to him with a petition that they intended to deliver to the king and wished to know the best method of doing it. They had offered it to him to read, but he had refused because the matter was not his business. Instead, he had gone to the king, who had told him the bishops could come when they pleased. Lloyd and Lake had then fetched the other bishops and gone to see the king. Questioning brought out that Sunderland did not know the contents of the petition at the time and had not seen it delivered.[49] Immediately after testifying, Sunderland left by a back way, fearing for his life. His testimony hardly changed the appearance of the case, as Pollexfen made clear in the court.

By that time, the defense had decided to open the wider issue, the alleged seditious character of the petition. Sir Robert Sawyer recalled the purport and wording of the petition, as well as the circumstances of presentation: The bishops had done nothing but what any man commanded to do a thing had a right to and be guilty of no crime. Sawyer read out the operative clause of the Declaration of Indulgence, by which the penal laws were supposed to be suspended. Did this clause have any effect? If not, the bishops had done nothing wrong; if so, great and evil consequences were to be feared.[50]

Just then a hurried exchange took place on the bench. Wright said to Justice Powell, "I must not suffer this, they intended to dispute the King's Power of suspending Laws." Powell replied, "My Lord, they must necessarily fall upon that Point; for if the King hath no such Power, (as clearly he hath not in my Judgement) the natural Consequence will be, that this Petition is not diminution of the King's Regal Power, and so not seditious or libellous." Wright gave way to this, though he disagreed with Powell's parenthesis: "I will hear them," the chief justice said, "let them talk until they are weary." That, Powell replied, was all he wished, "to hear them in defence of their Clients."[51] This exchange and Wright's concession probably made certain the verdict of the jury, if there had been any doubt before.

Sawyer showed that the bishops were warranted in petitioning by their position as spiritual judges and by the conscientious duty imposed on them under penalty of a curse by the statute of 1 Elizabeth I, c. 2, which made them guardians of the law of uniformity. "I allwayes lookt upon itt as the duty of an officer or Magistrate to tell the King

what is Law and what is not Law."⁵² Judges had actually refused to
obey royal commands when against law. Finch supported Sawyer
ably; there were to be no more blunders.

Counsel for the defense stood firmly on the ground that only the
king in Parliament could make, repeal, or suspend law. As Pemberton said, "[I]f the King may suspend the Lawes of the Church, I am
sure there is noe other Lawe but hee may suspend and if the King may
suspend all the Lawes of the Kingdome, in what a Condicon are all
the Subjects . . . for theire lives libertyes and propertyes. All at
Mercy."⁵³

The court and the counsel for the prosecution were impatient,
but defense brought precedents to show that Charles II and Richard
II had both required parliamentary authority to dispense with statutes. Laurence Halstead, keeper of the records at the Tower, attended
to render law French into English. A bill introduced into the House of
Lords in 1662 to give Charles II a dispensing power had not passed
the House of Commons.⁵⁴ The House of Commons had denied the
existence of the dispensing power in a resolution of February 14,
1672/73, and Charles II had withdrawn his own declaration, suspending the penal laws, as a result. The Commons's reply to James II's
speech to Parliament, November 16, 1685, showed the house's opinion that he had no such power.⁵⁵

This was real evidence about something, at last. Levinz summed
up ably and (for this trial) briefly. Delivery of the petition was not
proved; if delivery were proved, the petition was still no libel. In view
of the anathema with which the law threatened the bishops and the
doubted legality of the dispensing power, they had "al ye reason in ye
world to apply themselves to ye King." Finch said that he had no more
to say. Sawyer dealt with the statute of King Henry VIII enabling the
king to make law, a statute since repealed. Somers tied up the loose
ends of the cases of *Thomas v. Sorrell,* which he said denied the
suspending power, and *Godden v. Hales* (under James II), affirming
the dispensing power but (said Somers) denying the suspending one.⁵⁶

Attorney General Powys opened the summary for the prosecution with reflections on the manners of the counsel for the defense. As
for Richard II, his time was one of rebellion ending in deposition, and
talk about it was not applicable to this case. A House of Commons
resolution was that of only one part of the legislative body; King
Charles had never agreed that he had no such power. Brought to the
point by Chief Justice Wright, Powys took his stand on the legally
correct but morally indefensible ground that a libel need not be false

to be punishable, for the reason that it tended to disturb the peace. Petitioning was open to all, but did anyone therefore have the right to tell the king to his face that he was acting illegally? There was no greater proof of the tendency, said Powys, than the crowd in the court and the speeches which had been made, raising "discontent & jealousies, as if ye free course of law ware restrained & arbitrary will & pleasure set up in stead of it." The bishops might have raised their objection in Parliament, which was to meet in November, but nothing would serve them except to complain as they did, out of Parliament. The illegality of the petition proved its malice and sedition.[57]

Solicitor General Williams repeated much of the preceding argument, asserting that the bishops had no right to petition outside Parliament. Here Justice Powell said aside to Wright that this was a strange doctrine; "If that be Law, the Subject is in a miserable Case." But Wright let Williams go on; as he had given great liberty to the bishops' counsel, he was probably wise to do so. Williams was not convincing. In another exchange of asides with Powell, Wright denied that Williams was imposing on the judges: "[F]or my part, I do not believe one word he says."[58] Williams's auditors hissed when he sneered at resolutions of the House of Commons. Twice Wright found him far off the subject and brought him back again. Powell seemed to be convincing Justice Holloway, for he joined in Powell's practice of pricking the balloons blown up by Williams. People in court again hissed Williams when he said, not for the first time, that the bishops should have acquiesced in anything they were commanded to do against their consciences until Parliament met. Powys appealed to the court and the jury to take notice of the hissing.[59]

Chief Justice Wright now began to make himself safe with the king. Petitioning was a right of the bishops, he said, but should not be in "this reflective way." Justice Powell was less timid: The bishops had been commanded to distribute the declaration before Parliament could meet, and they could not disobey without explaining except in contempt. Serjeant Sir Robert Baldock, a minor counsel for the prosecution, argued for obedience, and Powell had to remind him that the bishops were charged with libel, not disobedience. (Everyone in the court must have known that though Powell was right, Baldock was near the true motive of the king in ordering prosecution of the bishops.) A few sputters more were emitted by Sir Bartholomew Shower and Serjeant Henry Trinder, who had done little to earn their fees, and the prosecution rested for all time.[60]

Wright led in the summing-up, so long postponed. Declarations in Parliament were not law; the dispensing power was not before the court. The jury had to decide whether the bishops had been proved to have published the petition and whether the petition was a libel. It was enough to believe that the petition quoted in the information was the one delivered to the king. If that was the jury's decision, and only in that case, the jury should decide whether the petition would "disturb the Governmt or make mischiefe or a Stirr among ye People." If so, it was a libel. Wright stated that he believed the petition to be such but asked the other judges to give their opinions.[61]

Justice Holloway told the jury that for anyone to say anything after the chief justice summed up was not customary, but this was a special case. He believed that the bishops' intentions and the circumstances should be considered. If the intention was only "to save themselves harmless & to Free themselves from blame in shewing ye reason of their disobedience to ye Kings comand . . . I cannot think it is a Lybell. It is left to you . . . but that is my opinion."[62]

Powell, speaking in his turn, could perceive no sedition or other crime "fixt upon" the bishops. A libel must be false, malicious, and seditious. The petition was not false or malicious; it had been decently and humbly presented. The objection raised against the dispensing power by the defense was a proper one, for he had made a careful search for a case which turned upon a valid royal dispensing power and found none. Powell saw no difference between the power to dispense with the penal laws of religion and that to dispense with any other laws: "[I]f this be once allowed of there will need no Parliamt all ye Legislature will be in ye King wch is a thing worth considering & I leave ye issue to God & yor Consciences."[63]

Justice Allibone, the only Catholic on the bench, took a high line indeed in supporting the king: "[Y]e Governmt ought not to be impeached by argumt nor ye exercise of ye Governmt shaken by argumt . . . no private man can take upon him to write concerning ye Governmt at all for what has any private man to do wth. ye Governmt. if his interest be not stirred or shakened [sic]. It is ye business of Subjects to mind only their owne properties & interest."[64] Petition was right only in one's own particular interest, not "to meddle with a matter yt relates to ye Governmt." Allibone strained a precedent of James I's reign, on a petition accompanied by a threat, to apply it to this case. Justice Powell corrected him from greater knowledge, but without much effect on Allibone's opinion. Allibone closed by agreeing that a libel need not be untrue and that "every Libel against the

Government carries in it Sedition" and repeating that the bishops had contradicted the actual exercise of the government.[65]

Wright offered the jurymen wine before leaving them to their work. They asked for the statute book and relevant papers, and the court allowed them all but the votes of the House of Commons. Then the judges arose, and the jury fell to considering the case. The bishops went, "with all the privacy they could, to their respective abodes." Again the people cheered them.[66]

The deliberations lasted all night, while officers of the court watched, and guards supplied by the defense counsel watched the officers, to prevent tampering with the jury. In secondary works the length of the process has usually been attributed to a single stubborn juror resisting acquittal, but this seems to exaggerate obstinacy to a high degree. It is more likely that the sources are correct that show the jury as beginning 7–5, or 8–4, for a verdict of not guilty, with gradual attrition during the night on the weaker side until only Michael Arnold (the king's brewer) held out.[67] It seems probable that Thomas Harriott, who had approved the repeal of the penal laws and test act, was one of those initially in favor of conviction. Who the others might have been can only be guessed. About midnight, and also about three in the morning, the discussions became so loud that people outside the jury room could hear the noise.

Argument was not the sole pressure. The practice of the time denied to jurors food, fire, drink, tobacco, and candles until they had agreed; the deliberations therefore took place mostly in the dark. We are told that Thomas Austin (he of £3,000 a year) undertook to answer any reasoning of Arnold's and threatened to stay there until he was no bigger than a tobacco pipe rather than find such a petition to be a crime. At four o'clock the water provided for washing had all been drunk, and Arnold stood alone in the face of the other eleven jurors. When he had given up hope that they would yield and (presumably) could bear hunger and isolation no longer, he joined the majority.

It was six in the morning of June 30. Word that the jury had reached a verdict was sent to the judges. The jury stayed together to obviate any attempt to influence its members either to change their minds or not to appear. The court reassembled at ten o'clock. Sir Samuel Astrey went through the formula for eliciting a verdict, and Sir Roger Langley, foreman, announced that it was not guilty, "At which there was a very great Shout."[68] Lord Halifax, we are told, stood up and waved his hat, and continuous cheering that could be heard at Temple Bar began. As the news spread throughout the City, so did the cheering: "[T]he crowd and the rabble, the shouts and huzzas yesterday, and the *Io Triumphe's* today were incredible," said a newswriter.[69]

Solicitor General Williams moved to have the shouters committed. A student of Gray's Inn was arrested, then reprimanded by the chief justice, who said he also was glad of the acquittal, but "your Manner of rejoycing here in Court is indecent." Wright advised him to rejoice in his chamber or elsewhere. Wright's son-in-law stood surety, and the young man was discharged. The court then rose, and the bishops went away.[70]

They went "with great shoutings & acclamations; their Councill with great applause. W. W. [Solicitor Williams] was hist as he went." People prayed that God would direct the bishops. Bishop Cartwright was called "a grasping wolf in sheep's clothing" as he left the court.[71]

For all the sharp, even bitter, exchanges between counsel, the careful hedging of Chief Justice Wright, and the blind prejudgment of Allibone, the trial had resulted in what we must call a just verdict. Its proceedings had been much fairer than some of those of the "Popish-Plot" period. There had been no bullying from the bench, though Wright had sometimes been testy. The prosecution had shown bad judgment; Williams, to whom the lead had fallen, has since been described as only a good second counsel. The jury justified itself in the end, however questionable its selection may have seemed in the beginning. The jurymen enjoyed great public esteem at the moment, except for the unfortunate Arnold, whose late conversion became common knowledge. The bishops were heroes.

The night of June 30 was boisterous, here and there riotous. Noblemen and gentlemen rode among the poor people, throwing money to them, "To drink the health of the king, the lords bishops, and the jury."[72] The capital was ablaze with light; fifty-six bonfires were counted between Charing Cross and Somerset House alone.[73] "Almost all the Papists in London had bonfires made at their doors, and in most places, and Myld. Arundel and others were made to pay for them. [Lord] Salisbury's servants came out, fired and killed a man, but the Rabble rallied and drove them in." The man killed was said to have been a beadle come to put out the fire, perhaps the head beadle of St. Clement's who was mortally wounded in Beaufort Street, the Strand, during the celebration.[74] Even the king had to endure a bonfire before his palace gate, in sight of the guards and against his orders.[75]

The mobs wounded several and robbed some. "Many will be called to an account," a newswriter told John Ellis. "Yesterday the Lord Mayor appeared before the King and his Council, to give account of those few bonfires which were made in the City by some of too fiery and indiscreet zeal."[76] James was said to have threatened the City of London with the quartering of troops; on the other hand, the soldiers were said to be contaminated by sympathy with the bishops. Terriesi, the Tuscan resident in England, thought the celebration greater than that for the birth of the Prince of Wales, at which "among other oddities, were . . . seen soldiers putting down their arms, and drinking the health of the bishops, drinking to the confusion of the pope, burning the pope [in effigy] etc."[77] The soldiers in the summer encampment at Hounslow cheered loudly for the bishops' acquittal when word came. James was struck by this, but remarked, "So much the worse for them."

In other cities, the people responded similarly to the news. Arthur Charlett, a fellow of University College, wrote from Oxford, "People in these parts will drink Bps Healths, and Bps Councill, and Bps Jury."[78] At Peterborough, the bells rang from three in the morning until nightfall for the acquittal of Peterborough's bishop (White) and the other six. (Peterborough's dean, Symon Patrick, was one of the leading supporters of the bishops.) The people (for once, one can use that word without exaggeration) had been alarmed and were now, probably against expectation, relieved. There were also bonfires at Exeter, Bristol, Gloucester, and Salisbury, a single Italian newsletter tells us.[79] Parish accounts often record payments made to bell ringers on this occasion.[80] In Somersetshire, a crowd celebrating the acquittal burned effigies of the pope and the new Prince of Wales.[81]

The bishops had various bills to pay. They offered the jury the usual fees and a dinner (altogether estimated to cost between 150 and 200 guineas); the jury declined the offer.[82] Barristers for the defense got £240 16s. all told; attorneys and solicitors a mere £5 18s. at the time, and £53 15s. in October. Officers of the court received £78 10s. Searching and copying records cost £64 19s. 6d. (£3 4s. 6d. more paid in October), gratuities £43 6s. 6d. Occasional expenses of many kinds came to £123 9s. 2d. (10s. more was paid in October). The grand total of costs of the defense was £614 8s. 8d. To pay that sum, the bishops taxed themselves 6 percent of their annual incomes. Later, each contributed in addition 10s. 5d. per £100 income to defray the small remainder.[83] As the bishops' annual revenues ranged from £350 (Trelawny of Bristol) to £4,000 (Sancroft of Canterbury), this was much fairer than equal division of the costs, which would have required Trelawny to contribute one-quarter of his income and Sancroft one forty-fifth of his. By taxation, Sancroft and Turner paid together nearly two-thirds of the total.

The Crown's expenses must also have been heavy, but James had the Crown's income to pay them. Another payment was a baronetcy for Solicitor General Williams. A third was the dismissal of Justices Powell and Holloway for their independent conduct at the trial. James had planned to win, not to lose; he had not wished his dispensing power to be debated; and he had no compunction about punishing men who crossed his plans. He also wished to punish the makers of bonfires to celebrate the acquittal who had refused to disperse on command. Catholic and "fanatick" (Dissenting) justices of the peace were set on to instigate proceedings against them in Middlesex, but the Middlesex grand jury, after having been sent to reconsider the matter four times, resolutely returned a bill of *ignoramus,* though "the proof was very plane against them." Thirteen of those tried at the Guildhall in London were condemned to whippings.[84] All the same, at Middlesex Quarter Sessions, Thomas Harriott, one of the former jurors of the bishops, repented and publicly retracted his consent to the repeal of the penal laws and test.[85]

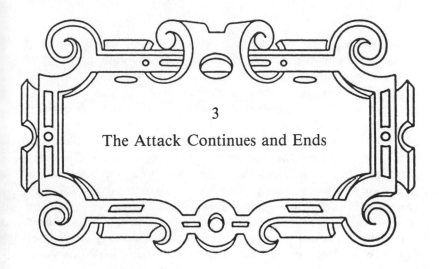

3

The Attack Continues and Ends

IT WAS VIRTUALLY CERTAIN to knowing observers that the king, though he had failed to convict the bishops, would also seek revenge on the new opposition among the lower clergy.[1] Parish ministers who had not read the declaration in their churches were open to the charge of disobedience. On July 12, James's Ecclesiastical Commission sent orders to all archdeacons and chancellors to furnish on the approaching August 16 the names of clergymen in their archdeaconries and dioceses who had not read it. The king's precise intention was not known, but obviously it was not friendly. A few days later, the news ran that Bishop Crew of Durham had suspended several clergymen, including his own chaplain, for that offense and that Bishop Cartwright of Chester intended to suspend clergymen for it, especially in his own city, "where the Dean [James Arderne, a Cambridge man of a Cheshire family] is affirmed to have promised the reading, and then to have lien sick a-bed when the day came, so that it was not read in the Cathedral."[2]

At the same time, the acquitted bishops and their sympathetic colleagues were leading a revival of Anglican piety, going to their dioceses and holding catechizings and confirmations. Sancroft and Frampton confirmed several thousands of children at Lambeth and Croydon, we are told. (The Catholic Bishop Philip Ellis and the Jesuit schoolmaster Andrew Pulton were then confirming "some hundreds" at their chapel at the Savoy.) Unity with Dissenters was furthered by conferences with them at which the archbishop and the clergy of London hoped to accommodate differences of ceremony, with the aim of proposing changes in the next parliament.

Sancroft himself prepared a statement of "[S]ome heads of things to be more fully insisted upon," for the guidance of the bishops in addressing the clergy and the people in their dioceses. Clergymen should often remind themselves of their vows, oaths, and subscriptions, and their obligations thereby; they should also be active and zealous in their duty and set examples of strictness in "all Holy Conversation." (Throughout the statement Sancroft chooses words carefully so as to avoid giving legitimate offense to his royal master.) Diligent catechizing to prepare children for confirmation and instruction on Christian belief and the obligations of baptismal vows should be "insisted upon." Ministers should perform daily services decently, affectionately, and gravely; such services should be as frequent as possible, especially on the days appointed by the rubric and the canons. They should prevail upon their parishioners to take Communion often and should offer it once a month, with preparation by preaching "for worthy receiving of it." Clergymen should remind their flocks at least four times a year that all foreign jurisdiction (the pope's) had been abolished and that they owed obedience to the king "in all things *Lawfull*" and "patient submission to the rest." They should show the "kindest respect" to the gentry and nobility for the help and "Countenance" they had given the Church of England and exhort all Anglicans to steadfastness in the faith, especially against *"Popish Emissaries,"* and to reformation of their lives.

The Anglican clergy should anticipate activity of "Romish Emissaries" around people on the verge of death by visiting the sick to give instruction, settle doubts, and comfort them, praying for them and preparing them to receive the Eucharist. Lastly, they should associate wisely and kindly with non-Anglicans to win them for the church, especially "our *Brethren* the *Protestant Dissenters"* — visit them, receive their visits, and persuade them to compliance with the church if possible, otherwise to walking "by the same Rule" and to belief that the Anglican bishops were the enemies of Roman errors, superstitions, idolatries, and tyrannies; ministers should also exhort Dissenters to join in prayer for the reunion of all reformed churches against the common enemies and for agreement in the truth of God's word, meeting in one communion and life "in perfect Unity and godly Love."[3]

The concerned bishops were thus to spread their views and encourage emulation of their actions throughout the country. But James II also took his ideas and policies to the people. In other times the itinerant justices of assize, appointed by the king and judging by his law, had served him as gatherers and disseminators of information. In the summer of 1688, James II resolved to have his judges take all occasions to persuade the king's subjects, "especially such as would be esteemed truly loyal and well affected," to support the king's Declaration of Indulgence and tell them that the king intended soon to call Parliament and try to get the declaration "past into a Law." (This device was to be applied at the same time as others, such as remodeling the corporations of towns and remanning the commissions of the peace in the counties.) The king could not doubt that "such as desire the common good" would assist him since the "advancement of Land" and the "improvement of the Trade and Manufactures" were concerned in it. The judges were to tell Anglicans that the king would keep his promises in the declaration and to encourage people of all beliefs to "live friendly together" and unite to effectuate the king's intentions for that "common good."

The judges were to remove fears and jealousies that might be insinuated by ill-affected persons, by showing that the king had for three years been a gracious prince with designs only for "universal happiness" and contradicting idle and false reports. People were to be persuaded that liberty of conscience had already increased British trade, just as it had furthered the increase in wealth of some of England's neighbors. And the judges should let everyone know that the king was resolved to trust, confide in, and reward all his subjects who zealously helped him to carry out his plans.[4]

This was a double attack upon the clergy: proceedings against the parochial ministers who had not read the declaration, coupled with the propaganda for the declaration in which the judges were expected to play a part (side by side with propaganda by printed sheets, pamphlets, and even books).

The proceedings, however, depended on archdeacons and chancellors for the furnishing of names of offenders. As early as July 24, an informant wrote to Lord Herbert of Chirbury, "I am credibly told that some of the Arch Deacons & Chancellors . . . have desired to be excused from that employ."[5] On August 6/16, the Tuscan Terriesi reported that nearly all of them refused to send names to the Ecclesiastical Commission and challenged its competence. Even the churchwardens of Oxfordshire, summoned to witness against minis-

ters who had not read the declaration, escaped questioning.[6] When
the commission met on August 16, it was to learn that "little or no
Inquiry had been made." Presentments of offenders came from only
five jurisdictions — Durham, Lincoln, St. David's, Buckingham, and
Chester.[7] (Buckingham was an archdeaconry, Chester the diocese, but
whether the reports for the others represent the whole dioceses or
archdeaconries of the same name within them does not appear.)
Several of the archdeacons and chancellors had gathered at Doctors'
Commons, the home of the doctors of civil law in London, to consider their defense for refusing to return names. Eight adopted the
plea that they had no authority to make the necessary inquiries
without episcopal visitation; six refused either to make that defense or
to render a return; three of those present gave way and presented
names; and one alleged that he had not been legally served with the
demand.[8] Others "sent up word, that they either never saw the Declaration, or saw it by chance, or saw not the order for reading it." This
was an uncertain account; the matter was kept private.[9]

A few parish ministers acquired the favor of the king, having
read the declaration as prescribed. One was Timothy Hall, of All
Hallows Staining, London. Him James nominated suddenly to the
vacant see of Oxford on August 18, though Hall had no degree beyond his Oxford B.A. or other distinction of any kind. Moreover, he
had been ejected from a parish in 1662, possibly as a Dissenter, and
was suspected of Presbyterian beliefs, though he was a conformist in
1688, and he may have had other shortcomings. His alleged inade-
quacy and servility made him instantly the scorn of the knowledgeable: "The B[ishop] of O[xford] fills every Mouth; I never knew any
under a more Universal Odium; The B[ishop] of C[hester, Cartwright]
is a St to him."[10] Another who had accepted such odium hoped for
suitable compensation — Dr. John Geary (or Gery), archdeacon of
Buckingham and prebendary of Lincoln Cathedral. He had two
Leicestershire parishes and may have read the declaration in one or
both of them, for he certainly read it somewhere, and other clergymen of Leicestershire would have nothing to do with him. He also
reported those in his archdeaconry who disobeyed. Acting on a rumor
that Bishop Barlow of Lincoln was dying, it seems, Dr. William Foster, chancellor of that diocese, solicited the earl of Huntingdon, an
ecclesiastical commissioner, on August 13 to ask help in getting Geary
promoted to Barlow's place. Foster made a merit of Geary's having
read the declaration. Huntington, a patron of Geary, may have received the application with favor, but Barlow lived longer than that

kind of merit. Geary no doubt bore up under the loss of a bishopric in the enjoyment of several other preferments.[11]

James is known to have acted at once against a minister who did not read—Dr. Francis Hawkins, chaplain of the Tower of London. His position was apparently held at the king's pleasure, and the king was pleased to remove him while the bishops' case was still pending. A far more respectable figure than Hall, Hawkins was a semidemimartyr for the Anglican cause. He was also a tiger for his rights and insisted on keeping his house at the Tower, which, he said, belonged to him. He did not starve, for he was also dean of Chichester and vicar of Willesden, Middlesex, and he continued to enjoy his freeholds in those places throughout the crisis.[12]

Dr. Thomas Wainwright, chancellor of Chester, reported the names of those who had read the declaration rather than those who had not, for the latter were too many.[13] No doubt, he hoped to profit from it. Bishop Thomas Lamplugh of Exeter had given written approbation to the bishops' petition, but had trimmed, complained his colleague Trelawny of Bristol:

> his Lorp. acting according to a settl'd maxim of his own I will be safe, had given order for ye publishing ye declaration, notwithstanding ye Bisp. of Bathe & Wells's, & my letters to him, & was at last brought to recall ym by ye deanes [Richard Annesley's] sending him word yt if he would betray ye church he should not ye cathedral, for he would rather be hang'd at ye doors of it, yn ye declaration should be read there or in any part of his jurisdiction, wch is large in ye county. ye gentry & clergy complained to me very much of ye. Bishps giving a church to the mayor [of Exeter, Sir Thomas Jefford] for his conventicle (in which ye declaration was read).[14]

The ecclesiastical commissioners were unhappy in their position. The group that met on August 16 included only one bishop (Cartwright) and one judge (Sir Edward Herbert, chief justice of Common Pleas), one die-hard courtier (the earl of Huntingdon), and the increasingly insecure earl of Sunderland. A letter from Bishop Sprat, an absent commissioner, informed those present that he declined to sit any longer to punish clergymen, especially "those of his own order, the Bishops." "Now, My Lords, the safty of the Church of England seeming to be exceedingly concerned in this Prosecu͠con, I must declare that I cannot with a safe Conscience Sitt a Judge in this Case upon so many pious and excellent men, with whom (if it be God's Will) it rather becomes me to suffer, than to be in the least

Accessary to their Sufferings." This was his feeling, though he had read the Declaration of Indulgence. Sprat asked not to be required to attend further sittings of the commission.[15]

Lacking cooperation from most of the chancellors and archdeacons, the commission ordered a visitation by all with "Ecclesiastical Jurisdiction" and adjourned to December 6. Its members probably did not expect it actually to meet again, and it did not. Shortly after this fiasco, Bishop Sprat was preaching before the exemplarily Protestant Princess Anne at Tonbridge.[16] There were to be no proceedings against the clergymen who had disobeyed the king's command as to the Declaration of Indulgence.

The other effort, to gain support by the persuasion of the judges, soon became one to discredit the bishops, though the king's written instructions did not mention them. No doubt there were other, perhaps oral, instructions, for the tone and content of the utterances of the different judges on all the circuits were fairly consistent (that is, the utterances of judges who had much to say).

As usual, the judges of the central common-law courts divided themselves among the circuits. Sir Richard Allibone went the Home Circuit with Justice Sir Thomas Street. At Croydon, Allibone charged the grand jury of Surrey on the need for love, unity, and liberty of conscience, closing with an argument that the petitioning bishops, though found not guilty by a jury, were still guilty. "Any man may petition in his private affairs to his Majesty; but what have we to do to petition about Government?" asked he, "for that which is so, 'tis a Libel, and of bad consequence."[17] These are Allibone's words, already familiar to us from the proceedings of the trial, but James's irreconcilability shows through them. A verdict was not final if the king did not like it.

Allibone did not live long enough to learn that his doctrine would not become part of the constitution. That same month, a hostile writer reported that he had caught "a great cold . . . in passing through the wilds [Weald] of Kent, as well as by his overheating himself by his vehemence in declaiming against the Bishops in his charge to the Juries."[18] He died shortly after.

Richard Heath, a baron of the exchequer,

> told the jury at Northampton that the Bps were guilty of a factious & seditious Libell, but were so crafty as to take care there shd not be evidence against him [sic]. He told them they must believe him because he was upon his oath. He advis'd them to bring the Bone-fire

men in as Rioters, but they found the Bill Ignoramus. He ask'd the Sheriff [probably Thomas Andrews, Esq.] whether he had got a good Jury. The Sh. said they were all Persons of great loyalty & honour. Upon wch the J[udge] sd, But I doubt whether they will do the King's business.[19]

The recently promoted Sir John Rotherham, a baron of the exchequer and former Whig, went the Oxford Circuit; he charged the grand jury of Oxfordshire and took the opportunity to attack the clergy in general for debauchery, laziness, and greed, and also to call the bishops' petition a libel. "Great exceptions" were taken against such tirades, and the gentlemen who usually trooped to meet and honor assize judges now more often stayed away; "at Berks and Oxford particularly, only the High Sheriff and his sons met them." The judges who were not hot enough, however, were not expected to hold their posts.[20] Grand juries' members were required to attend, but they showed independence (or rebelliousness) by refusing to express abhorrence of the bishops' petition and by attempting to indict Catholic justices of the peace.[21] James II had accomplished absolutely nothing by his attack; clergymen were no more cowed than the grand juries. Bishop Frampton preached before the judges at Gloucester "of ye consequence of stretching a Conscience for any worldly preferment, upon wtt [what] will profit to gain ye whole world & lose our own souls."[22]

Oxford University, which had once been a nursery of passive obedience, was now almost mutinous. It refused Timothy Hall the honorary doctorate that the king directed it to confer and that would once have been virtually automatic (for a new bishop without a doctor's degree).[23] All Souls College received a royal mandate to give to John Cartwright, son of the bishop of Chester, the college living of Barking (Essex) that the bishop had resigned "into the king's hand," so that the son might have it. Bishop Cartwright was then almost as odious as Timothy Hall, and his son was, like many bishops' sons, a snatcher of preferment with his father's connivance. (John Cartwright was already a prebendary of Lincoln and Worcester.) The college replied to the king that it would "consider of it." King James then kept the bishop in the living as before.[24]

The king's pitiless persecution of the legitimate fellows of Magdalen College continued. A number had already been dispossessed for refusal to turn out one president of the college and put in another, Bishop Samuel Parker of Oxford. On August 7, six still in place who refused to recognize the Catholic Bishop Bonaventure Giffard as president in succession to Parker were deprived of their fellowships on the pretext of nonresidence.[25]

The twenty-six fellows who had first been ejected were also barred by an order of December 10, 1687, from "any Ecclesiastical dignity, Benefice or Promotion," and those not yet in holy orders were barred from ordination.[26] This prohibition was highly inhumane as well as unjust. Most of the fellows had no prospect other than as scholars or as clergymen, and they had provoked the king by standing by college statutes to which they were sworn.

Without attracting much attention, it seems, several of the deprived fellows obtained nominations to benefices all the same and were instituted by appropriate bishops. At least two such cases are recorded in print: Charles Penyston, presented to the vicarage of Sandhurst, near Gloucester, by Bishop Trelawny as patron and instituted by Bishop Frampton; and James Fayrer, nominated to Downe, Kent, by the patron, the rector of Orpington, himself a nominee of the archbishop of Canterbury. As Downe was a peculiar of Canterbury, Fayrer may have been instituted by Sancroft himself. Both of these cases occurred only a short time after the issue of the prohibition.[27] If these three bishops were so bold in keeping the Magdalen men from destitution, there were probably other cases.

Bishop Frampton met a legal problem connected with the illegal possession of Magdalen College by intruders. The college owned, as All Souls and other colleges did, the right of presentation to college livings, generally reserved for fellows who had completed their studies and wished to leave the university for the active ministry of the church, in which they could (by the way) get married. On August 1, 1688, died Dr. Edmund Diggle, a former fellow in possession of the rectory of Slimbridge (Gloucestershire) in Frampton's diocese, worth £200 a year. Bishop Giffard, as president of Magdalen, appointed Charles Hawles, an ordained Anglican priest and one of the few legitimate fellows remaining in the college, to Slimbridge. Hawles went to Standish, where Frampton was staying, with documents signifying his nomination.

While waiting to see the bishop, Hawles made a clumsy attempt to tamper with the papers he had brought, which attempt Frampton's nephew, who was present, prevented. When Frampton appeared, Hawles offered him the papers; the presentation was signed by James Almond, made steward of the college by the intruders. He also presented an instrument authorizing Almond to make the presentment and signed by the intruded president, Bishop Giffard. Frampton asked Hawles where was Madaura, of which Giffard called himself bishop in his signature ("Bonaventure Epis. Madaurensis"). Hawles replied that he knew only that "the gentleman so subscribing was made President by the King."

Frampton deferred the institution of Hawles to the limit allowed by law while he sent to consult eminent lawyers, but he solved his problem himself. He noticed that Almond had dated the presentation one day before Giffard had authorized him to make it, which explained Hawles's wish to alter one or other of the two documents. Hawles returned, and Frampton positively denied him institution, but James II's quarrel with the church was patched over before Hawles's case could be brought to court.[28]

The legitimate, but ejected, fellows also wished to fill Slimbridge, and most of them favored nomination of Dr. Thomas Bayley. When they were in a position to do so, on the ominous Fifth of November (Guy Fawkes Day, celebrated to commemorate the detection of the Catholic "Gunpowder Plot"), they presented him, and Frampton instituted him.[29]

Hawles also obtained nomination to the vicarage of Willoughby, and the suspended bishop of Lichfield and Coventry may have instituted him, but his position there would have been extremely poor when the tide turned, and he resigned it in 1689.[30]

On Saturday, July 21, the old duke of Ormond died, leaving vacant the chancellorship of Oxford University and occasioning another clash between the university and the king. The duke had been a man after Oxford's heart and its staunch friend. His son, styled earl of Ossory, had made a great reputation as a soldier but predeceased his father. The duke died in Dorset, and the news went from there to Oxford. It was the duty of the university's convocation to fill the vacancy, which it proceeded to do as quickly as possible. It met on the morning of Monday, July 23, and may have considered the marquis of Halifax and the earls of Nottingham and Abingdon; a newswriter told John Ellis that all three had parties in the election. Nevertheless, consideration cannot have been long, for at about ten that same morning, convocation elected the second duke of Ormond, grandson of the first. The intention was certainly to escape the king's nomination of one of his obnoxious supporters. On July 24, a royal mandate reached the university, requiring the election of Lord Chancellor Jeffreys to be chancellor also of the university. Vice Chancellor Gilbert Ironside, of Wadham College, wrote to notify the king that the election had already taken place and to excuse the university from revoking its choice.[31]

James had had the experience of trying to reverse the election of a president of Magdalen College. Perhaps learning from the experience, he chose not to press the university but to have the young duke withdraw. Secretary of State Middleton wrote from Windsor to the earl of Rochester, a fellow Tory and former father-in-law of Ormond, asking the earl to let the duke know that he should decline the chancellorship or, if he had accepted it, resign it, as he "probably may not appear in publick for some time."[32] This explanation seems to allude to the new chancellor's youth, but Ormond was not so young that he could not appear in public. If James had looked back over his own life, he would not have found it odd to have been lord high admiral at twenty-seven or that he had made his illegitimate son a colonel and governor of Portsmouth before his eighteenth birthday. By his rank and family, Ormond was a personage and could hold high office without causing remark at twenty-three, as he then was.

Rochester and Ormond happened to be traveling to Windsor together on July 26 when a messenger stopped them to give Rochester Middleton's letter. On reading it, Ormond turned about and went home, obviously affronted, while Rochester continued on his way. The earl may be presumed to have represented the bad effect of the letter to the king, for on July 27 Ormond told the earl of Clarendon that Rochester had sent word that James "did desist in the matter of the university," with advice that Ormond should "make hast to wayt on his Maty."; the duke complied.[33]

Leopold Finch, the scandalous warden of All Souls College, was one of the first to congratulate the new chancellor. On August 23, a delegation from the university went to the duke's house in St. James's Square, Westminster, conferred on him a doctorate of laws, and installed him as chancellor. Afterward, he entertained "his noble friends, acquaintance, and the academians" in a temporary wooden hall set up in his garden, in a fashion "equall to if not exceeding any banquet made by the king." Eight hundred dishes were served. The "noble friends" were the marquis of Worcester, son of the duke of Beaufort and Ormond's brother-in-law; the earls of Oxford, Radnor, Shrewsbury, Devonshire (Ormond's uncle by marriage), Scarsdale (groom of the stole to Prince George of Denmark), Craven, Danby, Berkeley, Rochester, Roscommon, and Ranelagh (a cousin of Rochester's wife); Viscounts Cholmondeley, Lumley, and Falkland; and the heir of the duke of Queensberry, styled earl of Drumlanrig.[34] The king's attempt to prevent Ormond's installation and the wound to the duke's dignity so inflicted made it natural that a number of the most discontented notables of Great Britain should rally to him by eating and drinking with leaders of the church and the university.

Wise men about the king probably advised him to take a further step of reconciliation; in September he conferred on Ormond the Garter that had belonged to his grandfather after rumor had given it to several other men. That was perhaps supposed to have appeased Ormond completely and stopped his mouth.

It was one of the details of a new policy, adopted under a threat of invasion. The old one, preferred by James II, was one of demands followed by force when refused. What was remarkable was the series of refusals, each of which might be described as rebellion and was thought to be rebellion by the king: refusal to distribute the declaration, refusal to read it aloud in the churches, refusal to convict the bishops, refusal to report those who had not read, refusal to recognize a Catholic bishop as head of an Oxford college, refusal to deny the deprived fellows of Magdalen preferment, avoidance of electing a chancellor of Oxford University to please the king in such a way as nearly to refuse it, and refusal of the elected chancellor to demit his office on the king's direction. It was a chain of incidents in which the king's faithful servants in the Church of England were forced to disobey by his unreasonable demands and his harsh methods. James found resistance in other quarters also, as the reader will see, and learned nothing from it whenever it occurred, though he changed his policy to reduce the size of the opposition. When he did change, he found that the alienation was irreversible.

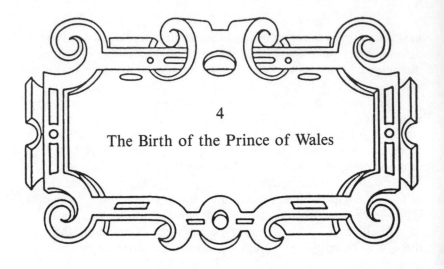

4

The Birth of the Prince of Wales

KING JAMES'S SECOND MARRIAGE had been childless. In the autumn of 1687, rumors that Queen Maria Beatrice was pregnant again ran around the court and reached the ears of many people outside. On December 23, after confirmation of the fact by her physicians, the king announced it to his Privy Council and ordered public rejoicing, so much was the sexual life of the monarch the business of the people in a hereditary monarchy.[1]

As the queen's "big belly" waxed and the king's measures became more extreme, the pregnancy was an omen (to Catholics) of a long-continuing enjoyment of power by Catholics and (to Protestants) of doom for Protestantism in the British Isles. For the daughters of James's first marriage, Princesses Mary and Anne, it meant postponement, if not negation, of their rights to succession if the queen gave birth to a male child.

As had happened once before when Maria Beatrice was with child, there was a hostile story that she and her husband planned an imposture to exclude Protestants Mary and Anne and implant in the line a boy who was not the son of the king and queen. To the spreaders of rumors it hardly mattered whose son the boy would actually be. Belief in the story presupposed complete lack of scruple in the queen, her husband, her bedchamberwomen, her physicians — entirely too many for an actual plot. The letters therefore blackened characters and aroused emotion to make the tale credible.

Anthony Wood, the Oxford antiquary, reported in his diary on January 21, 1687/8, a libel found by the butler of All Souls' College "containing an accompt of 3 women to be brought to bed and if any of the children is a boy, he must be nursed up and be King," which the butler delivered to a justice of the peace. On the day of thanksgiving for the pregnancy appointed by James's proclamation, Wood noticed that only two colleges, Christ Church (where Dean John Massey was a Catholic) and Magdalen (where many fellows were Catholics) rang their bells, though a few other colleges lit bonfires.[2]

Dispensers of written attacks on belief in James's announcement found ways to smuggle copies into the king's own quarters. Ambassador van Citters mentions a pamphlet (which he calls the third) found on a chair in the royal bedchamber on the morning of January 31/February 10, railing at the pregnancy and insinuating that "the Papal Nuncio has something to do with that."[3] The object of smuggling the pamphlet in can only have been to anger and frustrate the king, but the wider dispersal of these papers was to prepare for a charge of conspiracy and deceit if a son was born. (The birth of a son was essential for James's plans to lift the burdens from his coreligionists and Dissenters; it was now essential also for at least a few men who already hoped to overthrow him, for it would touch William of Orange's expectations and make him willing to help. It is a matter of speculation, though an interesting one, what James's enemies would have done if Maria Beatrice had borne James a daughter.)

Unreconciled Whigs, of course, needed no persuasion that James planned a crime against the law of succession and his own daughters; those who had proposed to exclude James from the throne had no great reverence for the order of succession and quite enough fear and hatred of the king to wish him deposed. Rather, the seditious papers chiefly aimed at conviction among the Tories, who did revere the succession and would support the right of any legitimate son of James's to precedence in the succession over his daughters—unless they could believe that the boy was not the king's son, that James himself was violating the rules.

His actions against laws made by Parliament opened the minds of some Tories to the possibility of a plot against the law of succession. His stubbornness against opposition from any quarter, even from his old Anglican supporters, made some think that he would manufacture a living male heir if he could not beget one. He and his daughters were so obviously at odds that Mary, the elder, submitted entirely to the wishes of her husband, William of Orange, that both opposed the king's wish to repeal the penal laws and test acts and that both supported the fellows of Magdalen College and the petitioning bishops. Nevertheless, some Tories refused to believe James capable of such a crime and could not see how anyone could believe it. On the day appointed for thanksgiving in London (January 15), the earl of Clarendon, the king's brother-in-law and uncle of the two princesses, attended St. James's Church: "There were not above two or three in the church who brought the Forme of Prayer [written for this special occasion] with them: 'tis strange to see, how the Queen's great Belly is everywhere ridiculed, as if scarce anybody beleeved it to be true: Good God help us."[4]

Printing was under such tight control in England that most of this material probably came from presses in the Netherlands. Previous efforts to have the Dutch authorities punish writers, printers, and publishers of attacks on King James showed that it was safe to write and publish there. Sheets and pamphlets printed in English could be shipped to consignees in England and distributed by them — of course, secretly.

James can have taken small consolation from the "inspired" addresses he received from here and there, expressing joy at the prospect of an addition to his family. Aphra Behn's *Congratulatory Poem to her Most Sacred Majesty on the Universal Hopes of All Loyal Persons, for a Prince of Wales* was published both in London and Edinburgh (where the king's own printer did the work). Some spoke of the pregnancy as a miracle (which is a thing impossible according to natural laws) and were sure that the miracle must end in the birth of a prince. Such talk was jarring to Protestants, some of whom ventured the thought that Catholics had sometimes contrived "miracles" and might do so again. Protestants were certain that God was not making true miracles against them and for their enemies. They were therefore inclined to accept the crude suggestions illicitly circulated.

How the prince and princess of Orange stood was in doubt, for signs from the Netherlands were contradictory. On the one hand, the English minister, the marquis of Albeville, reported, daily prayers were offered for the safe delivery of the queen and for a boy; on the other, "her R[oyal] H[ighness] grows daily more and more subject to the will of the Prince," and he had persuaded her that she could not rely on her father's willingness to observe the rules of the succession.[5]

There was some uncertainty about the place of the queen's confinement. Windsor and Whitehall were both mentioned. (The latter was rejected because the queen's quarters there were too cramped.)[6] The date of the expected birth was also in doubt; if conception had occurred on September 6, 1687, the child should be born about June 6; if, as the doctors thought, on October 6, about July 6.[7]

Nearing the end of her time, she received a severe shock. One of her bedchamberwomen, Mrs. Elizabeth Bromley, granddaughter of Justice Sir Richard Holloway, gave the queen a false report of the death of her brother, the duke of Modena, perhaps with malice. The next day, Wednesday May 9, she was in such a state that doctors feared a miscarriage. James was away at Chatham, but he hurried back to Westminster on that account.[8] The incident had no sequel, however. The queen was evidently satisfied that Mrs. Bromley had not been malicious, for she retained her in her position.

Princess Anne was one of the unbelievers in the pregnancy. If James died without a male heir, Mary of Orange would succeed; but Mary had been married to William for ten years without having a child, so that it was not at all unlikely that Anne would eventually be queen, either in succession to Mary or, if Mary died young, directly after James II. Anne could not expect so glorious a future if her stepmother had a son.

Moreover she detested her stepmother. She wrote to Mary that the queen was a hypocrite and a bigot, loved flattery, and was more generally hated than anyone. Ladies of quality came to the queen's court only when obliged to do so. Nevertheless, Anne said with a tone of long-suffering, she would show Maria Beatrice respect and give her no just cause for resentment. Anne did nothing to learn whether her stepmother was pregnant, though she had opportunities to find out. Alleging falsely that she also was pregnant, Anne left the court on May 17 for Bath, supposedly for her health.[9] As it later became known that Anne had not been with child, she has been accused of absenting herself of set purpose to avoid being a witness to the birth, persuaded by Mrs. Barbara Berkeley, wife of Colonel John Berkeley of the princess's regiment of dragoons, and Sarah, Lady Churchill.[10] The accusation seems just, and it is ironic that the charge of pretending pregnancy made against the queen is actually proved against her stepdaughter.

On May 29, Maria Beatrice was recovering from a cold. Her physicians were unwilling to take risks with such an important case. It was decided that she could not go to Windsor for her confinement because her health was weak; instead she should stay at St. James's Palace, though she was reluctant to use it because her experience of confinements there had been unlucky.[11] (None of her pregnancies had resulted in children who lived long.) On the king's orders, preparations began at once, and by June 9, "The Bed of State [was] set up there agt her Maties lying in—A Cradle of State is also made, both being exceeding rich."[12]

The following day, June 10, Maria Beatrice was brought to bed about eight o'clock in the morning; her son was born about ten.[13] The happy king knighted her doctor at the bedside, directed a mass to be sung with the Te Deum, held a meeting of his Privy Council as soon as possible, and ordered a proclamation of a general thanksgiving. Letters were to be sent to lords lieutenants of counties and to captains of warships for the same purpose.[14] On June 11, James wrote the news to Pope Innocent XI, whom he expected to celebrate the event.[15]

Public response was fairly good. As James Macpherson put it long after, "[C]ould faith be placed in addresses, no Prince was ever more beloved than James by his subjects."[16] Catholics of Magdalen College, Oxford, had the Te Deum sung on the day of the birth; Magdalen and Christ Church joyously rang their bells, and some citizens made bonfires; but the other colleges abstained, reflecting that Catholicism and the Crown might now never part. People at Leicester and Derby drank royal healths and rang bells on this occasion. At Gloucester, the Catholic mayor, John Hill, committed a churchwarden to custody because the bells of his church did not ring on arrival of the news.[17] The mayor of Maidstone bound over a "Person of Quality's" servant who tried to entice or intimidate the bell ringers to refuse to ring.[18] London's court of aldermen resolved to have conduits run with claret during the official celebration and taxed its members to pay the charge. On June 29, the mayor, aldermen, and sheriffs went to kiss the hand of the infant prince.[19]

Both universities decreed the publication of collections of verses written in honor of the event, and in due course two volumes appeared: *Strenae natalitiae academiae Oxoniensis* at Oxford and *Illustrissimi principis ducis Cornubiae . . . Genethliacon* at Cambridge (the latter title reminds us that the Prince of Wales was also duke of Cornwall). Most of the contributions were in Latin, but a number were in Greek, and some (at the end of each book) in English—these mostly by writers who also contributed verses in the ancient languages. One need not take all these effusions seriously; many of the versifiers later celebrated the revolution with equal enthusiasm. They were often very young students, availing themselves of a good opportunity for a first publication.

When *Strenae natalitiae* appeared, about July 9, Anthony Wood, a proud Merton man, tells us that nine contributions by Mertonians were published there, "more than any college or hall besides."[20] (Actually Christ Church led with sixteen pieces.) Six heads of houses and several future bishops were among the writers. What one does not find there is any piece by a member of Magdalen College, intruded or ejected, though at least two Catholic fellows of other colleges (Thomas Deane of University and John Augustine Bernard [or Barnard] of Brasenose) wrote verses found worthy of inclusion. Neither Obadiah Walker, master of University College, nor John Massey, dean of Christ Church, contributed, for whatever reason. The unknown compiler of the volume was probably influenced by unpopularity in the last two cases, but maintained a balance in that of Magdalen College.

The Cambridge *Genethliacon* is very similar. (In both volumes was a liking for comparison of the royal birth to that of Hercules.) Trinity College led in number of contributions, followed closely by King's. Seven heads of colleges showed their skill in versification, as well as several future luminaries of the church, a historian (Bevil Higgons), and a future suicide. The Catholic master of Sidney Sussex College, Joshua Basset, was among the heads contributing, and at least two other writers were real or suspected Catholics — Valentine Husband of Sidney and Clement Boult of Caius. A large number were later nonjurors.

The day of public rejoicing in and around London was June 19. Besides the arrangements made in the City by the court of aldermen, there was a celebration in Southwark for two regiments of soldiers there (the Scots Guards and the earl of Lichfield's regiment). They were drawn up together; the Catholic soldiers then went to their chapel and the Protestants to parish churches. That evening there were bonfires and the firing of guns. Officers were feasted, and "great quantity of ale" was given to the private soldiers.[21]

In the country, July 1 was the day. Many doubtless celebrated chiefly for the bishops' acquittal on the previous day. At Oxford, all colleges except Merton had bonfires; some had the special college entertainments called gaudies. Soldiers stationed there made a bonfire before the Cross Inn and fired carbine salutes. Many were "mad and drunk."[22] The *London Gazette* reported celebration at Banbury with bonfires and bell ringing; an anonymous contemporary added to the copy of the *Gazette* now in the University Library, Cambridge, "And the Pope burnt."[23] It had been observed in London that the acquittal caused more joy and excited behavior than the birth of the Prince of Wales.[24]

Abroad, the king of France rejoiced with the king of England.[25] The States General politely received James's formal letter notifying it of the birth of a son and dispatched congratulations by its ambassador, van Citters. The English minister, the marquis of Albeville, observed, however, that the price of Dutch East India Company shares fell by five points at the news.[26] Prince William sent his kinsman William Henry van Nassau-Zuilesteyn almost at once to compliment King James on the birth (and, privately, to learn the mind of the opposition). He had an audience for the purpose on the afternoon of July 1.[27] Kings Charles XI of Sweden, Joseph of Hungary (Emperor Leopold's heir), and Christian V of Denmark; Elector John George III of Saxony; and Duke Ernest Augustus of Brunswick-Lüneberg also sent congratulations.[28] The Spanish court at Madrid celebrated the event for three days.[29]

The earl of Middleton, who was present at the queen's delivery, described the new Prince of Wales as "handsome and lusty," and van Citters, who probably saw him later, called him "a well-formed prince."[30] His diet, however, did not agree with him, and his nurses (strangely) dosed him with an antidote for poisons and infectious diseases ("mitridate," the Modenese Ronchi said) and Spanish wine without first consulting his physician. The latter gave him some small remedy, and he recovered from his first troubles about June 15. The illness caused the king great fear.[31]

The queen's earlier children had taken milk and had died in infancy. The king, with the advice of physicians, decided that the Prince of Wales should not have milk but should eat a kind of water gruel. Ronchi reported that most at court accepted the resulting digestive problem as "a very common thing in babies"; they deprecated the alarm that some, at least, could not help feeling at every moment.[32] Such casualness seems suspicious; there must have been at least a few at court who were hoping the boy would die. The Tuscan resident, Terriesi, recorded more fear at court than complacency.[33]

The prince lived on through July; on July 27 he was well enough for an escort of many persons of quality to take him to Richmond (Surrey). Six companies of foot guards and two troops of dragoons also accompanied him there, where they made a small camp. Only members of his retinue could enter his quarters, for fear of smallpox, which was then rife.[34] (It was about this time, when he was "five or six Weeks old," that a later story would have had the real prince dead of

"Convulsive Fits" and replaced by a false one.[35] This story was apparently concocted for those who believed in the genuineness of the birth on good information but did not wish to be bound to support the claim of James's child.)

On August 6, however, the baby seemed to be at his last breath, after five or six days of sickness from failure to digest his food. The king then intervened, overruling the doctors and their fear of the evils of curdled milk on an infant stomach, and ordered that a wet nurse be found. The wife of a tilemaker was selected by a method suggesting a growing suspicion of the physicians; she nursed the prince, and he began to recover. James rewarded the tilemaker's wife richly with two hundred or three hundred guineas at once and an income of £100 a year. She was unaccustomed to the ways of the court; Sir John Bramston recalled, "[T]hey tell many prettie stories of the simplicity and innocency of this nurse."[36] By August 20, the recuperation was virtually complete, and the prince's attendants could often take him outdoors for fresh air.

Thus the Prince of Wales was born and did not die. His tiny but ominous existence continued the pressure on English Protestants to overthrow his father before it was too late, and that might be soon, for James had been laboring long to pack Parliament for the repeal of the penal laws and test acts. They feared he would pack all future parliaments and bring to an end the system of "mixed" government by king and Parliament that many Englishmen thought England's peculiar glory.

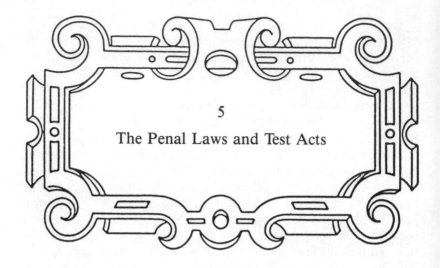

5

The Penal Laws and Test Acts

ON DISSOLVING his solidly Anglican Parliament in 1687 after prorogation from 1685, James had turned to Protestant Dissenters for help in the repeal of the anti-Catholic and anti-Dissenter penal laws and test acts that kept Catholics and Dissenters out of office and Parliament. His intention was to convene a parliament with a majority against the legislation he wished to repeal; he expected to find his majority among the most obedient Tories and among Dissenters, who stood to gain offices, political enfranchisement, and freedom of worship for themselves. As members were chosen by towns and counties, and local government was for the most part in the hands of Tories whom the king could not rely upon for this purpose, he found it necessary to make changes at that level.

James had other ends in view as well. He was concerned that the militia in each county should be commanded by a reliable lord lieutenant, assisted by reliable deputy lieutenants. Repression of riotous resistance to the central government in boroughs and cities would be difficult or impossible without obedient magistrates and municipal councils (corporations). But for James, repeal of laws which curbed, insulted, and menaced his coreligionists was becoming all-absorbing toward the end of 1687, for if he could not achieve at least this success, odds were great that his reign would confer no lasting benefit upon them. Thus he must make a majority in the House of Commons, and he was fully determined to do so.

Materials for a majority were there, enough potential members of Parliament put themselves at his disposal. Some Tories would still do anything he willed. Some Dissenters believed repeal would be as helpful to them as to Catholics and did not think the prospect of help bright in any other quarter. Some Tories might be unwilling but were in James's power through possession of offices, which they could not afford to lose and from which he had the power to eject them. Some Dissenters and Whigs owed him obedience in return for granted or expected pardons or remissions of fines for past offenses. There were men (of whatever opinion) with enemies, hoping for protection or power to take revenge; men with local goals to reach, such as patronage of a parliamentary borough or elevation in social status in their counties; and men who were simply greedy. Some of those available for the king's use were rising men, but many had such solid "interests" (bodies of consistent support in constituencies arising from old obligations, friendship, family connections, and local economic power) as to be sure of election without regard to national issues. As James was very powerful and prosperous, he could gratify if not all, a great many, securing for assistance toward his goal the personal interests of those who had them and backing with his own strength those who would be unable to secure election without it. His problem was to annul the interests of the irreconcilable, discover the interests he could bring over, and distribute his backing to carry elections in enough other constituencies to make a majority. Differences among circumstances of the many constituencies greatly complicated his problem.

The forty English counties returned two members each; the twelve Welsh ones each returned one. In them the electorates were large, and usually they were led by the greater local landholders, whose dependents, friends, and admirers were numerous. A combination of several influential landholding families behind a pair of candidates was often so strong that other aspirants found a contest not worthwhile. James had some support among this traditionally dominant class, but he could do little to add to it because the greater landholders were esteemed the most independent of local leaders and usually lived up to expectation.

However, James began with the counties his inquiry to learn how much support he had in the political classes of the nation. On October 25, 1687, he ordered lords lieutenants to ask their deputy lieutenants and the justices of the peace of their counties three questions; an affirmative answer to all would be agreement with royal policy. The first question was whether the respondent would be for repealing the penal laws and test acts if he were elected to sit in the House of Commons. The second was whether he would help in election of members who would support repeal. These were the crucial ones, those which were likely to draw negative replies. The third question was simply whether the man would live in friendly fashion with those of all religious persuasions. Those responding almost all gave acceptable answers to it, although one justice of the peace at York reminded the questioner that he was sworn to enforce the laws, which required action against conventicles and observance of the tests.[1] That question occasioned no serious difficulty.

On December 11, the *London Gazette* announced that the king had resolved to establish liberty of conscience by law and would "review the lists" of deputy lieutenants and justices, keep those who would serve him, and add to the lists the names of others who would serve.

Some lords lieutenants balked. They resigned, or the king dismissed them, because they would not ask the questions according to the order. Others postponed the unpleasant task until forced to perform it (many in January 1688). In the meantime, those to be questioned had time to consult and arrive at similar or identical answers they could give. Moreover, the lords lieutenants usually proposed the questions formally at county meetings; the respondents then seem to have had an opportunity to deliberate together before replying. Lord Jeffreys, visiting his county (Buckinghamshire), "found nobody to Catechise."[2]

The first important reports to come to the attention of van Citters, the Dutch Ambassador, were from the duke of Norfolk in the county of that name and the duke of Beaufort for his Welsh lieutenancies that "they continued to work in vain while nobody can see his way [*kan verstaan*] to the abolition of the test and penal laws or will elect persons who will want to agree to that in parliament."[3] That was before Christmas 1687. Two months later, Sir Paul Rycaut, a friend of Lord Clarendon, assured a correspondent in Constantinople that "scarce one man of estate in a County will promise to gratify the King in this considerable point." Some would allow the lifting of the test for James's reign, so that he could employ whom he thought fit, but would keep it for members of Parliament to prevent the establishment of Catholicism by law.[4]

Many of the answers survive, at least in such descriptions as

"Consents," "Refuses," or "Doubtful." Sir George Duckett published what he could find from manuscripts in the Bodleian Library.[5] Unfortunately, those for London, Middlesex, and several other counties are unavailable. John Carswell, working from Duckett, has made a table for English counties (thirty-three in number, the West Riding of Yorkshire being counted separately from the North and East Riding, and Bristol as the separate county that it was administratively). Carswell found that though the rate of consent was as high as 54 percent in Kent and 50 percent in Worcestershire and Northumberland, and that of refusal as high as 79 percent in Dorsetshire and 61 percent in Derbyshire, the average of each was much lower, and the doubtfuls "exactly one quarter of the sample," and many (231 of 1,276) were absent or gave no reply.[6] We could be surer of our ground if the one-word descriptions of the answers were fuller and nearer to the actual words.

Obviously, the refusal of the desired answer to the first and second questions, the king's mood being what it was, would mean removal of the refuser from his post. One might suffer further signs of his resentment. During the first months of 1688, the king removed hundreds.[7] Those who consented, that is, replied yes to all three questions, were continued in office and might be given rewards for their compliance. A deputy lieutenant or justice of the peace who never answered the questions was unfathomable by James's men at the time; later in the year, his mind might become evident in action.

For many of the doubtful there remain clues. Broadly, they either did not know how they would act as members or electors, except that they would choose the best men, loyal men, or good Anglicans, or they gave such ambiguous answers that the lords lieutenants could not make them out.

"Doubtful" answers would not please James, and the respondents knew that. When, as many did, an answerer said to the first question that if elected he would decide about repeal of the penal acts and tests according to the reasons arising in the debate in the House of Commons and therefore could not promise his vote in advance, that was not good enough. Twenty in Cumberland and Westmorland gave that answer, as did a number in other counties, especially Devonshire, where the list of such "doubtfuls" was headed by Sir Edward Seymour, Bart., of Berry Pomeroy, a leader of the opposition in the Parliament of 1685. "Doubtfuls" of this kind were really opponents; coordinated, organized opposition was "faction," and James detested it, even when "doubts" were expressed in the most constitutional words. Some seemed to propose compromise by agreeing to the repeal or alteration of the penal laws but not of the acts imposing religious tests for officeholders, or the other way around. (The difference seems to show the relative importance to the respondent of fear of Catholics and fear of Dissenters, though it is not absolutely clear.) James was not ready to compromise; those answers would not have satisfied him. Some were probably confused and others really doubtful.

The late Professor J. R. Western suggested that James and his agents might in the end have bullied many of the "doubtfuls" into support and that perhaps the king would have found particularly vulnerable some men alleging age and infirmity as excuses for failure to give any answer at all.[8] Where opposition was concerted, as in Devonshire, I doubt that enough changes of mind would have occurred to be of any use; many of the intimidatable were already intimidated, and it does not do to underestimate the obstinacy of the old and sick.

Deputy lieutenants and justices of the peace were replaced by Catholics, nearly all loyal supporters of the king, even though some thought him too hasty, and by Dissenters who were less commonly so. Documents do not tell whether they gave "right" answers to the three questions before appointment; that their intentions were known is probable. It seems that they were often men of inferior standing. By replacement, James no doubt improved electoral prospects in some counties, but on the whole he failed. Carswell says with reason that "although James had a not inconsiderable body of support, he had something like two-thirds of the land-owning classes against him, and half of these were not afraid to say so."[9] The Protestant landed gentry, which had included almost all rural J.P.'s, was too conscious of its position, too solid in the face of challenge, too mindful of the past. That an individual gentleman was not a justice of the peace did not much lessen his "interest" in the county.

"By contrast," writes Professor J. R. Jones, "when the three questions were put to men of humbler social status who were direct dependents of the crown — such as customs and revenue officers — the results were very different, and highly satisfactory from James's point of view." Professor Jones sees the municipalities, through the Crown's control of their charters, as dependencies.[10]

Here James's men made their most systematic and determined effort, over a number of months. In November 1687, a commission was set up to handle electoral business, requiring much correspondence and travel by agents and some expenditure of money. Sir Nicho-

las Butler, a London merchant converted to Catholicism from the
Baptist faith, was to earn great opprobrium for his part in the commission's work at London. A Catholic gentleman of good estate
(though said to be avaricious) and a solicitor by profession, Robert
Brent of Larkstoke, Gloucestershire, earned as much or more by su-
pervising the gathering of local information to feed the commission,
which made recommendations to the Privy Council.[11]

Traveling agents, equipped with horses at the king's expense and
paid twenty shillings a day, were to make contact with important local
people. They carried letters of recommendation, and acceptable men
with local knowledge should if possible accompany them to make
personal introductions. The agents were to find "very good correspondence" in each town, "men of prudence and int'rest" to receive
and disperse letters and papers for the king's cause. They were also to
trace the influences at work in each borough or city, find out supporters and opponents of the king, and make recommendations for
changes in town governments. In the course of the work, they were to
keep Brent, who would be at his chambers in the Temple, informed.
J. R. Jones credits Brent with "the detailed work involved in the
regulations and purges of the [town] corporations and the preparation
of elections," with Butler "doing much of the work in London,"
though "no evidence survives as to the relations or distribution of
functions between the two men."[12]

Whether an agent was a traveler for a region or merely a local
assistant is also not always distinguishable. Benjamin Dennis was certainly one of the agents for Cambridgeshire, Norfolk, Suffolk, and
Essex; Dr. Nehemiah Cox, a recusant physician of Lime Street, London, was employed for corporations in Wiltshire and Dorsetshire;
and Nathaniel Wade, a pardoned ex-captain of Monmouth's army, for
Somersetshire and Devonshire. The records show the names of at
least three other traveling agents, not so clearly assigned, and of local
assistants of the traveling agents for Shropshire and Cheshire. The
local assistants at Nottingham were Timothy Tomlinson, solicitor of
the borough's corporation, and Caleb Wilkinson, a Dissenting member of its common council.[13] There was also no bar against involvement of an enthusiastic amateur such as Henry Bridges of Wells, son
of Sir Thomas Bridges of Keynsham, former lieutenant in the Horse
Guards and aspirant to a seat in the coming Parliament.[14] In fact, for
local people to take collusive action against a town charter or report
the villainy of a postmaster (as Bridges, probably a Dissenter, did) was
useful to the cause.

J. R. Jones has shown how the boroughs were attacked.[15] Past tensions and disagreements within each had created factions, some of which could be used against others to settle scores and satisfy ambitions. In some towns the factions were divided on religious lines; elsewhere the divisions were personal or unclear. The independence of many landed gentlemen was rarer among merchants and tradespeople, who by their votes might control a borough or city but did not usually interest themselves in national questions. Already commonly dominated by borough patrons, they often did not reject royal patronage, which could be more materially rewarding.

The traveling agents made several tours of the boroughs in their regions. The first was no doubt intended to coincide in time (December 1687) with the putting of the questions to J.P.'s and deputy lieutenants, but in the event it preceded most of the meetings held for the purpose. The second led to reports submitted in April 1688, the month of the reissue of the Declaration of Indulgence. A third round of tours led to reports in June and July; and the last, intended to be so, to reports in September, in which the tentative choice of candidates hardened into statements of royal support.

On tours, the agents used oral persuasion and distribution of written matter, from which much was hoped. They reported in September that "the Books that have been Dispers'd have had very good Effect . . . though Great Endeavours have been Used by the [Anglican] Church party to Diswade People from reading of them."[16] Agents could recommend reward and punishment of individuals, particularly inclusion in and exclusion from borough government by "remodeling" (changes in the composition) of the governing corporations. Favor could be earned by support for the king, help in influencing voters and important townsmen, guidance in selection of candidates who could win, and standing for Parliament when and where the king's ministers requested.

The traveling agents and their local helpers were more successful than historians used to believe. They made some mistakes in recommending inclusions in corporations, so that changes had to be made later. (The several revisions of some corporations are believed by J. R. Jones to have been parts of plans for gradual remodeling;[17] this of course does not account for successive intrusions and extrusions of the same members.) Some candidates at first thought good had to be dropped as unacceptable or lacking local support. Members of the opposition were so strong in some places that they would almost certainly win. The reported inclinations of some proposed candidates to repeal the penal laws and tests were found to be exaggerated. In towns where Dissent was weak, agents were compelled to rely on Anglican support if they could find it, and Dissenting help in the campaign became weaker with the rally to the bishops on their arrest and trial. The agents were serious, however, and they learned from their mistakes.

Their reports are the only documents we have for judging their success in most constituencies, and not all of the reports survive. Though expecting the ultimate test of the elections and shielding themselves from possible charges of misrepresentation by candor in writing of constituencies in which the king's policy of repeal was a lost cause, they do seem to have been on the optimistic side, perhaps because they found Dissent strong and, as Western has suggested, assumed that Dissenters would generally favor repeal.[18]

Be that as it may, the extant reports from September show the agents' expectations that of 312 seats for counties covered and the towns within them, 223 would surely be won by candidates who would vote for repeal. If the agents expected to win enough additional seats among those for constituencies not covered by reports (a mere 34 of 201), James may have believed himself sure of a majority for repeal. A prediction of more than 34 seats from such constituencies would have made success seem less precarious. The agents believed success was probable, and James, who showed great faith in them by accepting many of their recommendations, must have believed it as well.

Those who detested or suspected the king's religious policy and feared the repeal of the penal laws and tests did not know as much of the expectations as we can, because none of the agents' reports were available to them, so far as we know. Some men the king relied on were cautious. Samuel Sanders (or Saunders), who was later recommended by James as a candidate at Nottingham, wrote to the earl of Huntingdon near the beginning of the campaign on December 19, 1687, that he deplored the public management of the three questions and hoped that only "some particular stiff men" would lose their positions as a result.[19] Thus a king's man feared his master might go too far.

On the other side, James Johnstone, who gathered news in England for the prince of Orange, wrote on December 8, 1687, that James would succeed only if he could get sheriffs to make false returns (a slim chance). Johnstone reckoned that sixteen of thirty-six sheriffs were Catholics, but many had estates "and declare that

whoever expects false returns from them will be deceived . . . several
[of the Catholic landed gentry] have refused to be Sheriffs or Deputy
Lieutenants."[20] Yet some of the Catholic justices of the peace and
deputy lieutenants replied to the first of the three questions (whether
they would be for repeal if elected to Parliament) as though they were
actually eligible.[21]

Barrillon wrote on December 22/January 1, 1687/1688, that the
leading Catholics favored repealing the penal laws and tests before
doing anything else. Quite possibly those best known to Barrillon did
so; they may not have thought the king's methods the best to obtain
the end. Throughout the campaign, most assumed that any Catholic
in office would follow the king at least passively, and the assumption
appears to have been correct. Dr. John Hiliard, chancellor of the
diocese of Norwich and a J.P. in Norfolk, complained on January 23
that "phanaticks" and Catholics were working to have him turned out
of the commission of the peace for refusing to promise to help elect a
favorer of repeal to Parliament. He mentions Lord Powis by name.[22]
Lord Powis was one of the most prestigious of Catholic courtiers.
This rise in Catholic assertiveness caused great alarm. Also, Lord
Petre, another Catholic, went into Essex as its lord lieutenant reluctantly, as a painful duty to the king, but nevertheless he "by the king's
command visited the country, as well as the corporations. He carried
divers gentlemen, Papists, with him in his circuit." Petre replaced the
Protestant earl of Oxford in the lieutenancy; he must have known the
unpopularity he would suffer as a result.[23]

Francesco Terriesi, the Tuscan resident, reported in his dispatch
of February 13/23 that the populace, though it would like a parliamentary session (from its fondness for novelty, he says),

> asserts continually that His Majesty cannot convoke it if he wants
> nothing from it but to succeed in his aforesaid plan, not so much
> because it insists that His Majesty has not taken the right road to
> success in it, as because . . . it will absolutely not concur in such
> royal wishes. . . .
>   And the continual libels on such matters, which the seditious
> publish every day, strengthen them in their opinion. Therefore the
> Hollanders, seeing how much these contribute to countermining the
> royal desire still go on vomiting from their country into this
> kingdom such a vast quantity of them that they render it completely
> infected with such poison.

Two thousand copies of a piece thought to be the work of Dr. Gilbert

Burnet had just been intercepted at the Customs House. Terriesi continued to believe that the general opinion and the opposition of great lords and others of influence made it impossible for James to succeed without using force.[24]

The French ambassador, however, saw only a temporary difficulty. He reported on February 17/27 that though there was a rumor that Parliament would meet in May, James's best-trusted ministers were not of that mind. There were not enough reliable people to carry the abolition of the penal laws and tests. Barrillon assumed that the king of England would prefer the wiser course over the apparently more dangerous one.[25]

To deal with seditious publications, James ordered on February 10 a proclamation for the enforcement of an act, 14 Charles II, "for preventing Abuses in Printing Seditious, Treasonable, & unlicensed Books and Pamphletts." The Stationers' Company was expected to help in searches for printing of unlicensed books and in seizures and arrests when such printing was detected.[26] The king's men in the post office intercepted unpleasing correspondence, such as that of Colonel Henry Belasyse with correspondents in Holland.[27]

To circumvent unwilling gentlemen, the king issued new commissions of lieutenancy for seventeen English counties, two of the ridings of Yorkshire, and all twelve Welsh counties in February and March.[28]

Terriesi, sympathizing with James's policy very closely, did not observe or hear of much benefit from the measures taken to carry it out. The king, he told the Tuscan *segreteria,* was losing the Anglicans without gaining the Dissenters.[29] The modern researches of Professor Douglas Lacey bear out Terriesi's estimate of the situation. By April 1688, moderate Dissenters and moderate Anglicans were reentering a coalition. The king's agents approved, with the description "right," sixty candidates also backed by Dissenters; nineteen of these had been exclusionists not many years before, and Lacey was of the opinion that they would probably have opposed repeal of the test acts even if elected with James's help.[30]

James had heard predictions that preparations would take as long as a year; he was therefore not discouraged by the rate of progress. When he reissued the Declaration of Indulgence on April 27, he stated therein his intention to call a parliament and his hope that it would show satisfaction with his policy of toleration. He conjured his subjects to "lay aside all private animosities . . . and to choose Such Members of Parliament as may do their part to finish what we have begun for the advantage of the Monarchy over which Almighty God hath placed us." He would hold a parliament in November at the latest.[31]

James offered various benefits expected from liberty of conscience. In the declaration itself he raised the possibility of increasing commerce, even "Commanding the Trade of the world." Van Citters reported at about the same time a bill proposed to improve the mint and another forbidding English seamen to enter foreign service, thus keeping them from enlisting with the Dutch in particular and reserving them for service in the English fleet and merchant marine. These bills were to be valued by the king and English merchants alike. James also planned a general naturalization of resident foreigners to stimulate industry and commerce by encouraging immigration of foreign merchants and skilled laborers. Huguenots, to whom James was more friendly than he admitted to Louis XIV's ambassador, were the probable beneficiaries in prospect.[32] A projected registration of lands throughout the kingdom would benefit landed proprietors; on the other hand, the building of thirty-five warships with funds derived from taxation on land would alleviate the financial burdens of commerce. A strict prohibition of export of wool would favor English woolen manufacture.[33]

If intended as distractions, these attempts to gain backing from diverse economic interests failed. The political classes were by that time well aware of the king's main purpose, and it was that purpose that they had to decide whether to support. In cautious words, many men must have said or written as Thomas Walker did to Lord Hatton on April 28: "I have sent yr Ld.sp the Declaration which tells Us when ye Parliament shall Meet; & what itt is the King Designs. which wee all prety well knew before." Walker wrote ironically of the king's statement that he would add strength to his army if necessary, that it was "a great Comfort to us all."[34]

It was observable by anyone in touch with events that James would use conventional or unconventional means to make a parliament that would do as he desired. On April 16, John Bagnold wrote from Derby that the undersheriff of that county had served a summons from the Court of King's Bench on the authorities of that borough to show by what warrant (quo warranto) Derby held its privileges. The state of factions there was such that what Dr. David Hosford describes as "the old loyalist faction" cooperated with the king by making a voluntary surrender. On April 26, Samuel Newton wrote in his diary that the mayor, five aldermen, twelve common councillors, and the town clerk of Cambridge were put out of office and their replacements installed.[35] Also in April, James's agents complained that revenue officers were not doing their bit for James's service; van Citters informed the States General on May 18 that nearly a hundred customs officers in the West of England had been removed for opposing repeal of the penal laws and tests.[36] And so it went on. In July, 1688, no quarter sessions could be held in Shropshire, "for want of Justices," as the king had removed so many. Shropshire in August had "but on[e] Justice of the Peace . . . & he is Carryed to Jale for debt: where the People are forced to go to him for there [sic] ffreedom, and ye Poore Devil cannot have it himselfe."[37] A modern historian assures us that in Derbyshire "a great many administrative-judicial posts [were] unfilled, staffed with men of limited influence or . . . placed in the hands of [men] unsympathetic to the royal cause."[38]

These are a few examples of the intense activity of the king's agents and the willingness to change the composition of local government on a grand scale, visible to everyone. The business irritated the political classes, and it frightened them as it seemed to approach success. Suppose that the recasting of the towns proved to be enough: In that case the king had won. Suppose it did not: The king could use his unusually large army to carry the day. James had threatened London with the billeting of troops after the celebration of the bishops' acquittal, and he was said to have made the same threat to the town of Queenborough to counter the opposing electoral power of Sir John and Caleb Banks. But that was only one method. Arrest of candidates, keeping opposition voters from the polls, armed prevention of elections where defeat was sure—these were all *possible, conceivable* to James, or his enemies could think they were. Were such thoughts in the mind of a correspondent who wrote (on July 31) that the army at Hounslow would soon break camp "in order to get to their winter quarters before the writs [for elections] come out"?[39]

There was here, of course, no effort for democracy, though sometimes for a larger or smaller electorate. James would usually want as voters the town corporation (commonly not large), the body of freemen (men with full town rights) if narrowly restricted, or the burgage holders of a small number of pieces of town property, because his agents could manage a small number more easily than a large one. The corporation had a strong attraction; James could put members in or out under many charters. If a large electorate would be unfavorable, Charles II and James had earlier used a new charter to restrict its size. In 1688, however, James's agents thought that Plymouth would be "right" if a reversion was made from election by the corporation (used in 1685) to the older "popular" election, apparently by the freeholders and freemen of the place. At Barnstaple, freemen living out of town for a year and a day had recently been disenfranchised, "the restoreing of whome to their freedomes without charge, by yr Maties order, with a Regulation, will secure this Election."[40] The decision depended on probable results, not on principle.[41] If the king could secure a large majority in one parliament to carry out his wishes, composition of electorates in future might become unimportant.

There were upholders of the antidemocratic principle. John Eston, a member of John Bunyan's Dissenting congregation at Bedford, and a future candidate for Parliament and mayor of the borough, lamented to the earl of Peterborough when the campaign was beginning (December 6, 1687), "that so much Democrasie is mixed in the Government, that thereby the exercise of ye Souvraigne power should be in any manner limited by ye suffrages of the common people, whose humours are allwayes fluctuating, and ye most part of them guided, not by reason, but deliberation like mere animals [*sic*]." Eston thought that changes of circumstances since the introduction of this democratic alloy made it necessary to eliminate it, he hoped in the next Parliament.[42]

A more specifically monarchist enemy of democracy left us a paper presumably intended for publication, though perhaps not actually issued. Said he:

> If by a Free Election men mean a Popular Election, I dread ye Consequences of such an Elecōn more than ye Other. . . . The Generality of ye People of ys. Nacōn are very incompetent Judges of ye Qualificacōns of Parliamt. Men . . . If by a free Election, men mean an Elecōn by Votes of men, sway'd and Regulated by ye Authority, and Advice of ye Inferior Clergy and Gentry [their Parsons or Land Lds] excluding ye Kg and his more Immediate Deputies in Ch[urch] and State, ye Bp., and Ld. Lieutenants, they mean an Elecōn, wch. indeed is no free Elecōn, for ye Authority of ye Particular Parsons, or Landlords over their People, or Tennants, takes off from their Liberty of Choice, & Freedom of Elecōn as much as ye Authority of a Kg. and their other Governours, for surely 'tis as bad for a Doe-bak'd Parson, and a Parboil'd Justice to prescribe to their Inferiors, as for their Kg., Bp., or Governour of their Country.[43]

This author obviously opposed both "popular" elections by large numbers of freemen of towns and forty-shilling freeholders in counties, the nearest in seventeenth-century England to democracy, and those dominated by private-borough patrons and not therefore controlled by the king directly or indirectly. Application of his views in practice would indeed have given King James the kind of parliament he needed, but only over the strenuous opposition of men who had places of honor and power in the existing system and saw those places as a species of property. James could act very foolishly, but he did not attempt to act on these views, though it is very possible that he agreed with them.

His general policy is illustrated by the experience of the borough of Nottingham. There he had two regulators, both local men; on their advice, he displaced all the municipal officials early in the spring of 1688. The replacements named to office appear to have been for the most part Dissenters; the new mayor (John Sherwin) had earlier been an active Whig. Dr. Hosford observes, however, that the most prominent Whigs "stood aside" from municipal office at that time, and some former officials challenged the authority of the new ones. The government decided to take away the charter granted to Nottingham by Charles II and thus end such challenges.[44]

In the meantime, the regulators and others considered what should be the terms of a new charter when the old one was forfeited. On June 21, Nathan Wright, deputy recorder of Nottingham, later a knight and lord keeper of the great seal, wrote of what the town could expect: "[A]ll the present members of the corporation are to stand, all the corporation's desires are granted, only in the business of the elections of officers of the town, Mr. Attorney General [Powis] will not be perswaded *to let the populace have any vote, as being a matter contrary to his Majesty's design,* and tending to a disturbance among themselves. . . . These are the terms upon which all charters are granted at this day, and none are to pass without them."[45]

The parliamentary franchise was not specified (as it happened, though at Nottingham it was wide, it did not include all adult male inhabitants). Apparently the general policy remained one of reducing the numbers of voters. George Langford, who had recently succeeded to the mayoralty on Sherwin's death, attempted to limit the vote for municipal office to common councillors; probably wishing to avoid unpopularity among burgesses of the town, he later reversed himself and raised a perhaps tremulous voice for the small rights of the "populace." For other reasons, the old charter was not forfeited, though by what must have been an administrative blunder, the town received a new charter on September 29. Only by use of superb ingenuity did the town government establish its legitimacy throughout the months that followed.[46]

Popular belief probably exaggerated the radicalism of James's policy toward large electorates: in February 1688, rumor had it that he would reduce the number of electors of Westminster from twenty thousand to two hundred.[47]

One cannot believe that James either increased or reduced the size of any electorate without alienating those whose votes were weakened or who lost their votes, and what he did not do but was thought to be doing was as threatening as what he did.

Even more outrageous to patrons of parliamentary cities and boroughs was a threat to their control of parliamentary elections in their towns. A number of patrons were still friendly to James—the duke of Beaufort at Malmesbury, the duke of Norfolk at Arundel and elsewhere, the earls of Bath (Plymouth) and Clarendon (Christchurch), and Viscount Montague (Midhurst). Against him were the earl of Bedford (Tavistock) and others. Whichever side they took, patrons were easy to offend, for patronage was valuable property, acquired by expense and effort, sometimes over many years, and meddling could destroy its value and make waste all the expense and effort. And meddling there was. John Brown, patron of Aldeburgh, initially opposed James's policy; the threat of a quo-warranto proceeding made Brown agree in April to elect two members of Parliament recommended by the king. Lord Bath, though James's servant, complained of the intrusion of Sir Edmund Nosworthy in boroughs where Bath had interests, which might have led to Bath's permanent loss of them to Nosworthy.[48] Needless to say, opposition patrons, such as Sir Edward Seymour, found loss of their influence particularly hateful. Electorates, on their side, disliked being told to reject the wishes of popular patrons, and an unpopular royal agent could make an electorate balk against the king. John Beare of Bearscombe, Devon, a patron himself, managed Honiton and Totnes through his interest for the king; the king's traveling agents left those boroughs alone. But Tavistock, the earl of Bedford's borough, was fair game for agents. They found that Dissenters there would vote for Sir James Butler, a man the king could accept, absolutely not for Beare, who was also acceptable to James as agreeing to repeal and had been suggested to them.[49] Something about Beare had turned Tavistock voters against him.

James sensed the heated atmosphere and hesitated at the very first to take immediate action against the seven bishops because some courtiers advised him to be mild to the petitioners and give them time to repair the damage they had done (as he saw it) by good conduct in Parliament. According to Barrillon, James's court believed the bishops to be allied with leaders of the opposition.[50] Their trial consolidated the Protestant factions and raised opposition in unexpected places.

The loyal borough of Grantham, Lincolnshire, neither very old nor very prestigious, had twice surrendered its charters to Charles II (in 1664 and 1684). Three years of James's reign had weakened its willingness to elect royal nominees. When, on April 25, 1688, the mayor, Robert Cracroft, received a summons of quo warranto, requiring legal justification of town privileges, the corporation prepared to fight the case. In June, the month of the royal birth and the bishops' trial, James removed Mayor Cracroft and five other incumbent aldermen, and substituted for them four supposedly suitably pliant men. One of these, Edward Secker, was elected mayor in August without reference to the king and thereafter behaved with a marked independence. Grantham probably lost its case, for the king granted it a new charter, sealed and enrolled in September, which omitted Secker's name and made one Edward Coddrington mayor. The new charter was a dead letter. Secker continued to serve, apparently without resistance from Coddrington. When the king later recalled the new charter, Secker was elected again under an older one and completed the usual term of one year.[51]

Here the solidarity of the governing class of a town asserted itself as surely as that of the gentry could. James's policy was so thoroughly offensive to a formerly loyal group, in and out of the corporation, that it hardly mattered which individual members of the group were actually included in the government. In September, also, James directed Captain Thomas Harrington of Boothby Pagnell, alderman of Grantham under the latest charter and member of Parliament for the borough in 1685, to stand for Parliament there again. Harrington had given affirmative answers to the three questions in November 1687. He never sat again for Grantham or any other constituency, though his local ties seem to have been good ones.[52] Grantham's mutiny was the equivalent of the return of *ignoramus* on the celebrants of the bishops' acquittal in Middlesex or the near-mutiny of sailors against the performance of Mass aboard James's warships — both in July — or the duke of Norfolk's uneasy expression of dissatisfaction in August.[53] This reaction had not a single cause but many, clustered about the king's religion and his religious policy, arousing the fear and the ire of his subjects.

The opposition worked on those feelings without difficulty in private and by underhand circulation of printed and manuscript attacks. Publications from the king's journalistic stable, in which the former Whig Henry Care was the hardestworking horse, matched the opposition in quantity and virulence of expression; the king's side had of course the advantages of open distribution and fuller financial backing. Perusal of such material is tedious, the detailing of it more so. Few of the writers were graceful or witty; strong prejudices are often apparent, sarcasm the common tone.

Writers for the royal cause might have shown, but did not show, the good feeling appropriate to a new era of religious toleration. Their opponents appealed to suspicion among Protestants. Two papers on that side stand out from the ordinary abuse. One is the well-known *Anatomy of an Equivalent,* by the marquis of Halifax, which demolished the proposal that Protestants give up the test acts in exchange for legal guarantees of Protestant security that would be protection as effective; Halifax showed that while the king had a dispensing power, he could dispense with a legal guarantee, and an unreliable future parliament could repeal it.

Another paper, short and effective, was written after the beginning of the proceedings against the bishops. It cut through the thin pretense that advisers had misled or misinformed the king in a series of rhetorical questions:

I. Whether any real or zealous papist was ever for Liberty of Conscience? . . .

II. Whether the King be a real and zealous papist? . . .

III. Whether the King, in his brother's reign, did not cause the persecution against the Dissenters to be more violent than otherwise it would have been?

IV. Whether he doth not now make use of the Dissenters to pull down the Church of England, as he did of the Church of England to ruin the Dissenters, that the Papists may be better enabled, in a short time to destroy them both?

V. Whether any ought to believe he will be for Liberty any longer than serves his turn?

VI. Whether if these Penal Laws and Tests were repealed, there would not many turn Papists that now dare not?

VII. Whether the forcing of all that are in Offices . . . to lose

their places, or declare they will be for repealing the Penal Laws and
Test, be not violating his own Declaration for Liberty of Conscience, and a new Test upon the people?

VIII. Whether the suspending the Bishop of *London;* the dis-
possessing of the Fellows of *Magdalen College* of their Freeholds;
the imprisoning and prosecuting the Seven Bishops for reasoning
according to Law; are not sufficient reasons [considerations] how
well the King intends to repeal his Declaration for Liberty of Conscience, wherein he promiseth to protect and maintain all his
bishops and clergy, and all other his subjects of the Church of
England, in quiet and full enjoyment of their possessions . . . [?]

IX. Whether the usage of the Protestants in France and Savoy,
for these three years past, be not a sufficient warning not to trust to
the Declaration, Promises, or Oaths, in the matters of Religion of
any Papist whatsoever?

X. Whether any equivalent whatsoever under a Popish King
that hath a standing army, and pretends to a Dispensing Power, can
be as equal security as the Penal Laws and Tests, as affairs now
stand in *England.*

*If any think fit to answer these Queries, they are desired to doe
it, as plainly and fairly as they are set forth.*[54]

By the time that these suspicions could be voiced, and in such words,
no reply was possible.

A good many justices of the peace in Yorkshire seemed to have
missed answering the famous three questions when they were first
asked, in early 1688. The city of York was violent in February:

> some men having gone to the chapel of a Jesuit, which had been
> erected there by favor of the liberty of conscience, they wished to
> throw it down and carry the Jesuit away, and they would have done
> it if they had not met some soldiers of the garrison, who all the same
> were not enough to subdue the number of the crowd . . . which
> cried out: no Jesuits, no chapel, no soldiers, who [the soldiers] were
> obliged to run there in a body and disperse the multitude with blows
> of swords and of muskets used as clubs.[55]

Lieutenant Colonel James Purcell, a Catholic, acted with "vigilancy
and care," and received official approval afterward, but the king was
displeased with officers and soldiers who inflicted immediate punishment on citizens of York by tying them up neck and heels and making
them ride the "wooden horse"; he suspended and confined an officer
who struck a citizen in the presence of the lord mayor of York. He left
the rioters to the justices of assize.[56]

It was at York, on July 17, that a new series of meetings to ask the three questions began (the others were at Ripon on August 9, Skipton on August 14, Leeds on August 15, Pontefract on August 20, York again on August 25, and Doncaster on August 30). Among those especially solicited were aldermen of several boroughs.

Trouble began at once. Thomas Raynes, lord mayor of York, with the deputy recorder and nine other aldermen, made practically identical answers to the first and second questions, referring decision on repeal of the penal laws and tests to "the best reasons I am capable of, when I heare the debates of the house," and stating that he would choose as members "men of good understanding, honest principalls and undoubted Loyalty, and also I believe will very well please the King." One alderman of York was compliant; one was tentatively disposed to repeal but unwilling to promise before hearing the debates; and one (Sir Henry Thompson, a former member for the city) agreeable to repeal of the penal laws, but not the tests, "made for the preservation of the Protestant religion, and the Church of England" in which he had been "born and bred."[57]

At Ripon, two justices, Sir Edmund and Sir Jonathan Jennings, holders of strong parliamentary influence in that borough, refused to acknowledge the commission of the questioners. The dean of Ripon admitted that his conscience would not permit him to support the Declaration of Indulgence. The mayor and the only two aldermen respondents skillfully evaded the first and second questions. At Skipton, three justices gave a common answer like that of the mayor and aldermen of York; two, another answer only slightly different. One of the three, Thomas Fawkes, and one of the two, Ambrose Pudsey, were members of the next Parliament. One respondent agreed to repeal only if that was the result of the debate in the House of Commons.[58]

At Leeds, the mayor, recorder, and twelve aldermen gave terse, almost identical answers: "The reasonable voates of the house" would guide them, and they would vote for loyal members of the "Church of England, as now by Law established."[59] At Pontefract, justices of the peace met about an hour before the questioners arrived; fourteen of them, of whom six had sat in the Parliament of 1685 and were also to sit in that of 1688/1689, agreed on a common answer to the first question, refusing to promise to vote for repeal before hearing the debates and asserting awareness "that the protestant Church may be deeply concerned herein as to its security, which Church wee are bound to support by all lawful means." To the second question, their joint reply was that "Untill such penal Lawes and Test may be made appear to be repugnant to the Protestant interest, we cannot contribute to" election of repealers. Another justice, who was absent, sent in a virtually identical reply later. Only eight justices, of whom three were Protestants, complied with the king's wishes. None of the Protestant justices complying at Pontefract ever sat in a parliament.[60] Moreover, the mayor, recorder, seven aldermen and town clerk of Pontefract jointly refused to promise before hearing the debates to vote for repeal; they also pledged themselves to vote only for candidates of known loyalty to the king and faithful to the Church of England. Four aldermen submitted to James's policy.[61]

Only one of seven responding justices of St. Peter's Liberty, York, gave the questioners satisfactory answers at a meeting on August 25. One of the aldermen of Doncaster was absent and one in jail when the questioners appeared there on August 30. The two who answered denied that they could ever be elected to Parliament and bound themselves only to help elect loyal persons who would "maintaine the Protestant religion."[62]

It seems that most of the members of the political classes of York and the West Riding of Yorkshire firmly opposed James's policy; the corporations had been remodeled and Catholic and Dissenting justices appointed, and temptation and intimidation had been tried.

Some other constituencies were showing the same spirit. The corporation of Norwich refused to "admit some of ffather Penns Crew . . . wth out takeing ye. Corporation Oaths." James had remodeled Bristol's corporation in January 1688; nevertheless, it refused him an address of thanks in April and ignored a royal mandate in October for admission of Dissenters as freemen without taking the oaths.[63] As late (or early) as June, the corporation of Plymouth declared that it would elect as members only Protestant Devonshiremen; the Anglican cathedral interest at Exeter still dominated that city, and several boroughs in the same county declared their attachment to Tory patrons. Four Devonshire boroughs managed by John Beare (Totnes, Tiverton, Dartmouth, and Honiton) were at that time "in great disorder and distraction about their new Regulations," that is, interference with their corporations' compositions. I suspect that Devonshire was another center of resistance, even though not one justice or deputy lieutenant had given a blunt refusal to the three questions.[64] Refusal to give a promise was as effective (and as much resented at court) as a statement of opposition to repeal. Reresby described the events in his own Yorkshire in these words: "[O]ur justices of the West Rideing had given their negative" to the questions. As the word of the Yorkshire phenomenon spread, others interpreted it exactly so.[65]

Twenty-four peers joined the effort of the local and traveling agents in the latter part of the summer, using whatever influence they had to assure election of candidates who would vote to repeal the statutes of intolerance.[66] About half of these lords were Catholics whose appearance in constituencies as royal agents and future powers must in itself have alarmed Protestants. Negotiations behind the scenes were confirming or setting aside tentative agreements on "right men" to stand for Parliament. The stiffness of the Yorkshire gentry, shared by we know not how many others, came just before James ordered (on August 24) writs sent out on September 21 for a general election. It was probably too late to change the decisions in most cases. Agents neither endorsed nor rejected some Yorkshire candidates—Viscount Downe, Sir Thomas Yarburgh, Sir Henry Goodrick, and Sir Michael Wentworth—but merely described them as probably successful, as the strong preferences of Yorkshire borough electors made clear.[67]

Although J. R. Jones holds that the agents were more competent and discerning than they have usually been thought, there is no denying that they made some mistakes. Besides Colonel John Darcy—a "glaring example," as Professor J. H. Plumb puts it—the surviving lists show a number of names that also appear on a list of James's opponents, probably prepared to gauge the support that William of Orange could expect in an invasion. I cannot reduce the number of these below eleven. And James fleetingly endorsed John Somers, one of the counsel for the bishops, for Droitwich, though he later withdrew the recommendation. This fallibility was not the fault merely of a few harebrained agents; errors are too widely scattered. Though at least three mistakes were made for Sussex and its boroughs and two for Suffolk and Sudbury, candidates for Nottinghamshire, Aylesbury, Wallingford, Newcastle-under-Lyme, Cirencester, Worcester, and Wendover were also sadly misunderstood.[68]

Two elements of uncertainty, then, are to be seen in the king's election campaign: (1) many of the constituencies were bound to choose candidates whose "interest" in them was powerful, no matter what James's agents did; and (2) some candidates were not tools, though the agents recommended them. The king never knew, nor shall we know, whether the campaign was a success.

His opponents feared that it would be and that a packed parliament would repeal the penal laws and tests and so strengthen the king's position that he would be forever beyond control. Remodeled obedient boroughs would return a majority of handpicked obedient members who would endorse royal decisions and enact them into law. If these conditions could be established, the king could turn against his Dissenting and high-Tory supporters whenever he thought the time right.

Only a handful of conspirators addressed to William the letter of June 30, usually termed the "invitation" to intervene, of which more will be said. For some time afterward, only small numbers of others were admitted to the secret. Among those unaware of the letter, there must have been a widespread and growing agreement with this part of its contents:

> [W]e do much doubt whether this present state of things will not yet be much changed to the worse before another year . . . by such . . . changes as are not only to be expected from a packed Parliament, but what the meeting of any Parliament (in our present circumstances) may produce against those who will be looked upon as principal obstructors of their [really, James's] proceedings there, it being taken for granted that if things cannot then be carried to their wishes in a parliamentary way other measures will be put in execution by more violent means; and although such proceedings will then heighten the discontents, yet such courses will probably be taken at that time as will prevent all possible means of relieving ourselves.[69]

If the signers had known more than they did, they would have worried more.

In the middle of September, the earl of Sunderland addressed many letters to lords lieutenants (such as the bishop of Durham for that county), other officials (Sir Robert Holmes, governor of the Isle of Wight; John Pratt, mayor of Berwick upon Tweed), and men with borough interests (Lord Newburgh at Cirencester), directing or asking support for candidates who the king hoped would do his will.[70] He also wrote to many notables, directing them to stand for Parliament with royal support: Roger Pope of Wollaston, Shropshire, a king's equerry, at Bridgnorth; Sir Lionel Walden of Huntingdon in Huntingdonshire; Sir William Villiers, Bart., at Leicester; Captain William Barlow at Haverfordwest; Colonel Charles Churchill, groom of Prince George of Denmark's bedchamber, at St. Albans; James St. Amand, the king's apothecary, at St. Ives; and many more.[71]

James nominated many officials, placeholders, and officers of his

army and navy, including Sir Charles Scarsborough, one of his physicians, at Grampound; Sir Christopher Wren, surveyor of the king's
works, at Plympton; Rear Admiral Sir Robert Holmes at Newport
(Isle of Wight); William Bridgman, a clerk of the Privy Council, at
Droitwich; and Charles Bertie, younger son of the second earl of
Lindsey and paymaster of the Ordnance, at Stamford, Lincolnshire.
Among those James is known to have directed to stand or for whom
he asked support, I have counted twenty-seven serving army officers:
one brigadier general, Sir John Fenwick, nominated for Northumberland; seven colonels (Fenwick among them); seven lieutenant colonels; three majors; and ten captains.[72] (Some others who are called by
military titles were militia officers, retired officers, or survivors of the
civil wars.) There was at least one naval captain (Robert Wilford at
Queenborough). The incomplete list of the agents' recommendations
in September contains several more names of officers who may or
may not have been nominated by the king. Others may have stood
with his support in boroughs and counties not covered by those lists,
as did Roger Kirby (or Kirkby), captain in the Coldstream Guards
with the rank of lieutenant colonel, at Lancaster.

    J. R. Jones has observed that the king's agents very often selected
for nomination in a borough men of the place or the immediate neigh-
borhood, much more often than voters usually did in elections.[73] That
observation is correct and readily explicable. Town corporations had
often been packed with outsiders to insure control; James could make
an appeal to local sentiment by presenting a candidate with strong
local associations. Also, James could encroach on patronized boroughs, where patrons had the habit of naming outsiders, with greater
ease when he put forward local men as his candidates. He did it, not
on principle but because it worked. The initiative in the practice did
not always come from his side; in June 1688, when agents canvassed
the Cornish boroughs, ten of them each promised "to elect two such
Members for the ensuing Parliament as their present Recorder shall
recommend, or approve of, provided they are of the Protestant religion, and their Countrymen [Cornishmen]."[74] (Here were the terms,
not entirely palatable, on which the king could arrange everything
with the recorders.)

    It was convenient to work even courtiers into this scheme where
possible. Thus William Chiffinch, page of James II's bedchamber,
was to stand at Windsor, where the court interest was powerful and
near which he had a house. As for others, the Whiggish and republican Major John Braman of Chichester was approved for that city by

the agents in September, as the Dissenter Sir Thomas Jefford was at Exeter, John Kingsford at Canterbury, John Aglionby at Carlisle, and Richard Slater at Nottingham.[75] Henry Stone of Skellingthorpe, three miles from Lincoln where James nominated him, was a generous donor to the city corporation and to a local school.[76] Oliver Montague and Sir Littleton Osbaldeston, as recorders of Huntingdon and Woodstock, were natural candidates for those boroughs; recorders had often been members for their towns in earlier parliaments. It was all the better when the local men had sat before. One could multiply examples to show the policy.

All the same, a local voter might not see things just as James wanted him to see them. James's candidates would really owe their membership to him, not to local people. Those who lost their right to vote at that time were not likely to take satisfaction in "representation" by men they had not chosen. And the connection of a recorder and his town might be feeble — both Montague and Osbaldeston had attained that position under new charters issued by James.[77]

James and his agents honored the convention that a candidate for a county seat in Parliament must have substantial landed wealth in the county. Sir John Hanmer, nominated for Flintshire, was a landed proprietor there as well as a lieutenant colonel in the army. Sir John Reresby in Yorkshire, Sir Samuel Barnardiston in Suffolk, Sir John Fagg in Sussex, and Cornelius Clarke in Derbyshire are other examples that bear out the rule. A proprietor of estates in two or more counties was happily situated. (Hanmer had property in Suffolk, Fagg in Kent, and Barnardiston was also a rich merchant with business in London.) It would have been remarkable if James had attempted to ignore this convention. As he did not control the county franchise, which was fixed by an act of Parliament and confirmed by generations of habit, he would certainly have failed if he had ignored the expectations of the enfranchised that their own "countrymen" should be their county members.[78]

There was plenty of resistance as things were. I attribute to late August or early September an undated letter to James Harrington:

> Mr [William] Sacheverell has refus'd a Deputation & Commission [as deputy lieutenant and J.P.]; I was in his Company. He has a face & mien wch promises the least of any I ever saw. A particular Exception has by the Kg been put in agt Sr Willoughby [Hickman] & his Co-Burgess [John Ramsden] from being chose for Hull; but they are resolv'd to stand. . . . The Judges every where made large Harangues on his Maties resolutions to be firm to his promises made

to the C[hurch] of Engd. There is no appearance of Gentry at the
Assizes, & they are glad to be contented wth very mean Persons for
Grand-Jury-men.[79]

Reresby, one of the best informants of his time, made terms with
the king before agreeing to stand for a Yorkshire seat. The lord mayor
of York would be active against him; the king was to show Reresby's
influence by putting the mayor out of office and putting in one of
Reresby's opponents, as the office made its holder ineligible for Parliament; and two of Reresby's friends should also be members of the
city's corporation. Reresby hoped this would not exasperate York by
making it "jealous that I was too deep in the Court interest." The next
few days made his cause seem hopeless; on September 16, the marquis
of Halifax advised him not to be "too earnest to be chosen, or at least
not to take the Court assistance too much."[80]

James proclaimed the election on September 21 and set the date
of assembly at November 27. His proclamation announced that he
wished this Parliament to establish liberty of conscience while preserving the Church of England. He conceded one hope of the Tories in
opposition: "We are willing the Roman Catholicks shall remain incapable to be members of the House of Commons, Whereby those
Fears and Apprehensions will be removed, which many Persons have
had, that the Legislative Authority would be Engrossed by them."
James reassured Anglicans and expressed his hope for election of men
who would help his work. He promised that elections would be fair.[81]
He said nothing of Catholic peers and the House of Lords.

Barrillon reported on September 18 that the king of England
planned to create a plurality for liberty of conscience in the upper
house by making many peers. Those specifically named for his promotion were mostly already peers of Ireland or Scotland; only Protestants would do.[82] We need not take seriously the report of the very
hostile Viscount Newport that Sunderland proposed ennoblement of
a whole troop of guards.[83] It is clear that James meant to establish
toleration by use of Protestants in both houses, though if necessary
tampering with the membership of the House of Lords. He also intended by this step to divide his enemies and increase his own
strength.[84]

Reports of a force being prepared for William of Orange for an
invasion of England were just coming to be treated as serious by
James II. The day after the issue of the proclamation, he had Sunderland notify at least some of the lords lieutenants to restore former
deputy lieutenants who had recently been removed and to notify Lord

Chancellor Jeffreys of the names of justices of the peace in their counties who should also be restored.[85]

Mails being what they were, the notifications of the election and of the restoration of removed officials arrived simultaneously at Lostwithiel for the earl of Bath, lord lieutenant of Cornwall and Devonshire. Bath was there to convene a meeting of the Convocation of Tinners, "which consists of most of the chief gentlemen of the County [Cornwall], who are principally concerned in the contents"; he imparted the news to them at once, "which created a general satisfaction and joy to them all." He wrote that the restoration would undo some of the damage done by the "regulators" (James's agents), and he struck a special blow at his rival in patronage, Edward Nosworthy, who had disturbed the corporations in his counties.

> As the case now stands, if they proceed immediately to election of Parliament men, there will of necessity be disputes in many places. Scarce a Corporation knows its own magistrates; some of the old ones displaced by mistakes and misnomers, most of the new unduly chosen by reason of their ignorance of the Constitutions in the several Charters, with many other errors. . . . All which irregularities might be reduced to their proper course in a fortnight's time or thereabouts; the days for electing new mayors throughout all the County by their Charters being within that compass.[86]

Bath's advice was particularly important because the towns of Cornwall and Devonshire returned sixty-six borough members, without counting the four members for the counties.

An unfriendly newswriter discerned a mood of hesitation just before the issue of the proclamation. He had heard by September 19 that "the writs for a Parlmt. are all seald but things are so yt they dare not put them out as yet: and when they do 30ty. Corporations are to have none their Charters being taken away." (The same letter carried the report that Colonel Richard Norton of Southwick, whom the king's agents had recommended to be a candidate at Petersfield, had gone with the king's enemy, Lord Lovelace, to Holland. Norton was a veteran of Parliament since 1645 who had consented to repeal of the penal laws but not to that of the tests.)[87]

Though the proclamation and writs were not yet issued, Sir John Knatchbull summoned a meeting of gentlemen of east Kent at Elham for September 20 to consider persons to be proposed "for his Majesties Service in the [Cinque] ports adjacent." About forty attended, and the meeting recommended candidates to several ports. On September 23, Sir William Rooke, sheriff of Kent, showed Knatchbull a writ for the election.[88] In Oxfordshire, Lord Norreys, eldest son of the earl of Abingdon, invited the gentlemen of the county to a feast at Oxford's Cross Inn, and some sixty attended it. The object was to secure the election of Norreys's uncle, Captain Henry Bertie, to be one of the members for the county. Bertie had evaded the three questions when asked; he had been a member of three parliaments.[89]

Possibly not all the writs for the election left the Chancery. The electors (with four candidates) of Essex turned out on September 25 at Chelmsford to vote, but the sheriff had no writ, and no election took place, wrote Sir John Bramston, who went home to his house in Greek Street, Soho, to find a letter saying that the writs had been recalled. But Bishop Lloyd of Norwich reported arrival of writs for elections in Norfolk and his own personal summons to the House of Lords. Lloyd thought Norfolk would return two independent baronets, Sir Jacob Astley and Sir William Cooke, both former members of the Parliament of 1685, but the boroughs in the county he believed to be too well regulated and intimidated.[90] In Yorkshire as in Essex: Ralph Thoresby of Leeds rode on September 30 with two aldermen of his town to Tadcaster where a crowd of West Riding freeholders estimated at three thousand was disappointed by the nonappearance of the writs for election.[91]

A royal proclamation dated September 28 was already on its way to the public to explain what was happening. An invasion from Holland was preparing; "some false Pretences relating to Liberty, Property, and Religion . . . may be given out," but the intention was to conquer James's kingdoms and subject them to a foreign power. The king therefore had to recall the writs for the elections. He had already declined foreign assistance, he said; he would rely on his own subjects. He ordered lords lieutenants, other officials, and subjects in general to repel invasion, and he forbade any help to his enemies.[92]

Recall of writs came too late to Queenborough where an election had already been held and two court candidates had suffered defeat.[93]

That the country was in great disarray was already apparent. James would be fully busy with meeting the crisis by strengthening his army and fleet, providing supplies, detecting conspiracies, and (above all) appeasing his Protestant subjects. Part of the last task was to be the dismantling of the structure that he and his had labored so carefully to build for the repeal of the penal laws and test acts.

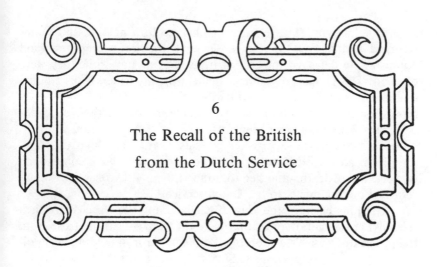

6

The Recall of the British
from the Dutch Service

FOR STATES TO MAINTAIN as parts of their armies units made up of
subjects of other states was common. According to a current economic theory, a government did well to substitute foreign mercenaries
for its own subjects, who might be better employed elsewhere.

The United Provinces had long kept Scottish and English regiments — two Scottish ones since 1586. In 1687, there were three Scottish and three English, officered and manned from their own countries. Many British gentlemen, even peers (such as the earl of Ossory,
son of one duke of Ormond and father of another) served in the
regiments during their careers; the service was reputable and less precarious than with British regular troops levied in emergencies and
(usually) soon disbanded afterward. The Dutch regarded their British
corps highly and paid them well. When at full strength, the units
mustered nearly four thousand effectives, a large and quite profes-
sional part of the Dutch army.

In 1685, King James requested the return of the troops for service against Monmouth's rebellion; the States General granted the request, according to Burnet with a little difficulty caused by opposition

This chapter first appeared under the same title in *The Historical Journal* 25
(1982). The author is indebted to the Cambridge University Press for permission to
republish it.

from Dutch towns.[1] The regiments embarked for England, and James returned thanks to the States General for its promptness and goodwill. He defrayed the cost of transport and pay while they were on loan. The Dutch government made a profit, which it distributed among the provinces that ordinarily paid the soldiers. The speedy repression of the rebellion, however, made the use of the troops unnecessary. This may have been fortunate, as they were not all loyal. Nine soldiers of the Scottish regiments drank the duke of Monmouth's health, to the authorities' knowledge. Two were condemned to be shot to death, another to suffer flogging. Afterward, James returned the regiments to the Dutch service.[2]

Relations between the king of England and the Dutch were then friendly; at the end of 1687, they were far from so. Strain arose from the prince of Orange's disapproval of his father-in-law's religious policy and from the refusal of the States General and the States (provincial governing body) of Holland to expel British political refugees, especially Dr. Gilbert Burnet, but also many Monmouth rebels and Rye-House plotters. Published attacks on James went unrepressed and unpunished in Holland. The Dutch East India Company's arrogance frustrated attempts to settle disputes about Dutch actions against English trade in India and the East Indies, greatly to the displeasure of the English East India Company. The nations were commercial rivals elsewhere as well, and both took trade very seriously. A grave annoyance to Dutch commerce was the depredations of Algerine corsairs in the Narrow Seas, and the shelter given those pirates in English ports.[3]

A special grievance was the growing disloyalty among the British in Dutch service, especially among the officers. As vacancies occurred, Prince William was filling them increasingly with men whose appointment James did not like. William would have wished to remove others excessively loyal to the king.[4] The prince refused to commission Catholics on James's nomination. That was a political refusal, for Catholic officers served in other units of the Dutch army; William intended his policy to contrast sharply with that of James. Moreover, the Protestant officers who owed their commissions only to William felt free, if so inclined, to speak disrespectfully of James and associate with his enemies.

The king would have liked to get such officers into his power and to deprive the States General and his disobedient son-in-law of the services of the six regiments. The means to achieve both ends was their recall to his service. At first he hesitated because his revenues were already stretched to pay the army he had. Six regiments would be a heartening addition to his strength against rebels or invaders, but they were more than he could pay. He might, of course, recall his subjects, dismiss many of them, and maintain a reduced number of regiments, or he might seek a new source of revenue for his enlarged establishment. Recall them he would.

The French ambassador was in his confidence. On January 16/26, 1688, Barrillon wrote to Louis XIV: "The recall of the troops from Holland is settled. Orders to execute it will go tomorrow . . . the King of England has spoken to the leading Catholics and then to the cabinet council with much firmness and loftiness. He went over again all that has been done since his accession to the throne by the States General and the Prince of Orange against his interests and even against his dignity. No one dared to contradict or to represent the inconveniences of the recall of the troops." Barrillon described James's speeches on the subject as exaggerating.[5]

The king did indeed request the return of the troops in a letter dated January 17 (O.S.), written in polite French, and referring to the Dutch readiness to comply in 1685. James's envoy at The Hague, the marquis of Albeville (who had an Imperial, not a British, title) would have instructions to provide everything necessary for their transportation. James said he was sure the States General would give all the assistance the envoy asked to make the embarkation easy and quick. He also notified the prince of Orange of the request.[6]

The earl of Middleton, secretary of state for the Northern Department, sent the letter to the States General, enclosed in the instructions to Albeville, by the hand of Colonel John Wauchope—since 1685, commander of one of the Scottish regiments concerned. How public the affair was at this early stage is not clear; Hoffmann, the Imperial secretary in London, was certainly informed of Wauchope's mission.[7] Albeville was to press not only for the release of the regiments but also for payment of arrears and freedom to bring away arms paid for by the soldiers. Captain William Davis, R.N., would go to help procure ships, and the regiments should begin embarking without delay. "It is not to be doubted, but that all the Loyall Gentlemen in the Brigade will give a dutyfull obedience to his Maties Commands." Those who seemed doubtful should be permitted to stay, "which will be a meanes to seperate the cleane from the uncleane."[8]

On January 24, Middleton sent by Captain Davis a letter to Albeville giving authority to contract for transport of twelve hundred persons to Harwich, seven hundred to Dover or Margate, and the rest to

Gravesend. Wives and children were included, and Albeville should muster the travelers before embarkation.[9] Some members of the London public began to hear rumors of James's request at about the same time, and van Citters allowed himself to mention the matter in an ordinary (rather than secret) dispatch of January 24/February 3.[10] The negotiation, such as it was, was conducted for the most part at The Hague.

Albeville delivered the request to the States General on February 6 (N.S.), and the latter decided to have the matter examined by its commissioners on military affairs, with the "most wise advice of His Highness the Prince of Orange."[11] D'Avaux, the French ambassador at The Hague, tells us that when the recall was first announced, "the Deputies of the Province of Holland and those of the States General said among themselves unanimously that it was necessary to return them . . . the Prince of Orange having knowledge of it spoke the morning of the next day to the Deputies of the States General with so much violence, and made them know his interests and his opinions so openly and strongly that they all changed their tune."[12]

On February 19, the commissioners reported, and the States General discussed the report. It resolved to reply to King James that if, "which God in his Mercy forbid!" he should need help, the States General would offer it "with as much readiness, willingness, and promptitude" as in 1685, but that the treaties and resolutions touching those troops did not seem to bind the Dutch government to return them to the king's service; on the contrary, the United Provinces had paid to have them raised, reinforced, and maintained from the enlistment bounty money onward; the Dutch had incurred most of the expense during the reign of Charles II, when the English government had contributed nothing. However, the States General would dismiss to the king's service any officers in those regiments who asked for release within a limited time. A letter to this effect was accordingly sent to the king.[13]

The resolution does not record the discussion, but there are some indications of what considerations the deputies raised. On February 8, for instance, the States General heard a petition from inhabitants of The Hague against returning the troops, calling attention to the considerable sums in arrears from The Hague and other places for recruiting and paying these troops. The States General had to consider the expense of settling accounts if it let the regiments go.[14]

There was also the example. Some Dutch deputies said that William of Orange was afraid that German princes whose subjects also served the Dutch as mercenaries might do as James did, "and so leave the States without a man."[15]

According to Daniel Johann Kramprich von Kronefelt (generally known as Kramprich), Imperial envoy at The Hague, the States General also discussed James's motives for the recall. That he made his request with Louis XIV's knowledge and approval was taken for granted. It seemed to many that his fundamental motive was to deprive the prince of Orange of the regiments, lest William go with them to England on the invitation of a parliament. No doubt James also wished to deprive the Dutch republic of parts of its defense at that time, when many of Louis XIV's actions suggested that Louis would attack it.[16]

Consideration probably caused the exclusion of the voluntary principle from application to enlisted men. Albeville reported on February 10 (O.S.?) that Gaspar Fagel said that he believed King James could probably have all who wanted to go if those who wished to remain were allowed to do so.[17] Prince William, however, would surely have considered that such a policy might leave the six regiments in shreds — a few men gone from one company, most from another — and recruitment, training, and discipline would suffer an enormous reverse. Barrillon wrote that the English court hoped for that to happen: "[T]hey wish only to disperse and separate this corps." Van Citters shared this opinion: "[T]he only object of the recall is to deprive others of the opportunity to employ them against the king."[18]

The prince, to be sure, said that he left the officers their liberty and had not spoken to them about staying, but, Albeville wrote, "[I] know others did in his name and by his order as i am informed by divers who were sufficiently catechised by his confidents and favorits."[19] Kramprich, keen for Emperor Leopold's interests, proposed to transfer the regiments intact to the Imperial army. The prince preferred sending emissaries to persuade officers and men to stay.[20]

James's proposal to recall the troops so alarmed the Dutch public that shares of the Dutch East India Company fell by 13 percent, as James was pleased to hear.[21] Amsterdam, queen of the Dutch cities and money market of northern Europe, joined by Delft and Dordrecht, was said by Albeville to want to return any of the British troops who wished to go, but Count d'Avaux heard that Amsterdam was alone among the towns of Holland in wishing to release them.[22]

James reacted at first to the refusal to surrender the regiments by holding council sessions for three days without a decision. His generals, and van Citters, feared he would break with the United Provinces, but the Tuscan Terriesi was sure that the king would prefer peace to making war, becoming dependent on his people, and giving up his religious project.[23] The English court was greatly embarrassed. Sunderland blamed the decision to recall the troops on the earl of Melfort's influence. Some said the disobedient soldiers who stayed in Holland should lose their property and (on paper at least) their lives, others that officers should be ordered to bring back the soldiers under their command, still others that the attempt at recall should be dropped. Van Citters lamented that he could not learn what decision was taken, "it being the more difficult since his majesty has chosen to remove one of the clerks from the office of the Earl of Middleton and to forbid him the court because he had revealed the king's decision about the recall of the troops (on which he was scrupulous) in question a little too early or prematurely, and especially so as to speak to me."[24] The clerk's name was Samuel de Paz; he had been born in the Netherlands, apparently of an Iberian Jewish family; he had become a denizen of England and had worked as a copyist and translator in the office of Middleton.[25]

Only the officers were told that they could choose between going and staying. According to the Polish minister at The Hague, a council of war called on them all to state their preferences.[26] Shortly, some of them began to go home. Middleton told Albeville to encourage them: "[F]rom that day [of departure] they are to be in the Kings pay, according to the severall Capacityes they are now in." He was to promise them money to clear their private debts, up to the amount which they could reimburse by deductions from pay over a reasonable time. The king offered substantial bounties for return, ranging from ninety-six guilders for an ensign to two thousand for a colonel. Albeville sent home a list of eleven debtor officers. One of them, Major Edward Wilson, was forcibly arrested for debt as his departure neared.[27]

One of the Scottish colonels was Hugh Mackay of Scourie, a soldier of great experience whom in 1686 James II had actually made a major general in the Royal Army.[28] At first, Mackay was minded to return; he had a Scottish estate as well as rank in the English service. Apparently he was then welcome at home, but he changed his mind, "being there let into the secret, as was supposed, of the intended Revolution."[29] If so (I do not suppose it), he was the first so trusted, for he wrote from The Hague on February 17 (N.S.) to ask the king's permission to remain in the Dutch service, because serving the king might strain his tender conscience.[30]

Major John Buchan certainly changed his mind. In early March,

1687/1688, Albeville listed him as "Just now come to town and Declared" for going home and also recommended him for advancement.
Buchan asked the prince of Orange on March 19 for leave to go. The
prince "ask'd him if he consider'd well what he did," and turned silently from him when Buchan stated his principle of obedience.
Perhaps William was franker in private; be that as it may, Buchan
remained in the service of the States General.[31]

William obviously resented the withdrawal of officers (though he
was later to employ many of them again). Captain John and Ensign
Charles Skelton, sons of Bevil Skelton, former English envoy at The
Hague, had served the States General. John Skelton was also an usher
to the princess of Orange. Though the family was Protestant, it was
closely associated with King James, and the father was obnoxious to
the prince. The two officers may have belonged to the faction in the
regiment that, Laurence Eachard wrote, "cou'd neither be safely kept
nor easily dismiss'd."[32] A little later than some of their colleagues,
both decided to quit the service and go home on James's command.
John hoped to keep his ushership, but William said bluntly "that
those that could not serve the States should not serve the Princesse."[33]

Some of the English in Holland may have been fearful that Captain Davis, the naval officer sent to arrange transportation, intended
to kidnap them and carry them back to England. Three Englishmen
stabbed but failed to assassinate Sir William Hamilton in early
March, apparently under the impression that he was Davis.[34]

The number of officers who returned has been variously stated,
from Bishop Burnet's thirty or forty, the sixty of Hoffmann and the
Historical Account of the British Regiments, to the seventy-five reported by Terriesi on March 19/29.[35] A painful comparison of
Dalton's army lists and those given by Sir James Ferguson yields
names of nineteen captains, four majors, one lieutenant colonel, and
three colonels; a total of twenty-seven of the rank of captain or
above.[36] A probably very partial count of identifiable junior officers
from several sources gives another twenty-seven names, not counting
those of twenty-two volunteers and a surgeon. The minimum, then,
would be fifty-four officers, senior and junior. As the junior officers
counted are listed only by chance and it is reasonable to suppose that
others who remigrated were not listed, I would conjecture a total of
not less than the seventy-five given by Terriesi.[37]

The king gave up hope, if he ever had any, of recovering the
regiments entire. Yet he thought he might get as many as two thousand ordinary soldiers to go home in spite of the ruling of the States

General that they must stay at their posts or be treated as deserters. Albeville opined that most of the soldiers wished to leave. That was just the opinion James held; he ordered Albeville to continue to negotiate for release of all British officers and soldiers who would go, denial of which would be against all precedent.[38] They were all "equaly my Subjects,"[39] and it was equally wrong for men of any rank to be kept from doing their duty.

He intended to put the two thousand men into his service, if so many returned; if not, he would add to them supplementary recruits up to that number.[40] They would form new regiments, finally fixed at three, and the returning officers would receive commissions equal in rank to those they had surrendered. The French king himself admitted the benefit to him of the recall; James suggested to him that France supply money to keep the new regiments in pay. Louis XIV was not sure at first that the benefit was quite enough to pay for.[41]

On March 2, 1688, James prohibited by proclamation the entry of any of his subjects into the services of foreign princes and states and authorized seizure by his governors and land and sea officers of offenders against the prohibition. On March 14, he proclaimed the recall of all British subjects specifically in the military or naval service of the United Provinces. The authority to seize offenders was repeated, except for those who quit the service and returned home. Proclamations directed at Scots were published at Edinburgh on March 22. Lord Middleton sent copies of the proclamations to Albeville for distribution among the English and Scots in their garrisons.[42] Had this proclamation been enforceable, the United Provinces would have lost six regiments; actions to enforce seizure of the British at sea or in the Netherlands, diplomats saw, would provoke war.[43] Seizure of four Scottish seamen from a Dutch warship, over the protests of the Dutch commander, in the previous December, under the instructions usually given to naval commanders, had troubled the States General so much that it had ordered an admiral to sea.[44] Actual seizures of reluctant British soldiers, however, seem not to have occurred.

As it was, many of James's subjects did their best to escape, and some actually got away. British diplomats abroad had orders to help them and authority to spend money to do so; some officers were sent to Liège and Antwerp to persuade those in garrison at Maastricht to go home. Yet James did not want subjects back who might be disloyal. He ordered that only the willing should be encouraged.[45] He would have done better to omit the threat from his proclamations.

The promise to make military places for the returning officers was exactly fulfilled. About the middle of March, he gave a friendly audience to the sixty or so officers who had arrived by that time; he announced his decision to raise three new regiments and fill them with the officers and "the common soldiers who are coming."[46] He issued commissions throughout the rest of the month almost sufficient to officer the regiments, whose colonels were to be John Hales, John Wauchope, and Roger McElligott — for English, Scots, and Irish, respectively. Later commissions filled the few gaps.[47] Most of the officers retained their former rank; there were some twenty-three promotions, including the commissioning of former sergeants and volunteers, and one seeming demotion, a former captain becoming a lieutenant and adjutant. (Later, when James further enlarged his army, he promoted still more.) The few returned officers who did not obtain commissions perhaps did not seek them.

Albeville obeyed his orders to continue soliciting the release of the whole force. On March 1 (N.S.) he submitted a memorial giving three precedents: of British troops transferred by the exiled Charles II from the French service to the Spanish, of a Scottish regiment recalled from the French service in 1665, and of British troops recalled from France after the marriage of William III of Orange to Mary.[48] After reference to a committee and with the "wise advice" of the prince of Orange, the States General professed ignorance of the treaty obliging it to give up the troops on James's demand.[49]

The earl of Middleton had already (February 28) dispatched to Albeville a copy of a recently discovered agreement about the troops, signed in 1678 by the prince (for the States General) and the earl of Ossory (for Charles II), which the envoy was to use to obtain the surrender of the troops to the king. The prince objected that the States General had never ratified this capitulation. Middleton asserted in a letter of March 13 (O.S.) that the prince had had the authority to conclude such a binding agreement ("very different from Nationall Treaties") without ratification. The earl had private doubts on the matter but ordered Albeville to proceed as though the agreement were binding, and Albeville presented a memorial to the States General on April 5 (N.S.) with a copy of the document of 1678.[50]

More officers seem to have been going than William could contemplate without worry: "If the prince had known that so many officers would have declared," wrote Albeville to James that March, "i can assure your Matie he would not have given them leave as he did, no more then he does to the souldiers." The envoy recommended certain officers for loyalty and self-sacrifice but warned him that Captain Emanuel Scrope Howe, brother of Sir Scrope Howe, ought to be searched for "important papers" when he reached Harwich. (Emanuel may have visited England at this time, but he did not leave the Dutch service.)[51] "They generaly say here, that your Matie intends them no good, and that you are in no capacity to do them harme: that the prince will be ready and prepared for all accidents that may happen in England."[52]

John Cutts, a young Englishman in debt but expectant of an inheritance of £2,000 a year, had been friendly to Monmouth and had served since as a volunteer in the campaign for Buda in 1686.[53] He was not commissioned in the British troops in Dutch service before the recall. Perhaps Albeville had suggested that Cutts ought to go to serve the king. Be that as it may, Cutts wrote from Loo (William's country house) to Lord Middleton on April 12 (N.S.) that he regretted that he could not serve James at that time. He would do anything for him, "were not the present measures of State visibly opposite to the Principles, and Interest of that Religion, which is dearer to me than all things in this World, or than Life it self."[54] On April 17, he received a commission as lieutenant colonel of one of the British regiments. The day before he was actually commissioned, James Kennedy, the Scottish agent at Rotterdam, heard that Cutts had sent the newly promoted Captain James or Jacob Ferguson and a lieutenant to Rotterdam that evening with orders to seize "all officers or cadets [volunteers] that are going for England, tho' they have passes"; Kennedy told them to go home by way of Zeeland or Flanders, presumably to evade capture.[55] Clearly, William would never let enlisted men go if he would not keep his word about officers, and by that time the States General agreed with him. As for Cutts, such adaptability as he showed was bound to get him into the Irish House of Lords (as indeed it did).

The States General gave its final answer to Albeville's importunities in a resolution of April 23, 1688. It defended its right to enlist men and the right of free men to enlist voluntarily in its service; it retained only British subjects who had so enlisted. It challenged Albeville's version of the facts as to what had happened in 1665, alleged complete ignorance of the capitulation of 1678, refuted the claim that the capitulation had gone into effect, and stood on its previous decision to keep the troops.[56]

Van Citters reported to his masters of the States General on May 7 (N.S.) that he knew from Lord Middleton that King James was "exceedingly displeased" with that reply, but he also heard that nothing further would be done on the matter.[57]

British common soldiers, however, came away without leave. Barrillon hoped that James's encouragement to return and proclaimed prohibition of service in the Dutch forces would soon scatter these units in such a fashion that they would no longer be reputed British.[58] Indeed, the Dutch emotional reaction to the prohibition explains a threat to chain men up who even asked to go home.[59]

The first reference to returning enlisted men was made by Terriesi; one sergeant and fourteen common soldiers had returned by March 9/19.[60] In April, Albeville heard, "som souldiers are fled away by way of flanders, but they will not have it spoken of." He had a citizen of Den Briel in south Holland hide a sergeant and three soldiers until they could get aboard a packet boat and hoped to do the same again.[61]

Such elopers were rigorously pursued. But the governor general of the Spanish Netherlands, the marquis of Gastañaga, sympathized with the fugitives, although there was a treaty with the States General providing for reciprocal return of deserters. When a captain in the Spanish "Porter's" regiment arrested two, the governor offered to send him to England as a prisoner.[62] On May 27, five Irish soldiers who had left the Dutch service at Berg-op-Zoom reached Brussels. They were stopped at the gate, brought to the governor of the city, taken to Sir Richard Bulstrode, the English envoy there, lodged by him, and sent to Nieuport to board a packet for home. Bulstrode's letter showed that he helped many more, and a Jesuit at Antwerp, Father Visconti, helped at least twelve deserters in May with money and passports, though Antwerp was not safe from pursuit across the border.[63] Parties as large as ten or twelve deserted, especially Catholics.[64] The tendency was serious enough to affect Danish and Norwegian officers and cadets in the Dutch service; several were tried for plotting to desert in August. Two of the cadets were boys who had served at Albeville's celebration of the birth of the Prince of Wales, "which was taken in very bad part," a newsletter tells us; they were fortunate to get off.[65]

According to a procedure laid down by William Blathwayt in May, officers and soldiers coming over produced certificates or otherwise satisfied David Crawford, the chief deputy commissary; they would then receive full pay from the date of leaving the Dutch service until "otherwise provided for or disposed of by His Maty." Those fit to serve were sent to the headquarters of Colonel John

Hales's English regiment of foot for the time, though a few, perhaps Irishmen, were sent to Colonel Roger McElligott's Irish regiment and given preference in promotions.[66]

However many enlisted men may have wished to leave the Netherlands, evidence now available would not support an opinion that a high proportion of them actually did so and enrolled in James's new regiments. The men so enrolled must have been chiefly new recruits, for the most part without military experience and needing training and discipline; each recruit received a guinea as enlistment bounty. James succeeded in getting money from Louis XIV to support them; in April, Barrillon had orders to pay over the money when the regiments were nearly up to strength, and in July he actually began doing so.[67]

The Irish regiment of McElligott differed somewhat from the other two. In the first place, James planned from the beginning to raise its ordinary soldiers mostly in Ireland, rather than by recruiting returned soldiers. The master general of the Irish Ordnance was to furnish its arms. It set up its headquarters at Chester, the easier to receive recruits who seem to have come from James's Irish army, from across the Irish Sea. By June 9, McElligott had two hundred men more than the planned strength (thirteen companies of fifty privates each).[68] Generally, these new Irish soldiers seem to have been Catholics.

At that time, Catholic Irishmen were objects of suspicion, when not of panic. Rumors went around in late June that McElligott's regiment "took free Quarters on the Gentlemen about Chester."[69] Captain Peter Shakerley (or Shackerley), governor of Chester, himself a Protestant of a Cheshire family, was disturbed to hear rumors from other places, "that this Regimt of Coll: McElligatts here in Garrison had sett This City on Fire, & Committed many great and hainous abuses to the Country, there is nothing of Truth in it, for on the Contrary there haveing been lately ye Annual Fayr . . . there has not been any disorder or injury don by any of ye Souldiers dureing ye same; but their deportment has been wth Honesty and Sobriety." Shakerley admitted that four or five had been "very irregular" at first, but making them run the "Gattloop" (gauntlet) and committing a few to jail for "haynous Felonious Crimes" had made the remainder "verry Regular."[70]

That the Irish soldiers "did nothing in the night time" was not a remarkable incident; it was remarkable that people would believe any wild tale about Irish depredations upon the English.

What moved common soldiers to run the risks of desertion and attempt to return to England? The second proclamation, with its threat of kidnapping and punishment, goes some way to explain. Fear of perpetual exile to avoid punishment would have been hard for many of the British soldiers in the Netherlands to face. James's offer to them of alternative employment of the same kind and at the same rank (or, as it often proved, a better one) was also important. A newswriter put the additional motive clearly, while exaggerating its effect upon the soldiers:

> [L]ately a party of English soldiers in making their escape for England had declared there that nothing else but the welcome news of his Majesty's resolution to keep a standing army in England and just payments had encouraged them to hazard their flight, and all and every one of the six regiments were resolved to follow them one time or other, which had obliged the States to order them more narrowly to be watched, and had caused one that ran away from his colours at Breda, and was retaken, to be hanged to deter the rest.[71]

These are material considerations.

There must also have been among the fugitives those who returned for no better reason than that the king bade them to, and they had been taught from every pulpit in their country to do his bidding; they could hardly imagine doing otherwise. These common soldiers were not politicians but simple Christians of their kind and day, and they believed that they owed their king loyalty and obedience as a Christian duty.

They were not alone in their belief. If d'Avaux's testimony is correct, and he was in a position to get correct news, many members of the States General at first favored release of the troops, and the governor general of the Spanish Netherlands fully sympathized with James's intention. William of Orange himself, when he had it in his power to avenge disloyalty to the Dutch service, not only did not do so but employed at least fourteen of the officers who had turned their backs on him when the king called them. Probably he never blamed officers or men for desiring to go; he saw only that he and the States General could ill afford to let them go. William was a prince with the prospect of becoming a king, and he saw the general advantage to princes and kings of unquestioning obedience among their subjects. He was also a general and statesman who knew the particular need of his army and state. He did not hesitate to put the need before the advantage, but he did not later retaliate against subjects who had been caught in a conflict of commands.

There was for William's benefit a counterflow of British subjects wishing to enter the States General's service or to ingratiate themselves with the prince.

James Kennedy wrote from Rotterdam on March 6/16 that a fugitive had just given him notice "that ther is a project in England, and elsewhere, to bring over recruites hither, to the 6 Regiments, Underhand, and as if it wer workmen, or ordinary passingers."[72] He wrote again, a month later: "Ther come dayly some of the English and Irish officers over to this Country, to seek service, but its a hard matter for me to find out their names, having no power to examin Masters of English and Irish Ships (as I have for the Scots)." The Scottish officers still in Holland said that Dutch recruits were hard to find to fill up vacancies in the British corps, and "none dare open their Mouth to make any of the Officers (that have stayed here) sensible of their fault; all is immediately caryed to Court . . . Thers Spyes over all, who watch, and observe not only Mens words, but their very looks."[73] About the same time, Albeville reported the coming of Scottish seamen to enter the Dutch fleet.[74]

There is an interesting case of remigration. John Cunningham had been sergeant major of Balfour's Scottish regiment in the Dutch army but received a major's commission in James's cavalry in 1685 during the regiment's stay in England. In May 1688, he wrote from Cambrai to someone close to the prince of Orange that he wished to leave the British service and reenter that of the States General, which he had only left on the king's command; his motive was "that religion I was borne and am to dye in."[75] Albeville took notice of him on July 25: "Cunningham Major of Horse in his Maties service was in France with the Kings leave, from thence he went privatly into England, and from thence came privatly hither. He pretends that the consideration of his Religion forc'd him hither. . . . whosoever declares against Your Matie is thought here to be very religious, tho he hath no religion at all."[76] James replaced Cunningham with another man on July 1; a Dutch document of October lists him as commanding a company of Scottish foot in the Dutch service.[77]

Several indications of departures from England to serve the Dutch Republic are available.[78] The total result, by July 16/26, according to Terriesi in London, was that each of the British regiments in Holland was said to have 150 more soldiers than it had had before the recall.[79]

The news of James's son's birth was a blow to men who were putting all their hope in the prince of Orange. Albeville then saw members of the States, courtiers, and "officers of the Brigade of his

Maties subjects, with so great consternation and deiection in their faces, that it would have added to my ioye, if it could receive an increase."[80] But that was only temporary.

Other British subjects were in the Netherlands who did not enroll in the regiments. These were sympathizers with William who had come over to give moral support or fearers of James's seeking protection. If William came to an invasion of England, the able-bodied among them would serve in newly raised English units (as many did). Some went openly to William's court and shunned Albeville; others called on the envoy during their visits to The Hague. Some skulked secretly in Dutch towns and saw William and his associates, if at all, by night. Albeville, increasingly kept distant, still had his ways of finding out some of those who had come over.[81] For example, Lord Wiltshire, eldest son of the Whig marquis of Winchester, was at The Hague that summer and was observed to visit the prince's house at Honselaarsdijk, though he had had a pass from James II to go abroad[82] and relations between king and prince could hardly have been worse. Wiltshire's father commended him to the prince.[83]

They were all waiting for something to happen. In the course of the summer, it became plain that the English and Scots were indeed to go to England with Prince William and not to James's service. They were the first units to go ashore at Torbay.

7

William's Union
with the Dutch Opposition

THE PRINCE OF ORANGE could expect, if James persisted in alarming his subjects, an invitation to intervene in English affairs and would accept it if the invitation seemed to promise enough support. Yet he could not do so without gathering support at home.

The United Provinces of the Netherlands was a federal republic. William was not a monarch there, but head of its first family, captain general of its army and admiral general of its navy, *stadhouder* (governor) of five of its seven provinces, and possessor of very great wealth. He could muster many adherents of his house and command the military resources of those provinces. He held other prerogatives, such as appointment of magistrates in Utrecht, Gelderland, and Overijsel; he was "first noble" of Zeeland and, through the deputation of his cousin Willem Adriaan of Nassau, lord of Odijk, was all-powerful there.[1] He had such influence that he could rely on a majority of the States General. All that, however, was not quite enough, for he had to deal with the city of Amsterdam and with the anti-Orange party in the country.

Amsterdam was possibly the wealthiest city in Europe. Its burgers paid a high proportion of the taxes of the province of Holland, and Holland contributed nearly 58 percent of the income of the central government. Its wealthy ruling class, the "regents," formed a municipal oligarchy knit close by blood, marriage, and common financial interests, allied with similar groups in other cities. Leading members of the class occupied governmental offices at Amsterdam; the most trusted and respected were annually elevated or reelected to the group of four *burgemeesters,* free of control of the *stadhouder.* The *burgemeesters* called meetings of the city council (*Vroedschap*) and decided what matters should come before it.[2]

The regents were not united on all subjects. Some families traced their positions to the era of revolt against Spain or earlier and tended to conservatism in religion. Another wealthy group had risen through commerce with Protestant ports in the Baltic in the seventeenth century and interested itself powerfully in the Reformed Church.[3] There were other differences, and division among patrician factions gave William III his opportunity. After 1672, he was unchecked by democratic opposition and could expect support from some of the oligarchs of Holland. "What he did," writes D. J. Roorda, "was merely to make use of those regents who were prepared to further the policies which he stubbornly pursued. If need be, he was not reluctant to benefit from corruption."[4]

The persuasion or seduction of part of the regent class would not suffice for the plan to invade England. Before William could ask and get help from the States General in such a difficult affair, and before he could leave the country with confidence in its safety, he must be sure of overwhelming support from all who mattered in the complicated government of the United Provinces, and that would not be easy to obtain. William's policy was exclusively concerned with foreign and military affairs; however good it was for European liberty and equilibrium, it conflicted with the short-term, highly commercial, and therefore irenic concerns of the republic and with the wishes and financial interests of many of the regents. He had tried to make the government dependent on his will to fulfill his purposes, even introducing authoritarian abuses to combat the license of the period preceding his stadhoudership.[5] He had thus made enemies whom he could neither remove nor subdue, to add to those habitually suspicious of the Orange family. He needed reconciliation.

The revocation of the Edict of Nantes in 1685, by which Louis XIV deprived his Protestant subjects, the Huguenots, of their freedom of worship and conscience, made for just such a reconciliation as William needed, for Louis was William's great enemy and the disturber of equilibrium, and the prince could say with conviction, and most of the regents could agree, that the king of France meant to destroy Protestantism everywhere. Thousands of "refugees" (the

French word now entered the English language in this connection) streamed into the Netherlands, stopping there or passing on to other places of safe settlement, for Louis XIV had not given most of them leave to go—he considered them fugitives from justice and subject to his laws if he could catch them. They were bitter, and they were not helpless. Some had illegally brought or sent funds out of France; even in the first months of the emigration, these sums were reported to reach an immense total.[6] Moreover, some of the Huguenots were experienced former officers of the French army. Thus French money and men could be had for William's cause and against the common enemy and object of hatred.

To the officers among the Huguenots, William extended his protection, for he intended to employ them in new regiments raised for the purpose (just as James created new regiments to employ his subjects recalled from the United Provinces), but he could not persuade the States General to agree to increase the size of the army. He was irritated; he was also unwilling to allow such good material to pass into England, say, or Brandenburg. He announced at The Hague that he would pay the expenses of the French Protestant officers out of his own purse, assigning eighty thousand guilders for the purpose.[7]

Evidently, on that subject the *stadhouder* and the States General did not see with one vision. A larger army would mean more power for the prince and more public expenditure. Amsterdam was the home of opposition to both. As the French ambassador, Jean-Antoine de Mesmes, count d'Avaux, was constantly at work on the regents of the city and like-minded groups elsewhere, it was no wonder. D'Avaux was an able diplomat, served by good intelligence, with influential friends at Amsterdam. (He was also already critical of some aspects of French policy.) A chief aim of his work, which one can call intrigue if one likes, was to prevent augmentation of the Dutch army or navy. (On November 22, 1686, he happily reported that the *burgemeesters* of Amsterdam had resolved on actually reducing the war budget [*staat van oorlog*] of the coming year by three million guilders, saving the money by reducing the salaries of generals and releasing from service many junior officers.)[8] In August 1687, partly no doubt because of d'Avaux's work, the Amsterdammers declared "very boldly" that they would never consent to the prince's request for support of nine thousand additional seamen in the fleet.[9] At the end of 1687, apparently, William's needed reconciliation was not accomplished.

In 1688, however, Louis XIV blundered, his enemies profited, and the Amsterdam authorities changed their minds.

Everyone acquainted with the United Provinces knew that the Dutch economy was built on foreign commerce. Perhaps next in importance to trade with the Baltic was that with France and in goods imported from France. War against France would virtually end such trade; moreover, war would put at risk every Dutch ship trading to the Mediterranean or to the East or West Indies. William III's plans must eventually lead to war. Not only Amsterdam but other Dutch cities would feel the effects upon commerce, and many private fortunes might go to ruin. The United Provinces had experienced such consequences, and the invasion of Dutch soil, while at war against France from 1672 to 1678.

Commerce was related to the religious question, for Dutch Protestant merchants were used to free movement in France without religious interference. (It was a shock to the States General and others to learn that French authorities were making religion a pretext for meddling with Dutch men and ships in January, 1688).[10]

The last great offense to Dutch trade began in a small way with a French restriction of the import of herring to those treated with salt from Brouage, a French salt-producing town—a restriction so tight as to amount to a prohibition of foreign catches. When the news of this step reached the United Provinces in September 1687, the States General complained to d'Avaux. It seemed a breach of the Franco-Dutch commercial treaty then in effect, but King Louis blandly instructed d'Avaux on October 9 that it was a mere police measure and had nothing to do with the treaty.[11] Neither, apparently, had long delays in French customhouses nor confiscation of foreign goods nor postponement of sailings in France.[12]

Dutch merchants and their government did not agree, as d'Avaux observed in a dispatch of November 6, in which he also mentioned new disputes between William and *"Messieurs d'Amsterdam."* D'Avaux confessed his fear that injury to the herring fishery, which supported more than sixty thousand persons, would bring the prince and Amsterdam together. In retaliation, Dutchmen proposed to lay impositions on French wines and syrups imported into the United Provinces. On November 19, Marquis de Seignelay wrote to assure d'Avaux that the Dutch would not cut off a trade in those commodities, which they carried on in northern Europe, and make useless two or three hundred ships employed in carrying them.[13] They did raise the duties on imported soap, oil, and whale fins. Louis in return put into effect a tariff schedule of 1667, raising the duties on woolen cloth from Holland, whether carried to France in Dutch vessels or in others. Seignelay wrote to d'Avaux that the king of France would not revoke his decision, even if the United Provinces renounced its recent tariff increases.

D'Avaux wrote later, looking back on events, that "there were the first causes of resentment we gave to the Dutch, which were greatly augmented afterwards, as will be seen."[14] He referred, no doubt, to the further prohibition of importation of Dutch cloth into France, which forced the town of Leiden to complain in March 1688 of the impending destruction of its chief industry. Leiden renewed its complaints to the States of Holland with support from the Corps of Nobles of that province, speaking through Pensionary Fagel, and without much opposition from Amsterdam or Rotterdam.[15] (The Dutch nobility was for the most part of the Orange party.) By July 29, the French ambassador had to write that the Amsterdammer regents were convinced that England and France were resolved to destroy their religion and, above all, their commerce.[16] This conviction was forcing cooperation with the prince. The Danish envoy at The Hague, Christian von Lente, had observed a few days before, "The Prince of Orange is more absolute in this country than I had believed, and he gained a short while ago a very important point in making the city of Amsterdam consent to the levy of a certain number of sailors."[17] D'Avaux reported to his master on August 26 that the commerce of Holland had diminished by more than a fourth and that people there were "very soured" against France.[18]

Nevertheless, as late as September 2 the States General was sending a message by courier to Willem van Wassenaer, lord of Starrenberg, its ambassador to France, that he should urge Louis XIV toward reestablishment of commerce between the two nations. D'Avaux thought Pensionary Fagel might thus try to obtain a refusal, to justify to the province of Holland the obstruction of French trade in the United Provinces.[19] The ambassador urged on Marquis de Croissy the importance of giving satisfaction to Starrenberg. He wrote also to King Louis: "[I]f these gentlemen were satisfied on commercial questions, they would not give the Prince of Orange freedom of action as they do, and I believe I have correct information that he has persuaded a good part of the *Messieurs d'Amsterdam* [probably the city council] that they cannot reestablish their trade except in actually preparing for war."[20]

D'Avaux's advice was fruitless; Louis XIV tightened the screws on Dutch trade further. At the end of September, he ordered his officers to stop and take possession of all Dutch ships in French ports.

Fifty-five were detained at Bordeaux and its neighboring ports, Blaye and Libourne; twenty-nine at La Rochelle; the total for all ports has been given as about three hundred. According to Professor Baxter, "[T]he sailors were . . . offered the choice between popery and the galleys."[21]

The regents had been more inclined to oppose William than to support France.[22] When Louis XIV attacked their trade, it may have been difficult for some of them to fall in with the Orange party; few indeed felt compunction about parting company with the king of France.

Perhaps, as Professor Andrew Lossky says, "the tariff restrictions on Dutch trade were meant to frighten Louis XIV's former Amsterdam friends after the policy of cajolery and bribery had failed and the Amsterdammers had come to an understanding with William III."[23] Lossky's assertion has two weaknesses, however. First, the regents of Amsterdam in late 1687 were by no means firmly united with William, to the latter's disgust. The tariff restrictions drove them to cooperate with him by giving assistance—for example, the nine thousand seamen they had initially refused to allow him— less grudgingly than they otherwise would have done. Second, Louis's determination to stick to the orders he had given, even if the Dutch made concessions, though probably unknown to the regents at the time, would have frustrated any long-term agreement with them, so that "frightening" them would not have made sense. More likely, Louis punished his friends and enemies alike in adopting his policy, which after all had something to do with mercantilist principles; and, of course, though doubtless frightened, the Amsterdammers did not panic. They rationally struck at Louis by helping to elevate his enemy, the prince of Orange, to the English throne.

On various grounds, many ordinary Netherlanders had long disliked the king of France. His bad faith in failing to observe the Treaty of Nijmegen; his arrogance toward all his neighbors; his support of Danish King Christian V's aggressive policy; his dishonest ways of getting money—all those were lively causes of dislike in 1688, but by far the most emotional reaction was to his persecution of Protestants, French and foreign, especially since the revocation of the Edict of Nantes.

Huguenot propaganda aroused a large part of the hatred and fear of Louis XIV. Many Huguenots had settled in Holland, encouraged by the generous assistance of Dutchmen, officials and others, even diplomats,[24] and they wrote many attacks on Louis XIV, some in French and some not, as heated and resentful as one would expect from victims for religion's sake.[25]

D'Avaux observed the effect of the continued and well-publicized persecution on the minds of the members of the various governing bodies in the United Provinces. He passed on a recommendation that Louis XIV relax his laws toward persons for whom the Amsterdammer authorities interceded: "[O]ne could not believe the good effect that would make throughout the city if Your Majesty did them some kindnesses from time to time; . . . that would efface the annoyance that affairs of religion give them, and win the hearts of the chief citizens, who would be still more inclined to Your Majesty's interest when they saw the honor Your Majesty had for their city."[26] Louis was remarkably stiff in such cases and seldom yielded. Dutchmen who had acquired French nationality he treated as badly as born Frenchmen. Even those who had not done so were not permitted to leave freely.[27]

D'Avaux also noticed the effects of sermons delivered by French Protestant ministers in Dutch churches. As he wrote later,

> During the time preaching ministers discoursed in the pulpit that French ships had been found loaded with Protestants, unwilling to change religion, who were being sent to America for sale to the savages, and said that if the King [of France] had conquered Holland, all the Dutch Protestants would have been treated the same. That business made a great commotion among the people and produced very unpleasant effects. A minister from Orange [then under French occupation] whose legs were crippled, had himself carried into the pulpit as if a man who could not walk, and testified that his infirmities were caused solely by the bad treatment he had received in France because of his religion.[28]

The concern in the Netherlands for foreign Protestants reached upward to the highest level, as when, in January 1688, the States General considered collection of money for the Vaudois (Waldensians) of the Piedmont, persecuted by Louis's satellite, the duke of Savoy.[29] James II was lumped with other Catholic monarchs as at least a potential persecutor of Protestants; and the Catholics of his court were thought by van Citters in no sense kindly disposed toward the United Provinces.[30] The authorities in Holland did not wish to expel Gilbert Burnet and other British exiles, in part because they did not wish to give aid to what appeared to be religious persecution. They were not free agents; d'Avaux reported in August that the city fathers of Amsterdam "excused themselves to their friends for being so embittered . . . about trade; . . . they dared not do all they pleased, and even . . . the preaching ministers had so strongly roused the people against them about religion that they risked being massacred if they opposed the Prince of Orange's plan."[31] Though those officials naturally continued to wish to please d'Avaux and therefore put the best face they could on their conduct, there was much in what they said. As for massacre, the brothers de Witt had been butchered by a mob in the streets of The Hague no further back than 1672.

The more closely James seemed aligned with Louis, the more fearful he made the Netherlanders. When the cathedral chapter of Cologne, in January 1688, chose as coadjutor and expected successor for its aging archbishop a French puppet, William Egon, Cardinal von Fürstenberg, James applauded, though neighboring states felt menaced, the United Provinces, militarily accessible from the direction of Cologne, particularly so. When the archbishop died, James favored the election of Fürstenberg to take his place.[32] His attitude seemed to indicate a secret alliance between England and France. In the summer of 1688, moreover, it became known that the king of France had offered the king of England a naval squadron to help ward off attack. Though James declined the offer, Dutch and French Protestants regarded it as another sign of a secret alliance—perhaps against Protestantism.

No such alliance existed, and all attempts then or since to find one have failed, but many in the Netherlands believed in it; they had special reasons to be sensitive. The two fleets of England and France, if combined, could easily outnumber the fleet of the United Provinces. The army of James II could be used either to suppress risings against his Catholicizing policy or to forward the aggressive designs of Louis XIV. Alternatively, Louis might lend James a force to wipe out Protestantism. The States General heard that his officials in June had ordered the children of Lutheran congregations around Mont-Royal, the new French fortress on German soil, to attend Catholic schools so as to grow up Catholics.[33]

Worst of all, British resources and men would not be disposable for the common cause, resistance to French aggression. That was not tolerable to William of Orange. He had managed his internal policy, wrote Robert Fruin, "so as to make the republic subservient to his European purpose," at some cost to constitutionality and freedom. Soon he would intervene for the same purpose in England.[34]

William was fortunate in the choice of *burgemeesters* at Amsterdam in February 1688. Joannes Hudde remained in office from the previous year; he had as colleagues Nicolaas Witsen (his cousin), Cornelis Geelvinck, and Jean Appelman. Of the four, only Appelman was a Francophile; the others were inclined, if it was consistent with the city's interests, to cooperate with the prince of Orange.[35]

We have seen, from the point of view of the French envoy, the rise of conflict between Amsterdam's interests and the policy of France. At the beginning of summer, William decided to take Hudde, Witsen, and Geelvinck into his confidence, using his own man, Everard van Weede, lord of Dijkvelt, as an intermediary for the first approaches. Witsen, for one, was probably not surprised; early in 1688 he sat in the body called the *Gecomitteerde Raden* and heard Pensionary Fagel suggest that the prince of Orange was thinking of an expedition to England. H. M. Tromp of Delft had privately told Witsen that "the Prince seemed to wish to play a little Monmouth."[36]

Dijkvelt was of course fully informed of William's plans, so far as they were made. He had in early 1687 been the prince's representative in England, almost a spy. He sent secretly to the three trustworthy *burgemeesters* of Amsterdam during June 1688 to speak with him. Geelvinck was not in the city, but Dijkvelt communicated to the other two what he knew of the situation in England, all in deep secrecy. He brought out the danger to the Dutch Republic in the supposed close alliance of James II and Louis XIV. Witsen and Hudde admitted the danger, but they still could not agree that armed intervention was necessary, preferring to rely on Providence. Dijkvelt asked whether it would not be better to attack than to be attacked, but the two *burgemeesters* feared the Catholic powers' resentment and advised waiting until the next spring. The country could not be left defenseless and leaderless without the utmost peril of French invasion.[37]

Dijkvelt showed particular confidence in Witsen, summoning him two days later to the prince's house in The Hague and saying to him, "*aut nunc, aut nunquam,* signifying that the work must be done now or never." Witsen prayed to God for wisdom and reluctantly went. Dijkvelt told him on his arrival that the magnates of England (perhaps the seven who signed the "invitation" to William) favored the prince, whose plans could hardly miscarry. After Hans Willem Bentinck, William III's closest friend, had corroborated the assertion, the still pessimistic Witsen had a private interview with the prince himself. The latter denied having come to a conclusion about invasion but revealed where he could get the money he would need — a fund about to be raised to repair fortifications. He could do the work overseas in a week or two and saw no special difficulty in it. Witsen did not agree, as he saw an obstacle as to William's and Mary's claim to the English Crown, which was evidently being discussed. The prince thought the king of England would use any time allowed him to strengthen himself further; therefore, the invasion could not wait until the next spring. The enterprise should be his alone, not the republic's, and all he wanted was support. Witsen raised financial objections. The discussion became too long for one day.

Resuming on the next, the prince came to the point of asking whether Witsen would stand by him if he could succeed without personally involving Witsen. The *burgemeester* asked leave to consult Hudde and Geelvinck at Amsterdam. He went, then returned to state the joint opinion of all three that they could advise neither for nor against the "great work"; they would advise as individuals an understanding on the subject, which would be consistent with their oaths and duty. They believed, however, that such an understanding would not pass the city council of Amsterdam. Witsen would not promise to press the matter in the council. He told Grand Pensionary Fagel that God might well take care of England, as a matter of religion, but Fagel replied that men might and ought to use the sword for religion: "So our fathers did, establishing the state on religion."

Witsen still resisted. The prince said again that he had not decided what to do but that he would prepare, raising money and recruiting seamen without giving the States knowledge of his plans. All these discussions remained a deep secret, kept from most men in the government.[38]

The Cologne election crisis was making a good deal of noise, and the Prince of Wales survived his first weeks. In August, Bentinck, who had recently represented William in negotiations with several German states, went to see the *burgemeesters* at Amsterdam. Hudde was sick, but Bentinck did see Geelvinck and Witsen at Witsen's house, though he knew as little of the city's intentions on departure as he had known on arrival.

The king of France had taken one more step to alienate the Dutch, provoking them especially against King James. On September 9, d'Avaux acted on instructions and informed the States General, regarding the military and naval armaments the prince made in the United Provinces:

His Majesty [of France] . . . cannot believe that Your Lordships are engaged in such great expense inside and outside their state, that they take into pay and bring into their country so many foreign troops; that they send to sea such a numerous fleet at so advanced a season, and prepare so great an apparatus of war, if they have not a

formed design commensurate with the magnitude of the preparations.

All these circumstances, Sirs, and so many others,
. . . convince . . . the King my master that this armament concerns
England; that is why his Majesty has ordered me to declare on his
behalf that the relations of friendship and alliance that he has with
the King of Great Britain will oblige him not only to support them,
but also to regard as a manifest breach of the peace and an open
rupture with his crown the first hostile act committed by your troops
or by your ships against his Britannic Majesty.[39]

An unusually large crowd was present at the delivery of this
memorial. The States General seemed to expect a proposal for compromise on commerce, made to divide the proponents of peace from
the adherents of the prince of Orange. The presiding deputy had
actually prepared a general answer for such a proposal and used some
words from it in an improvised and disconnected answer to Louis's
threat of war. D'Avaux thought the disturbed countenances of those
"in the secret" showed that William did intend to attack James II.[40]

They might have shown something else — conviction that the secret alliance between France and England existed, based on d'Avaux's
very words. As d'Avaux presented another memorial the same day to
say that Louis XIV had extended his protection to Cardinal Fürstenberg's claim to be archbishop of Cologne and the cardinal's subser-
vience to France was notorious, the two memorials seemed to make
parallel prohibitions and put James in the same light.

J. R. Jones has written that Louis did not intend to carry out his
threat, "either by an invasion of Dutch territory that would divert
William from invading England, or by giving James any significant
aid. . . . [T]he memorial could not be expected to prevent William's
invasion. As d'Avaux had indicated in his despatches, this could be
undertaken with the resources already at William's disposal."[41]

I disagree. If the memorial had frightened the States General into
denying permission for the expedition, William could hardly have
gone. William had not yet laid hands on all the additional funds he
would need, and he could not touch them without the States General's
approval. As that body did not yet know where the French army
would march in the approaching hostilities, it might under different
circumstances have been frightened. D'Avaux's chief effort in his relations with his master was to try to persuade him that circumstances
were becoming less favorable.

The memorial must be seen as a bluff, which failed, though the

French king may have anticipated failure. It did not alarm the States General more than the French danger to Protestantism or the damage inflicted by France on Dutch trade. Instead it brought the unpredictable city council of Amsterdam into the Orange camp. It was in September that William opened his plans to the States of Holland and thus to discussion in the city council. After deliberation, the council resolved on September 26 to support the prince of Orange without conditions. Until that resolution, no one was sure how the Amsterdammers would go.[42]

By that time, the French troops were in motion throughout their recent conquests, following Pope Innocent XI's decision against Fürstenberg in the election at Cologne.

It was chiefly Louis XIV's doing, really, though James had given great offense in the Netherlands by recalling the troops and licensing publication of the tract *Parliamentum Pacificum* (of which more later). "To be involved in an undertaking which must lead to a rupture with France," wrote the historian Sirtema van Grovestins, "it was necessary that Holland feel doubly offended in its religious sympathies, and, above all, in its interests as a commercial people."[43] It was Louis who persecuted Protestants with prison and galleys; it was he who hindered Dutch commerce and seized Dutch ships; it was his agents who circulated the rumor that he and James were allied; and it was he who threatened the republic in such a fashion as to provoke war rather than to deter it.[44] The outcome was the commencement of a war in which an expected neutral combated France. One wonders what Louis could have been thinking of.

He knew that there would soon be war. As it happened, the proximate cause was the disputed election at Cologne and Pope Innocent's decision. Several other causes would have done as well (including the expedition against England), for the true meaning of "inevitable war" is the obvious result of a general bellicose mood in the governments of several countries. Nowhere was the ruler's bellicosity stronger than in France. As for the Netherlands, Albeville wrote on September 7, "[T]he people generally every where [are] mad for war both against England and France; those of Amsterdam more then any."[45]

Louis also knew the special anxiety of the United Provinces (above all, of the province of Holland) for "its interests as a commercial people." He had deliberately set out to injure those interests by issuing new tariff regulations and other hindrances, just as he set out after the Cologne election to injure the Holy Roman Emperor

Leopold by war, just as he had set out to injure Protestants and alarm Protestant sympathizers by religious persecution.

He knew, no one better, that if his diplomatic bluff failed, the point of Dutch attack would be Great Britain. His spies and diplomats provided that knowledge. He cannot have wished to see James II's overthrow, having so much to lose by it. One can only conclude that Louis behaved so arrogantly either because he could not stop himself or because he could not see the necessity of self-control. All might go well: James might beat off an attack but suffer such great harm to his position that he would have to drift in an orbit around France for the foreseeable future.

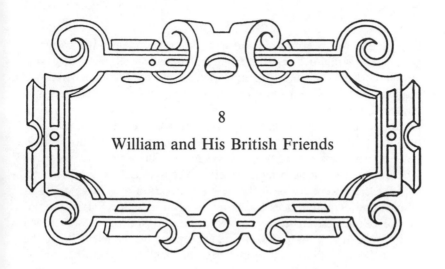

8

William and His British Friends

PRINCESS MARY OF ORANGE, was (until June 1688) heiress presumptive to the English Crown and its powers, but all who knew her knew also that she submitted completely to her husband. In the years since their marriage in 1677, the apparent certainty of Mary's succession to her father had encouraged the pair to make plans. Actually, William had made the plans and Mary had accepted them when they had enjoyed the prospect for nine years: He "had resolv'd within himself, as he said afterwards, *Not to be a Gentleman King,* to hold a Crown by the Courtesy of his Wife . . . without he might be secur'd in it for his Life." Dr. Gilbert Burnet, for whom no intrusion or presumption was too great, acted as William's go-between to broach the subject with Mary. Burnet advised the princess that it was her duty as a wife to obey her husband in everything. Mary, a natural dependent who adored her husband, was "all Obedience, and ready to allow the *Natural* Rights of a Husband, and decline the *Civil Rights* of a Sovereign."[1]

One does wonder what William would have done had his wife said no, having the ambition and use for power that he had, but so it was, from about 1686, that William and Mary had disposed of the royal power that they both expected to fall to Mary.

There was everything to be said, then, for William's becoming acquainted with the English system of government and with the

Englishmen who were important to it. Correspondence and converse were easy; William knew the English language well. Several of his Dutch courtiers also had English connections through wives or mothers: Hans Willem Bentinck through his wife, for instance, and Nassau-Zuilesteyn through wife and mother. At least a few English notables, such as the second duke of Ormond, were in an equivalent position (Ormond's mother was a Dutch kinswoman of the prince). And the better instructed William was in English affairs, the better for all concerned when he became in effect the monarch of the country.

Yet there were perils in the active cultivation of a large circle of friends and acquaintances by a man in such a position. It is a commonplace, but nevertheless true, that factions and persons excluded from favor in a monarchy will find their hope in the heir if he or she will let them. William had in fact been in touch with members of the English opposition before his marriage, when he was only a member of the royal family by his mother's birth.[2] Discontented associates of the heir, if detected in conspiracy, could make his position next to impossible; if conspiring but not detected, they could trouble the incumbent ruler. This could be especially true if the heir was also discontented, and in 1688 both Mary and William were discontented indeed.

James II had wished to convert both, but particularly Mary, to his own religion. He would do it for the good of their souls, be it understood, and it was (or should have been) a wish of perfect charity. James had also a political motive, however—the desire for security of his Roman Catholic subjects in their recent gains during at least the next reign. Conversion of the next heir could influence the political classes in the campaign for repeal of the penal laws and test acts. Of course, he also hoped to make more converts among other Protestants by showing them such an example and reminding them that Catholicism was (so to speak) a religion with a future. Anyone but James, whose reliance on Providence and his own authority was greater than a rational mind can easily grasp, would have known in advance that the attempt would fail. But James made it and, having failed, made a second suit to his daughter and son-in-law for approval of his intention to repeal the anti-Catholic laws.

William was also heir to the great Protestant tradition of his family, fairly tolerant for the seventeenth century. Dutch Catholics usually suffered no great oppression, and William did not indiscriminately dislike Catholics, but the English Parliament had passed the laws, and James's motive in wishing to remove them did not accord with the wishes of most Englishmen of the political classes. James's persistence in his course meant trouble for everyone, including James and his heir; certainly if William admitted inclination to repeal, he would become personally unpopular. He, and of course Mary, opposed repeal. James, unfortunately for himself, would not leave them alone.

After the issue of the first Declaration of Indulgence in the spring of 1687, a number of exiled Dissenters took advantage of the proffered liberty of conscience and returned to Great Britain. One of these was a Scottish lawyer named James Steuart. Finding life at home more free and enjoyable than before, he wrote enthusiastically to Dissenters remaining abroad, urging them to return home under the protection of the declaration.

Steuart wrote to (among others) William Carstares, a Scottish Presbyterian divine who had once plotted with the earl of Argyll. (Both Steuart and Carstares would be leading figures in postrevolutionary Scotland.) In 1687, Carstares was a chaplain of William of Orange and in close touch with Hans Willem Bentinck, William's closest friend, and Gaspar Fagel, the grand pensionary of the province of Holland. Carstares, who had been legally tortured in Scotland, told Bentinck and Fagel about Steuart's letter, commenting on the liberty of conscience: "[T]he fear . . . I have of a storm after this calm, and the sad experience, I have had of the crueltie and treachery of some of those, concerned in the government of that Kingdom [presumably Scotland], make me have an aversion from being within reach of men, from whom I have suffered so much." Approval by William of repeal of the anti-Catholic laws was out of the question. Carstares told Bentinck that he had answered Steuart's suggestion of the step to this effect: "[N]othing will move him [the prince] to allow the takeing away of laws that seclude Papists from publick offices." Carstares believed that Steuart was writing at James II's desire, and Steuart, offering Carstares a meeting *incognito* in Holland, added, "If you have a secret permission from The Hague [i.e., from William], it would promise more." Carstares was cautious in his reply.[3]

William considered the correspondence in conference with Fagel, Carstares, and Burnet. Fagel then drew up a letter in his own name, dated November 4, 1687; Burnet made a translation and sent it to Steuart.

The prince and princess of Orange, Fagel wrote, had already declared themselves to Albeville against religious persecution and in favor of as much liberty of conscience for Catholics as they had in the United Provinces. They were willing to concur in a legal freedom of worship for Dissenters and the repeal of some of the anti-Catholic penal laws but not in repeal of the test acts "or of those other *Penal Laws* . . . that tend to the security of the Protestant Religion"; reason and experience showed that Protestants and Catholics, "mixed together in places of Trust and publick employments," could not live peaceably. Exclusion from office was not serious punishment. As James had laid down that penal laws against Dissenters would be repealed only at the same time as the test, "the *Roman Catholicks* are only to blame for it, who will rather . . . that they and their posterity should lie still under the weight of the *Penal Laws*, and exposed to the hatred of the whole Nation than [be] still restrained from a capacity of attempting any thing against the Peace and the Security of the Protestant Religion." Protestants should be wary of attempts by Catholics to give first place to repealing the test "to clear a way for bringing in the *Roman Catholics to the Government*, and to publick Employments: in which case there would remain no relief for them [Protestants] but what were to be expected from a Roman Catholic Government."[4]

Steuart received Fagel's letter and passed it to Sunderland, Melfort, and King James, who was not happy with it. The gamble that William would change his mind had never been a good one, and it had failed. Worse than that, it gave the enemies of James's religious policy an opportunity to publish the opinion of the prince and the princess. Previously, it had been expressed only in conversation or other private communications.

Steuart, at least, seems to have recognized that he had made a mistake; he tried to persuade Carstares to suppress and destroy his letters.[5] But the Orange party had Fagel's letter printed (beginning in the middle of January) and a large number of copies distributed, in English, Dutch, German, French, and Latin. Anyone who remained ignorant of William and Mary's views either was illiterate or did not care about the religious controversy. Still, the damage to James was limited.

James was not pleased with the effects of his own error. I do not know how directly his displeasure affected John Northleigh's *Parliamentum Pacificum,* published in the following March (1688). The earl of Sunderland, a secretary of state, certainly licensed the book for publication, and the license seemed to many an endorsement of its contents. Northleigh already had a position as a controversialist be-

fore this subject came up; he may merely have seized an opportunity
to please the king.

The title refers to the Convention Parliament of 1660, or "Heal-
ing Parliament," that had favored a large measure of religious liberty.
Northleigh wished for another such parliament to establish toleration
by law. His argument did not at all require him to bring in foreign
considerations, but he attacked the United Provinces' protection of
Gilbert Burnet (who had taken on Dutch nationality) and thus offended the States General: "Those that never yet dealt so fairly with
Princes, may be suspected for such a superfluous Faith, to one that
puts himself upon them for a Vassal."[6] Worse, he doubted that
Princess Mary's opinion was correctly set forth in Fagel's letter and
even hinted that Fagel had not really written the letter. He was sarcas-
tic on Fagel's statement that exclusion from office was not serious
punishment. He asserted that Dutch Catholics participated in government in some provinces and towns as well as in the army (which Fagel
had admitted) and called participation a reward for services in rebellion and the establishment of independence. Should Catholics in
England not have as good reward for services to their lawful sovereign? He suggested that Burnet was the real author of Fagel's letter
and that Mary had nothing to do with it.[7] Translators rendered
Northleigh's book into French and Dutch, perhaps into other languages.

The States General took up *Parliamentum Pacificum* quickly. At
its session of April 9 (N.S.), 1688, it decided to protest against it to
Albeville at The Hague and to order van Citters to protest at the
English court.[8] Fagel also took offense at Northleigh's book. He was
the chief executive officer of Holland, a man of great standing in the
Dutch republic. He knew very well what Mary's views were, and he
disliked the suggestion that he had misrepresented them or allowed
some lying scribbler to use his name for that purpose.

Fagel therefore wrote another letter recounting the history of the
question, acknowledging his authorship of the original Dutch version
and stating that the prince and princess of Orange had examined both
Dutch and English versions before he sent the letter to Steuart. Sunderland had known very well when licensing *Parliamentum Pacificum*
that Fagel's letter was authentic. Fagel included in his published second letter an acknowledgment he had made to Albeville of the
authorship of the first one. He said he hoped Sunderland would recall
the license and punish the author. To avert a charge that the second
letter was spurious, he had his printer add an attestation that Fagel

had delivered it and ordered it published. He also appended extracts of Steuart's letters (probably to Carstares) to bear out his account. One dated August 26, 1687, said quite plainly that Steuart wrote with the king's permission, "and a Return expected by him."[9]

Northleigh had also attacked Gilbert Burnet. The future historian of his own times had not yet reached his full stature, but he had fully developed vanity and sensitivity. He replied to Northleigh with a swinging attack on the author, Charles II, James II, Jesuits, and Catholics in general. He pretended to fear that James's promises would "bind him till after a short Session or two," when a parliament packed by James's known methods would release the king from them: "[T]he Old Laws *de Heretico Comburendo* might again be revived," and James would "deny nothing to a Loyal and Catholick Parliament," as Charles had not denied to his Cavalier Parliament laws to punish Dissenters. Fagel's first letter had ended the dispute about liberty of conscience by its offer of repeal of some of the penal laws: "[T]he question is now no more, which Religion must be tolerated, but which Religion must Reign and prevail." The king might pension Catholics whom exclusion from office would ruin; Burnet was sure that Parliament would agree without a contrary vote to reimburse him. He defended the United Provinces on the charge of rebellion against their legitimate sovereign (one to which the republic's oligarchs were open and by which they were therefore easily offended), on the abandonment of Luxembourg to the French, and on the precipitate separate diplomatic action the Dutch had taken in the peace negotiations at Nijmegen in 1678.[10]

Burnet alleged himself suspicious of some plot against Mary's place in the English succession and pointed out that *Parliamentum Pacificum* cleared her of the wish to disturb the English state but did not clear William. The repeal of the test was intended to encourage people to become Catholics. It was

> to set up an Office at F. *Peters* for all pretenders [to offices], and perhaps a pretender will not be so much as received, till he has first abjur'd: so that every Vacancy will possibly make five or six Proselites. . . . And as for the two Houses of *Parliament,* as a great Creation will presently give them the majority in the House of Lords, so a new set of Charters, and bold Returns, will in a little time give them likewise the Majority in the House of Commons.

It would then be easy to overturn the Anglican establishment; Burnet hinted that the king and Parliament might also alter the succession to the Crown.[11] He did not try or need to try to prove his insinuations; they agreed very well with suspicions already widespread among literate Protestants. He was very likely unjust to King James, but James should have blamed himself for having given Burnet and others such an opportunity. If the king had taken Carstares's word as to William and Mary's views in the summer of 1687, he could have avoided all this.

Burnet's *Reflections* appeared in English and Dutch, if not in other languages. Thus all the principal publications of the controversy were available to those most concerned on both sides of the North Sea. They must have contributed in some degree to William's gains of support in the province of Holland and the city of Amsterdam. They certainly damaged the reputation of the English government for truth telling and cast discredit on the vulnerable Sunderland. Protestants uneasily awaiting the end of the queen's pregnancy were not soothed by Burnet's hints that James wished to change the succession. The king had few sympathizers in the controversy except (possibly) d'Avaux.[12]

James did not accept the States General's complaint against Northleigh, van Citters wrote on April 20/30. "His Majesty the other day gave the said Norwley [*sic*] the complaints brought against him, whereupon he, so I know, told some of his friends that he had asked His Majesty's protection, and was assured of it just as Doctor Burnet [is] of that of Your High Mightinesses."[13]

Burnet was not in fact secure in Holland; he feared kidnapping into England and was usually cautious and private in his movements. In March, a newswriter reported that he never went out in the evening and always had four gentlemen with him at that time; suspicious persons were sometimes observed near his house.[14] In April, however, he was seen to go out more frequently, as though confident of the protection of the authorities. On his side, Northleigh never had anything to fear, though he would have been unwise if he had visited the United Provinces in 1688. Fagel was dead within the year, having helped William in many ways, but in none more publicly or more effectively than in raising the prince's reputation for staunchness in the defense of the Protestant religion.

More than two hundred years ago, P. L. Muller posed three views of the expedition of William of Orange in 1688: Macaulay's, the salvation of English constitutional liberty; that of some earlier historians, expression and fulfilment of William's personal desire for power; and Ranke's (shared by other contemporary historians), "an

act of very great European significance, which may only be viewed
and judged as such." Muller rejected the first and second views and
accepted the third: "[W]e must . . . seek the motives for it [the expe-
dition] in European policy."[15]

I cannot see how to reject or hold any one of these three views. If
James had not attacked English constitutional (and religious) institutions, or had not been thought to do so, William would have lacked
support among the political classes. If William had not keenly desired
power, he would not have refused the role of "the queen's husband" as
he did and as he had said he would do. Yet it seems irrefutable that
William and his closest Dutch advisers were guided by their views of
what a "European policy" should be. European policy probably mattered more to William than the other motives, but it probably mattered a good deal less to most of his English friends.

There is a tone of wonder in Charles Hornby's statement of his
own quite accurate understanding of this policy:

> [A] *Revolution* in *England* was become of absolute Necessity, if not
> to us, at least, to some of our Neighbours. The vast scheme of
> making *France* the Seat of an universal Monarchy . . . was so suc-
> cessfully prosecuted . . . that the Arms of that Country had for
> many Years been the Terrour of *Europe,* and without the Assistance
> of *England* there was no resisting their Progress . . . King
> *James* . . . refused to enter into any Alliance to the Interruption of
> the Peace these Parts of *Europe* enjoy'd in his Reign . . . all the
> Confederacies that could be made were too Light without the
> Weight of *England* in the Scale, and without her Strength an un-
> equal Match for the Power of *France,* then in its most flourishing
> Condition. . . .
>
> An impatient Sense of the Difficulties he [William] had to
> struggle with, and an Ambition of making a Figure at the Head of a
> Force sufficient to curb the growing Power of France, and snatch
> the Laurels from that Monarch's Brow, set a keener Edge on his
> Appetite to the English Crown, which a Concurrence of Circum-
> stances both here and abroad now conspired to Place upon his
> Head.[16]

This must have seemed remarkable, and not only to Hornby:
England underwent a revolution because its king did not observe the
European interests that chiefly influenced the prince of Orange and
the anti-French party in Europe. Modern historians have come to
accept that as natural; to most Englishmen of the day it would have
seemed very unnatural had William announced his most important
motive to them before setting forth.

As it happened, his English followers had motives just as real, which he could share and make his own. He was indeed a staunch Protestant, though a Calvinist; he did deplore the persecution of the bishops;[17] he did favor government by agreement between king and Parliament over either James's government without Parliament or the prospective parliamentary dependence on the king. He had a direct interest in the succession to the Crown. These ostensible grounds for William's actions were important in the situation and acceptable to many Englishmen, as the prince knew at the time.

Early in 1687, Everard van Weede, lord of Dijkvelt, had paid England a visit as representing both the prince and the States General. He and William's kinsman Willem van Nassau, lord of Zuilesteyn, who went to England several months later, made and maintained personal contact with possible supporters. Some British magnates, and their sons, crossed to the Netherlands, paying their "duty" to the prince of Orange on reaching The Hague or whichever of the prince's country houses he dwelt in at the time. Aside from the tendencies of some of these tourists to oppose his will, James had not much to complain about, and there was no breach between him and his son-in-law. William's refusal to approve the repeal of the test acts certainly worsened relations, as did the attempt to recall British subjects in Dutch service. Publication of Fagel's first letter and the spread of knowledge of the prince's opposition to recall made the differences public. At the same time, Protestant subjects in England grew progressively less favorable to the king and therefore more inclined to sympathy with the prince.

About the beginning of February, a curious thing happened: The marquis of Halifax; the earls of Danby, Shrewsbury, and Dorset; Lord Lumley; Henry Sidney; and other Protestants of standing received anonymous letters, varying slightly but generally following this example: "You have very honest principles between Man and Man; but so corrupted and pernicious in Religion and Loyalty, that without you soon make your peace with God and the King after this 27th of Jan, you have not many days to live. Make use of this friendly caution, and repent before repentance is in vain."[18] Terriesi, sending an Italian translation of one copy to Florence, observed that such things were blamed by Protestants on Catholics, as consistent with their teachings, and by Catholics on Protestants, as consequences of their malice.[19]

It was not to James's advantage that such letters were sent. One might suspect that some Protestant or Protestants sent them to other

Protestants, whom perhaps they did not like, to help make James
unpopular; or some imprudent Catholic or Catholics may have sent
them without authority from James, genuinely believing that they
were doing their cause good. One cannot exclude the third possibility,
that James authorized the sending, though he ought to have known
better. Evidence is lacking to decide among the three possible origins.

After this burst of threats, some important persons removed
themselves abroad, particularly to the United Provinces – not as exiles
or fugitives, but voluntary expatriates until better days. While there,
they showed their respect (if no more) for the prince of Orange by
calling on him, though as relations between James and William
neared the breaking point, some were too cautious to do so openly.
They were also in a position to meet officers of the English and Scottish regiments there, and the political fugitives of the Rye-House and
Monmouth episodes. The press in Holland was nearer to a free one
than any other in Europe; booksellers openly sold, and the visiting
English openly read, the works of Burnet and other opposition
authors that censors did not allow to be published in England. Albeville complained in June, however, that he had trouble obtaining a
copy of one: "[I] gott [it] this day, but not without art, the printer,
who is an Englishman, makeing difficulty to sell it to every body."[20]
The only caution seems to have been to keep such matter out of the
hands of King James's agents.

Albeville was expected to keep an eye on the British in the country, and he reported their actions home. Sir William Hamilton pro-
fessed "zeal and fidelity" at dinner with the English envoy, but "one
Murray a pernicious little man keeps him [Hamilton] company too
often."[21] Lord Macclesfield stayed privately at Amsterdam in late
April. At the same time, Sir John Guise, a Mr. Trenchard, and the son
of a London alderman named Stanniard were at Rotterdam, and
Albeville heard they were going to William's house at Loo. James
Douglas, earl of Angus, the eldest son of the second marquis of
Douglas, went to Loo on arrival from England, and people in Hol-
land expected several great English lords soon.[22]

Albeville was not always perfectly informed. He reported in the
middle of May the presence of a Mr. Tippin, "who was sherif of
Yorkshier formerly: I am informed he is a disaffected man." Thomas
Tipping was indeed disaffected, but he was from Oxfordshire, not
Yorkshire. In the same letter, however, Albeville correctly reported the
arrival in disguise of Philip Bertie, younger son of the earl of Lindsey,

"to be a gentleman to her Royl. Heighs.," Princess Mary.[23]

The British then residing in the United Provinces were particularly sensitive to surveillance. One or some of them slipped an anonymous letter under Albeville's door, threatening bloody vengeance for any future harm done to the writer or writers, who reminded Albeville of the murder of Lieutenant Robert Thompson (in 1678, by Thompson's brother-in-law Samuel Hunter, clerk of the cheque at Sheerness), the attempt (of the previous English envoy Bevil Skelton) to kidnap Sir Robert Peyton from Holland, and the recent stabbing of Sir William Hamilton. The writers attributed all of these violences to the English government. Albeville complained of the threat, which really disturbed him, to the States General.[24]

Albeville was not to blame for his instructions. Sir Richard Bulstrode at Brussels did exactly the same: "I am told from a very good hand that my Lord George Savile [third son of the marquis of Halifax] at his being lately at Antwerp did use very undutifull expressions both ag[ains]t His Maties Person & Government, & from thence he is gone into Holland," Bulstrode wrote on June 2.[25] Unofficial observers also took note of the presence of British "men of quality." An anonymous newswriter wrote of Lord Wiltshire, the marquis of Winchester's son, that he "was also today [June 24] at Honselaarsdyck," one of William's houses.[26] That William's court was the mecca of the British malcontent was beyond disguise. Even some who had formerly been sent away (as Sir William Waller had been sent to Hesse-Cassel in January) were seen again at Amsterdam and The Hague.[27]

William of course corresponded with friends in Great Britain, though he could use the posts for nothing confidential, as letters to suspected persons were sometimes opened in the post office.[28] He sent and received messages by safe hands, such as Dijkvelt and Zuilesteyn. Much conveyed by word of mouth has been lost, but it seems certain that many such messages, as well as some of those preserved in writing, were simply assurances of esteem and willingness to serve the prince and princess of Orange. It was safer, to be sure, to confide more secret things only to the messenger's memory. Captain Emanuel Howe, nephew of the marquis of Winchester, carried a letter from William to the marquis and returned with Winchester's letter of thanks dated February 20, 1688; Howe probably carried in his head something too dangerous to set down on paper. He also served as a messenger for the earls of Devonshire and Shrewsbury.[29] From what survives, it is clear that many sources informed William about events in England; he could judge the extent of their commitment more by what their messengers said than by what they carried in writing.

We have what William then had not — the light which comes from subsequent events. Winchester, Shrewsbury, and Devonshire, and above all Danby (who corresponded separately in the spring of 1688), later supported William's cause; on the other hand, the marquis of Halifax trimmed until a late day, though he had sent his son, Lord George, to kiss William's hands. Arthur Herbert was a correspondent who took his risks early; the earl of Clarendon expressed as deep devotion but really adhered to King James.[30]

Admiral Edward Russell was a true supporter of Prince William; in April 1688, he was at The Hague to learn his leader's intentions. William said that he would be ready to go to England in September if invited to intervene by "men of the best interest."[31]

Barrillon, in London, heard something of these comings and goings, but as late as May 28/June 7 described them as intended "to take measures with the chiefs of the party opposed to the court and to concert with them a plan for a league against France." Those chiefs had been asked what would happen in England if a war began against France.[32] Quite possibly, clandestine correspondence did deal with these matters, among others.

Whigs and Tories were both among the most committed. The Whig party had begun as an anti-Catholic party, staking everything on the exclusion of the duke of York from the throne in the years 1679–1681. A few months of James's favor had not made it forget the years of persecution that had preceded them. The Tories, Anglican defenders of James's right to succeed, left his side on the subject of his treatment of their church. Stripped of offices for refusing to repeal the penal laws and test acts, outraged by the persecution of the bishops, alarmed by the subversion of Anglicanism and property rights in the universities, many Tories were in touch with each other for help to the deprived fellows of Magdalen College, support of the bishops in their trouble, and a common resistance to repeal. Yorkshire was a principal center for the last-named form of cooperation. It was no coincidence that the great leader of rebellion in the North was a Yorkshire Tory.

Yet some of the Tories still required persuasion to participate, or even acquiesce, in a military expedition and rising against the king; all that teaching of nonresistance had had its effect. A crime greater than the prosecution of the seven bishops was needed to justify that. Opposition leaders had to suggest to them, then convince them, that James II was scheming to violate the rules of royal succession by imposing a fraudulent birth upon the public and presenting a strange child as heir to the house of Stuart and the Crown of England.

They began their campaign with the announcement of the queen's pregnancy and tightened its intensity as the event neared. Princess Anne adopted early a belief convenient to her, scoffed at the "pretense," and made her views known to Princess Mary and her own little court. To feed the rumor-loving public, sheets and pamphlets were smuggled in from Holland, full of scandal and invective.

William did not believe everything he heard, but it suited his plans that Englishmen should believe that Maria Beatrice was not with child. Before the Prince of Wales was born, he said nothing of belief or disbelief. As he was obviously an interested party, it was better for ridicule of the pregnancy to seem to originate elsewhere.

The marquis of Albeville, as English envoy, received news of the royal birth with bubbling enthusiasm. Because the earl of Middleton had omitted to send word by express messenger, "The news was over all the Town before i received my letters."[33] (Others, if not Middleton, must have sent expresses to The Hague.) From Rotterdam, James Kennedy reported that his deputy had ordered a display of flags as a celebration by all British vessels in port. "The Scots obeyd, all of them, but not one English Master would doe it, refusing the same scornfully."[34] Albeville, planning a large celebration at The Hague, asked for instructions on inviting the prince and princess of Orange. After several days' delay, Middleton wrote him that the king would not have them invited on that or any other occasion.[35]

The prince and princess nevertheless sent Zuilesteyn to England a second time, as we have seen, with the stated object of paying their compliments to the king and queen on the birth of the Prince of Wales. Barrillon heard in London that William's first reaction was to send no one but that he was advised to send either a compliment or an army to England. Princess Mary also had her half brother prayed for in her chapel.[36] Zuilesteyn had his audience on the afternoon of July 1/11.[37]

Privately, the emissary served as William's agent among the opposition. (D'Avaux became aware of this part of his mission and believed that he had a large sum to help form a party for the prince in England.)[38] While waiting for the day of his audience, Zuilesteyn expressed to several of the more important malcontents the prince's willingness to help them, but only if assured of substantial assistance from inside the country. (Yet the prince seems already to have decided on an expedition.)

A group of them furnished the necessary assurances on June 30, 1688. Henry Sidney drew up and signed (with six other signatories) what has usually been described as an invitation for William to intervene.

Except by implication, it was not quite that, as others have pointed out.[39] Rather it was a statement that the public in general ("nineteen parts of twenty of the people") was dissatisfied with the government and would rise if given "protection," presumably by an army from abroad; "the greatest part of the nobility and gentry are as much dissatisfied," and "some of the most considerable of them would venture themselves with your Highness at your first landing"; in the army and navy, "not one in ten . . . would do them any service" against the prince. It was urgent that William act before a packed parliament met or James decided to achieve his ends "by more violent means," after which the situation would be beyond remedy. The signatories promised, if the prince could "give assistances this year sufficient for a relief under these circumstances," to "attend upon your Highness upon your landing, and to do all that lies in our power to prepare others to be in as much readiness as such an action is capable of." They left the preparations and the informing of the States General to the prince, but they told him, "[Y]our compliment upon the birth of the child (which not one in a thousand here believes to be the Queen's) hath done you some injury," as the supposedly fraudulent birth was "certainly one of the chief causes upon which the declaration of your entering the kingdom in a hostile manner, must be founded on your part, although many other reasons are to be given on ours." The subscribers requested the prince, if he thought fit to make the attempt, to let his supporters know when all could be ready.

Besides Sidney, the earls of Shrewsbury, Devonshire, and Danby; Lord Lumley; Bishop Compton of London; and Edward Russell signed the letter, not with their names but with the numbers used to stand for them in William's cipher correspondence with England.[40]

Ranke long ago drew attention to the absence here of any reference to deposing the king or any other specific change in the government. Too many Tories would have been estranged from the prince by an unpalatable announcement of intent to encroach upon the monarchy. As Charles Hornby later said:

[T]he Stomachs of these Babes were not able to digest the strong
Doctrines of deposing Kings, so they were to be fed with Milk, there
was no harm ment [sic] to the King! God forbid! But there being no
hopes of preventing the Ruin of the Kingdom but by a free Parliament, nor any obtaining that as Affairs then stood, the Prince was
to come and put all Things in Order; and when the House was Swept
clean, he it seems was to be set by, like a Broom behind the Door.[41]

Besides, specific changes could only be proposed in Parliament; announcement would be premature and perhaps offensive to Whigs as
well as Tories.

Sidney wrote a letter of his own to accompany the "invitation."
He explained that the earl of Nottingham had "gone very far, but now
his heart fails him, and he will go no further." Sidney doubted Nottingham's excuse of "scruples of conscience" for not signing. (Actually, the earl had consulted Dean Stillingfleet and Bishop Lloyd of
St. Asaph on the matter.) Zuilesteyn would await an answer to the
letter of the seven before returning to Holland, in the meantime going
"into the country for some days" to avert suspicion.[42] Arthur Herbert,
the one-eyed veteran of naval service broken by James on the religious issue, though not very religious, was going to Holland to serve
William; he carried the two letters with him. We are told that he went
disguised as a common seaman as he left the country against the
king's express wish. Zuilesteyn lingered in England until late in July;
James gave him a diamond ring said to be worth £300 on his leave-
taking. The emissary also carried away letters from Halifax, Nottingham, Shrewsbury, and Bishop Compton.[43]

The prince did not need urging. He had probably decided as early
as April to venture over to England; he had talked of the possibility to
his Dutch confidants even earlier. He had received reports that if he
did not rescue the Anglican Church, "the nation would become des-
perate and act for themselves, which . . . will be equally prejudicial
to the Prince, whether they succeed or be ruined." Success might
mean the establishment of a republican government.[44] He raised that
consideration as an explanation of his course of action, but his European policy was so important to him that only his timing of the
expedition may have been affected by a possible republican movement
or premature rebellion, unless he used it to help persuade Mary to
consent to the dethronement of her father after Zuilesteyn's return
from England. We know that she used the emissary's report on return
as justification for her consent.[45]

William's preparations—diplomatic, naval, and military—for his expedition do not concern us here. Let it suffice to say that they advanced rapidly.[46] By late September, as the reader has seen, the king was sure enough of the intent to invade England to feel compelled to abandon his plan to elect a packed parliament and carry the repeal of the penal laws and test acts. He also decided to take positive steps to reassure his alarmed subjects, beginning with the Church of England, and to persuade the United Netherlands not to send the expedition.

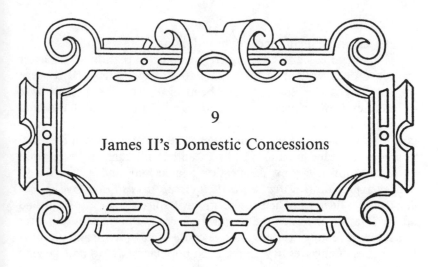

9

James II's Domestic Concessions

"IT PLEASETH HIS MAJESTY," said a newswriter on September 21, "to give every day some mark or other of his gracious intention to preserve thc Church of England as established, and thinks fit to convince the Bishops of it in the first place."[1] On that day, the daily ration of favor was an innovation. The king sent for Bishop Peter Mew and that evening for Bishop Turner, who was in the country; he also asked for others to come up to court. Lord Dartmouth, the king's intermediary in dealing with Turner, urged him to go up to London "for the service of our Master, & of ye kingdom," which might be in danger.[2]

The occasion was the publication of the king's declaration of September 21, announcing his intention of repealing the penal laws and test acts, with reassurances to the Church of England. Bishop Ken, who had to hasten up to town, was optimistic about the summons, although he had not yet seen the declaration.[3]

Bishop Turner arrived in London early. On September 26, at noon, he received a "civil letter" from an unnamed person of quality at court, inviting him to that person's lodgings that evening. It was apparent that this was an arrangement for a convenient interview with the king. Turner reluctantly consented, with the proviso that the meeting not be concealed, as people would come to know of it in any case. Thus it was in the royal bedchamber, surrounded by people, that James received Turner at 8:00 P.M.; he silently "wafted" the bishop into his closet, a small inner room adjoining.

James professed to be completely reconciled to Turner by a letter the bishop had written to Lord Dartmouth expressing kind concern for the king. "The Bps & I have been old friends, & if such have differd they may easily be good friends again." Turner said that he and his colleagues had regretted having to oppose the reading of the Declaration of Indulgence in the churches. The king replied that they had misunderstood his intention; he had wanted only that the declaration be better known. But his recollection heated him, and he "let fall ye cutting expression *ye have raised such evil spirits as I doubt ye cannot lay again.*" Turner applied the term "evil spirits" to those who had advised James to order the declaration read; the bishops were "at worst but ye remote occasion, not ye cause of all yt noise and tumult." But as they "unawares had gotten such popularity we wd now be glad to keep it a while for his service." He said that he hoped the king would ask nothing which would lessen their credit and reduce their utility. He was himself zealous for James's "honour and safety," and he was sure the other bishops were "very desirous of a composure [settlement]," if the king "wd but give us a ground to work upon, & to satisfy his good subjects."

James asked Turner's opinion of the recent declaration, supposed to be intended to effect reconciliation. The bishop said it needed further explanation, for its words suggested that Dissenters might be admitted to care of souls in the Church of England. James replied that his lawyers had taken the words from the Act of Uniformity. He assured Turner that the difficulty could be cleared up; he intended no more than to relieve Dissenters of the penalties imposed by the Act of Uniformity for not attending Anglican churches. Turner mentioned several Catholic converts then retaining Anglican livings: the vicar of Lynn Allhallows, Norfolk; the vicar of Putney; and one in Essex;[4] "a Cure of Souls is a Trust allwaies very considerable." Turner held that dispensing with the law in these cases encroached not only on the Act of Uniformity but on the rights of patrons of livings to nominate ministers. This was not even to mention the deanery of Christ Church and the mastership of University College, Oxford, or the mastership of Sidney College, Cambridge. James promised coldly that there would be no more such cases, but he did not wish to undo what he had done, and Magdalen College, Oxford, had been insolent. Turner offered to prove that Lord Sunderland had suppressed a "most humble Supplication" the fellows of Magdalen had put into his hands. James grumbled that his predecessors had done as much as he; he ought not to be grudged one of so many colleges "for the breeding up of ye poor Catholicks." Turner answered that the king's advisers would have been "more thrifty of his interest" if they had persuaded him to use his own money. James returned to the contents of the declaration; its barring of Catholics from the House of Commons ought to satisfy the Church of England's wish for security.

Given permission to speak frankly, Turner denied that the Anglican bishops could serve the king on the basis of that declaration. It did not exclude the Catholic peers from the House of Lords, and such reputed Catholics as Sir Solomon Swale, Sir Thomas Strickland, and Sir Edward Hales had taken the oaths of allegiance and supremacy, and were thus eligible to the House of Commons. They were not Catholics when they took the oaths, said the king, and should not be thought so until they rejoined the Catholic church. All the same, Turner insisted, "very many" Catholics had taken the oaths during the "Popish Plot" crisis and still attended Mass.

James acknowledged that Catholics had "their Latitude men," though few could conscientiously go so far. He also would be frank. He would allow the test to stand; though he would not have consented to it as a fresh enactment, he would not press for its repeal. The blunt bishop objected that if the holders of offices and places of trust were exempted from the test, "all Mankind might foresee & foretell, whoever they were who had in their hands the Executive power of the kingdom, & the administration of ye government, wd soon have the Legislative." At this the king grew angry and said that would be to suppose him and other Catholics "perfectly mad," which, Turner reflected silently, was no more than some of them had been. Indeed, James continued, "King & Parliamt. must be all supposed to be mad men, to let any one Party grasp at so much more than fell to their share." He protested that he was resolved to support the Church of England.

After this, he told the bishop his news of the threatened invasion. He denied that he intended to call in French forces to subdue England; if he did, France could not send them and make war on the empire at the same time. He trusted his own forces would be enough to deal with the Dutch. Turner left the royal presence and sat up all night recording what was said.[5]

On September 27, James proclaimed a general pardon to his subjects, except for treasons overseas and certain heinous crimes. The pardon retained a formula from one issued in 1686: "We do hereby . . . Pardon, Acquit, Release, and Discharge all Our Subjects

(except Bodies Politick and Incorporate)" and such other persons—
thirteen are named in the pardon—as were excluded specifically.
The bishops were suspicious of this general pardon. Bishop
Turner, in an undated letter to Sancroft, mentions a passage which
could be taken as excluding the whole clergy from the benefits of the
proclamation. Evidently he refers to the exception of bodies politic
and corporate. When Lord Godolphin sent Henry Frederick Thynne,
holder of several offices, with a message that the bishops should make
proposals for the public security, for "whatever was now fitt to be
askt by us [the bishops] wee might have it granted at least by degrees,"
Thynne learned of this objection to the pardon. "Hee stood amaz'd
and ran away to *Whitehall* about it."⁶ Shortly after, Bishops Sprat and
White wrote that they had brought the subject to Lord Chancellor
Jeffreys's attention; Jeffreys had replied, "Tis the usuall expression in
all acts of Pardon," and it did not exclude the clergy from the pardon.
Godolphin had already told the king, and Sancroft did not need to
say much about it, though he did talk with the king about it on
September 30.⁷ James issued a second general pardon on October 2,
extending his grace to "all and all manner of Bodies Politick or Corporate."⁸ The king was obviously willing to do a great deal to remove
the bishops' suspicions.

At least seven of them met with him at 10:00 A.M., September 28.
It was plain that he wanted their support, but he hardly knew how to
go about getting it. He lectured them on their duty and uttered general expressions of goodwill toward the Anglican Church, but he was
too busy to receive a set of points to be discussed, signed by eight
bishops. The meeting contented neither side, though the earl of
Middleton thought that James's announcement of the reinstatement
of Bishop Compton made the bishops present happy.⁹ A report went
round that one of the bishops said, on leaving, "*omnia bene*" (all is
well). The same day, James proclaimed his cancellation of the calling
of Parliament in view of the threatened invasion.¹⁰

Sancroft, at the time the meeting was summoned, was suffering
from "the gripes." By September 30, he had apparently recovered, for
he had an interview with the king. The latter said he hoped that he
had satisfied the bishops. The archbishop replied that they were satisfied as private persons but not as to the public. James then appointed
another meeting for October 2, postponed under pressure of business
to October 3. At that time, the bishops had a full audience and made
points orally. On the king's command, they adjourned to reduce them
to writing. That afternoon they presented a memorial for the king's

consideration; Sancroft read it out. The king was advised (1) to put county government into the hands of qualified persons (Anglican nobles and gentlemen); (2) to dissolve the Ecclesiastical Commission and not establish another; (3) to refrain from issuing dispensations enabling unqualified persons to hold office in church, state, or the universities, especially offices with cure of souls, and to restore the president and fellows of Magdalen College, Oxford; (4) to set aside licenses or faculties allowing Catholics to teach "publick Scholes" and to grant no more such; (5) to "desist from the exercise of such a Dispensing Power, as hath of late been us'd" and allow Parliament to settle that question; (6) "to inhibit the four forain Bishops, who stile themselves Vicars Apostolical" from invading the jurisdiction of the Anglican bishops; (7) to fill up vacant Anglican sees in England and Ireland and other preferments "with men of learning and pietie," particularly the archbishopric of York; (8) to supersede all "further Prosecution of *Quo Warrantos* against Corporations" and to restore their charters and privileges as the bishops had just learned James had done for the city of London; (9) to issue writs for "the calling of a free and regular Parliament" in which the Church of England would be secured, "a due Liberty of Conscience" provided for, and also security of liberties and properties of James's subjects, and mutual confidence would be established between king and people; (10) to permit the Anglican bishops to offer arguments for his return to the Anglican Church. Sancroft, Compton, Mew, Lloyd (of St. Asaph), Turner, Lake, Sprat, Ken, and White signed their names to this paper. (Lloyd, not present at the meeting, must have signed earlier.) James expressed disagreement only about Parliament.[11]

According to a newsletter, the bishops also asked the king for an explanation of some words in his proclamation calling Parliament. These words dealt with repealing legal clauses which inflicted penalties for Nonconformity on persons promoted to Anglican benefices. He explained that he did not intend to make all the penal laws of religion void; he had left the writing of the proclamation to Lords Jeffreys, Sunderland, and Middleton, "as fully & Amply in favour of the church of England as they could which his Matie. resolves to maintain In all It's rights and properties."[12] (Jeffreys told Lord Clarendon that he had drawn it, and Sunderland, Middleton, and Dartmouth had agreed on it, but Godolphin "had broken from them, by endeavouring to trim, and to find out softer words than he [Jeffreys] would have had.")[13]

It will be observed that the restoration of London's charter had been announced before the bishops gave their advice. The effect of the action was that London would have the charter it had had before loss of a legal battle under Charles II. The City celebrated with the usual bonfires to show its joy, and Jeffreys performed the ceremony of restoration on October 6. Within a few days, the City had chosen a new mayor, sheriff, and aldermen, all very calmly, under the old charter. The mayor, Sir John Chapman, was acceptable to the king.[14]

In his Privy Council on October 5, James declared his intention of dissolving the Ecclesiastical Commission and ordered Jeffreys to take the necessary steps. He met again with several bishops on October 7 and asked them to appoint a public fast and compose special prayers on the occasion of the threatened descent on England. He then seemed displeased with the paper submitted on October 3. On October 10, he received the form of the prayers, and he notified the bishops the next day of his approval.[15]

He continued to deliberate on further steps. Early on October 16 he summoned Sancroft to confer with him at 10:00 A.M. Presumably, the archbishop kept the appointment punctually. The king excused his own failure so far to restore the fellows of Magdalen College or the charters of other corporations. The archbishop mentioned vacant sees and benefices in Ireland that ought to be filled. Then James revealed the real reason for the meeting. He was certain that William of Orange was coming to invade the country, and "it would be very much for his service, and a thing very well becoming the Bishops, if they would meet together, and draw up an Abhorrence of this attempt of the Prince, &c." Some discussion followed as to which bishops could be found quickly. At last Sancroft asked and received permission to speak freely and said that he did not believe the prince really intended to attack England; the bishops, therefore, need not make such a declaration. James did not press the matter. The next day, he announced in council that he was proclaiming a further restoration of liberties and charters to corporations.[16]

Barrillon wrote to Louis XIV on October 1/11, early in the attempted reconciliation, "The Episcopal party shows good intentions toward the King of England's side, but it is to be feared that what is done in favor of the bishops and the Anglican Church may make all the Nonconformists, who had for some time declared for him, be lost to him." But by October 4/14, the Frenchman believed James's step to be necessary. The Nonconformists were not powerful or united enough to defend the royal authority, and their old habit was opposition to it. Therefore, the court made a show of reconciling all factional interests: Anglicans would content themselves with the government, churches, benefices, and public worship, and all other sects would have freedom of religion without risk of penalties or prosecutions.[17]

Some there were who wished the king and the bishops apart. One was Bishop Lloyd of St. Asaph, now almost James's declared enemy, who told Lord Clarendon on October 7 that "he was very well pleased he was not here [for the meeting on October 3], for he had no mind to go to the King." Another was Princess Anne. She told Clarendon on October 12 that "she wished the Bishops were out of town; 'for,' said she, 'it is plain they can do no good. The King will not hearken to them, and they will but expose themselves by being here.' "[18] A third was John Evelyn, who wrote to Sancroft on October 10 that he feared consultations of the king with the bishops were intended to divide Protestants.[19]

James did not throw over the Dissenters, even now. He consulted on October 14 with four Presbyterians, on the fifteenth with six Independents, and on the sixteenth with some Anabaptists to explain his attitudes towards those sects and the Church of England. He assured them that he stood by his promises of liberty of conscience. Ronchi, however, was writing almost simultaneously that the king of England would restore the fellows of Magdalen College and make Bishop Ken archbishop of York to please the bishops.[20]

On October 20, Bishop Mew, visitor of Magdalen College, appeared in Oxford, "attended by a thousand horse and all ye Coaches of this place," with people in the streets blessing him because he was to restore the fellows of the college during his stay. But at nine o'clock the same evening, he received a summons to see the king at ten in the morning of the twenty-first and obediently left Oxford without effecting the restoration.[21] He seems to have used little judgment, and James was angry at him, but literal-mindedness may have been the only safe attitude in dealing with a hot-tempered man who sent commands to appear without adequate explanations. Mew suddenly returned to Oxford on October 24 to execute his mission. Next morning, he went to prayers in the college chapel, "being met at ye College gate by Dr Hough [the deprived president] and most of the old [deprived] Members of yt Society: all which being done they went into ye Coll Hall, where the Bishp called for the buttery Book and haveing first struck out all the names of the Popish Fellows and Demys, order'd Dr Hough to be enter'd President, and the old Fellows, Demys, Chaplins, Clarks, and Quiristers to be placed as formerly."[22]

Thus a "colony" of Catholics that had recently been transplanted from the seminary at Douai was expelled, with other Catholics. Only one of the Douai group had entered even his surname on the college books. It is unlikely that any of the Catholic members witnessed Mew's actions; they were all reported to be in London by October 6.[23] One "old" fellow, Robert Charnock, lost his position because he had become a Catholic.

Captain Humphrey Langham, of Belasyse's former regiment in the Dutch service, brought over a parcel of copies of William of Orange's declaration of his intention in the invasion, which the captain left with a pardoned former supporter of Monmouth in London on October 31/November 10. The ex-Monmouthite took the parcel to the earl of Middleton, and the authorities seized Langham, brought him before the king's council, and sent him to Newgate Prison.[24]

The declaration contained a statement that "a Great many Lords, both Spirituall and Temporall" had invited William to intervene in English affairs. This avowal aroused James to discover whether William was telling the truth. He sent for Sancroft, but the archbishop was not at home. On November 1, he saw Bishop Compton, read him the passage, and asked him about it. Compton's position would have embarrassed a man of less assurance, for he was the only spiritual peer who had signed the letter interpreted as an invitation. He did not exactly tell a lie; he said he "was confident, the rest of the Bishops would as readily answer in the negative [to a question about an invitation] as myself." James professed belief that the bishops were all innocent. (He was not unsuspecting, but he preferred suspicion that William had lied to suspicion that Compton or any of his episcopal brethren would violate their oaths to him.)

"Next he told me," Compton recorded, "he thought it requisite, we should make some publick Declaration of our Innocence in this matter, and likewise an Abhorrence." Compton asked to see William's declaration, but the king refused. Compton remarked that "this was a matter to be consider'd." James then said he would have the archbishop call the bishops together.[25]

So he did, and Sancroft, Compton, Crew, Cartwright, and Watson presented themselves at Whitehall at ten o'clock next morning. Viscount Preston was there with a copy of the prince's declaration. The king stated the purpose of the meeting and his belief that no bishop had invited the prince. Sancroft at once denied that he had done so. Compton said he had given the king his answer the day before. The other three quickly (and honestly) followed Sancroft in denial.

King James then pressed for a written statement to the same effect, which he would publish "for his service" – an "Apology" for themselves which he asked them to prepare and have the archbishop convey to him for approval. Then Sancroft could send it to the absent bishops for their agreement. He closed the conference with a suggestion that "you express your dislike of the Prince's design" in the statement, "to which (though he said it twice) neither the Archbishop, nor the Bishop of *London,* (nor any of the other three, as far as is remember'd) return'd one Word."[26]

Assembling the stronger bishops was a problem. Crew, Watson, and Cartwright were useless now for any purpose, and they were in the way of the others. Most of the latter were in the country. Sancroft, Sprat, and Compton decided to send to Bishop White, who was not far off, to meet with them on November 5. Before White arrived, Lord Preston asked Sancroft to hasten the preparation of the written denial of the invitation to the prince. White was in London on the fourth and met with his summoners as planned the next day. They reached complete agreement. The earl of Clarendon, who saw them together at dinner in Lambeth, learned that "they had no mind to make a Declaration [against the expedition] under their hands, except the Temporall Lords would joyn with them."[27]

At least one of the concerned bishops, Lloyd of St. Asaph, had gone into hiding. John Ince, Lloyd's attorney, wrote advice to Sancroft to find a "safe place."[28]

White, Compton, Sprat, and the archbishop went together to Whitehall on November 6. Bishop Watson attempted to join them, though he did not know their thoughts, but Sancroft asked Lord Preston aside for a private audience with the king, and Watson was therefore not present. In the royal closet, Sancroft said, "Sir . . . we have done all that can be expected from us in this business. Since your Majesty has declar'd, you are well satisfy'd in our Innocence, we regard not the censures of others." White and Sprat then took their first opportunity to deny having any hand in inviting William; they said they knew of none who had. Gladly accepting these protestations, James asked for the paper he had wished them to prepare. Sancroft replied that they had brought no paper as it was not necessary or proper; they cared not at all for any opinion but the king's.[29]

James was excited and anxious. He needed such a paper, had

expected one, and thought the bishops had promised him one. (Later in the interview, he admitted that people would not believe a publication of his own saying that the bishops denied inviting William.)[30]

The bishops, on their side, were evasive and determined to avoid writing for the king. They would not acknowledge that the prince had issued the declaration: "[S]carce one in 500 believes it to be the Prince's true Declaration."[31]

"No! said the king with some vehemence, then that five hundred would cut my throat, or bring in Prince of O to cut my throat." To which the bishops ejaculated, "God forbid." They went on to say that the "false" reference to invitation by spiritual and temporal lords showed that the declaration was not William's, for such an obvious falsehood would soon be exposed. James did not think the prince would "stick at a Lye." The bishops excused themselves from "a business of State, which properly belongs not to us," and Sancroft reminded the king of the violent prosecution to which he and other bishops had been subjected for petitioning about affairs of civil government outside Parliament; even after acquittal, James's judges had aspersed them "as seditious Libelers." James said he thought all that well past; the bishops' counsel had used him uncivilly, for that matter; but if he asked the bishops for advice on affairs of state, there could be no danger in giving it.[32]

It soon became apparent that the king would not be satisfied without a statement of abhorrence of William's expedition and that the bishops would not give him one. They suggested summoning the temporal lords to consult about the matter. The king believed that some of those lords had caused the bishops to change their minds. The latter denied it and asked whether James had asked lay peers to do what he had asked of the bishops. James admitted that he had not. After a little more argument, he gave up: "[T]his is the last time: I wil urge you no farther. If you wil not assist mee as I desire, I must stand upon my own legs, and trust to myself and my own arms."

The bishops promised to assist the king with their prayers and offered to serve him as peers, either in a parliament or in an assembly of such spiritual and temporal lords as were in or near London. Bishop Sprat tells us, "This was not hearken'd to; and so we were dismiss'd."[33]

The bishops were not straightforward, and neither was James. It seems to me that there was a reason given by neither side for the refusal to declare abhorrence of the invasion. Such a statement would have been a blow at William, whom the bishops had at the time no reason to fear or to dislike. Compton, of course, had signed the letter to William. The others present could not approve the expedition, no doubt, but (perhaps through Compton's working on their minds) preferred to do nothing. It is possible that they agreed with many other Protestants that William's presence in the country was necessary for the protection of the church, rescue of the king from evil counselors, and adoption of "measures more consistent with the feelings and wishes of his [James's] people," as George D'Oyly supposed. How many of the absent bishops would have agreed with those present we cannot know, though Sprat's cooperation with Sancroft, White, and Compton may have been one of several changes from support of the king. That many temporal peers were keeping neutral in this period was obvious to several observers.[34] If the bishops were to deliberate jointly with them, James would win no victory but would have to receive a petition for a free parliament signed by a number of peers.

These events make evident that James's concessions never fully reconciled the concerned bishops to the king. They knew well that they owed the concessions to William's threat; if the threat disappeared, James might cancel or forget the concessions. One should emphasize "might"; nobody can say with certainty. The rancor and fear remaining from unjust prosecution and the abuse showered on them by the judges on circuit disposed the concerned element of the Anglican Church to suspect the king and to walk warily near him, and resentment of their success in resistance and of their popularity shows itself clearly in remarks James made, even during his efforts at reconciliation. He said bishops were safe in dealing with state affairs when he asked them for advice, and they probably could have trusted him then. But how long after survival of the crisis would it be before he found his own best security in reducing them to impotence and taking advantage of their vulnerability? And so they prayed for the king's safety and health, but also for God to "inspire him with Wisdom, and Justice in all his Counsells" and to "Preserve and establish that holy Religion, we profess, together with our Laws, and ancient Government."[35]

Bishops Compton and Lloyd of St. Asaph were in touch with opponents of the king, who probably feared that their prestigious colleagues might actively take James's side. There are signs of busywork by these two bishops against the king. Lloyd was unwilling to go to meetings with James in the autumn, and he had probably been working up a spirit of opposition in his diocese since his acquittal.[36] Despite that, James accepted the bishops' denials of inviting William

at face value, but the passage about the invitation (perhaps deliberately inserted for the purpose by William Harbord) did cause a difference over publishing a contradiction and statement of abhorrence,
and thus revived the animosities of the previous spring and summer,
to the prince of Orange's advantage.

Bishop Sprat, in an apology for his conduct, wrote of the effect
of refusal to write an abhorrence, "His Majesty parted from us with
Indignation. And thereupon the Jesuited Party at Court were so vio-
lently enraged against us, that as we were credibly informed, one of
the Chief advised in a heat, we should all be Imprisoned, and the
Truth should be extorted from us by Violence."[37] (Sprat may have
exaggerated his past peril; he had much to apologize for.) At least a
few outsiders learned that "Something very bold was said, for neither
party was pleased, by their countenances at parting."[38] This was the
lamentable state (for James) of relations between the most eminent
members of the established church and that church's supreme governor: The bishops would not be tools, and the king could see them as
nothing else.

One who had been a true tool at last turned in his hand. Early in
November, Bishop Crew refused to sit in the Privy Council with
Catholics. He was under something of a cloud at court but continued
to be admitted there. On November 14, he presented to the king a
paper of advice to withdraw his protection from Catholic chapels that
caused disturbance, offer the see of York to a more deserving man
than Crew himself (who had been mentioned for it), replace the
Catholic John Massey as dean of Christ Church, Oxford, allow the
fellows of Sidney Sussex College, Cambridge, to elect a qualified
master in the place of Joshua Basset (a Catholic), and call a free
parliament as soon as possible.[39] These requests were all obnoxious to
James, although he at the last yielded to all of them (Massey left
Oxford on November 30, and James tried to name a replacement for
him on December 8; the king authorized a new election at Sidney on
December 1.) The conciliatory policy had failed to obtain support
from the more conscientious Anglicans, and James's predicament had
begun to lose him the adherence even of the venal.

The king made political concessions, as he made religious ones,
because he was certain that the Dutch intended to attack him in his
kingdom, and he made them against his will. Probably the first of any
importance was made on or slightly before September 22, when he
authorized lords lieutenants to reemploy former deputy lieutenants
and justices of the peace who were willing to serve again.[40] These were

certainly in great part Protestants whom he had removed to further the repeal of the penal laws and test acts. Reemployment of them was one of the signs that he was abandoning that campaign. He made another conciliatory step in the first and second proclamations of general pardon. A third was the restoration of the charter of London; a fourth (as much a political concession as a religious one) was his attempt to win back the alienated Anglican bishops.

The country was seriously upset. There were rumors that James had sent for French troops for repressive purposes. Some credulous people may have left London in fear of the French.[41] Many Anglican gentlemen were discontented and sore at their treatment over the three questions. The lower clergy was as suspicious as the bishops and even more fearful. The Dutch threat, Deane Monteage wrote to Viscount Hatton on October 2, "has mightily alarum'd our Citty [London] so that some Goldsmyths [who also served as bankers] have declined payments, & others are likely to follow [;] the very tradesmen themselves though they have money by them will not part with it on any termes for goods they bought some time since." Two goldsmiths (Moor and Thomas) shut up their shops on October 1. That month, the law courts were "thin and empty of business."[42]

The ordinary person heard only rumors, some deliberately spread to damage James II. Readers should be aware that official documents and private letters cited in historical works were closed to almost all living when they were written. The *London Gazette* was neither frank nor full. Many of the manuscript newsletters received by well-to-do people who paid for them originated in the office of the secretaries of state and were subject to political control. How was anyone to know what was happening? Many could have asked this question: "What is there in this Buzze of ye Dutch fleete [?] . . . none can Resolve it that I meet wth."[43] Was there to be fighting? No one knew. The Modenese Ronchi wrote to his duke that the princess of Orange, who had never left off writing to her father, was rumored to be going with the invasion fleet.[44] That suggested that peace would prevail.

The country was generally quiet in the early part of the waiting period. Some rarely seen magnates, such as the duke of Somerset, went to court to give assurances of their loyalty; others (the duke of Newcastle, the earls of Derby and Lindsey, and Lord Wharton) sent letters. Many remained in the country, and some were reported to have gone to the Netherlands.[45]

It was particularly important that London should remain loyal and calm. James restored its charter in order to appease it. The bishops' paper, submitted on October 3, contained a list of other practical steps toward recovery of public support or at least lessening the public estrangement. Some such steps were necessary. Van Citters reported that at the first proclamation of general pardon by the king's herald, everybody present kept silent. (No doubt the fifty-seven convicted persons at the Old Bailey who were released because of it felt some pleasure.)

And not only bishops read the king's proclamations with suspicious care: Sir John Lowther of Lowther noticed that the king excepted four more named persons from the second general pardon than from the first: "[C]ertainlie, those that were once pardoned, could not be declared criminall ffor the same offences." (One of the four, Laurence Braddon, was James's prisoner; the king did not wish to release him or to waive future opportunities of punishing the other three.) Lowther also objected to James's exception of all who had been excepted from Charles II's pardons, not noticing that the same reservation had been made in the general pardon of September 27.[46] In short, as Terriesi wrote with his authoritarian bias on October 8/18, "All the steps that His Majesty has taken . . . have been of no other use than to gain for him the ridicule of the people, and to make them say that it will be necessary that he make greater ones: as in fact it will be necessary without its being the least bit grateful to him about it [senza che esso glie ne sia di cosa minima riconoscente]."[47] All the same, such of the king's supporters as Sir John Reresby and the earl of Bath, recommending restoration of the old charters of York and Exeter, must have believed that some concessions would bring gains in strength.[48]

The dissolution of the Ecclesiastical Commission and the promised restoration of the fellows of Magdalen College may have been a little reassuring, but London was still not appeased. Alderman Sir William Pritchard, lord mayor at the time of the quo-warranto proceedings against the City under Charles II, declined to serve when the charter was restored. Sir William Turner (a Nonconformist), Sir Robert Clayton (a Whig), and Sir James Edwards, all former mayors, refused to serve unless the court judgment removing them were reversed by another court judgment, and Barrillon believed that all three men were unwilling to serve against the prince of Orange. Sir George Treby only reluctantly allowed himself to be reinstated as the City's recorder.[49]

Charles Duncombe was a London banker-goldsmith who had

gained great wealth under Charles II and James; the latter had made him an alderman of the City. In October, James called upon him and another financier, Richard Kent, for a loan of £140,000, of which Duncombe seems to have been made responsible for £100,000, an enormous sum for any one lender at the time. Both Duncombe and Kent were said to have "aledged his Majesty owed them a great summ, and [that] they have noe money left." James's needs were pressing, and he must have pressed his bankers, for Duncombe, no doubt thinking the debt would prove to be a bad one if the king was defeated, went into hiding. Van Citters reported on October 29 (N.S.) that the parties had compromised the affair; Duncombe was to lend only £20,000. James was highly shocked at his unwillingness.[50] (His rival inspired great confidence and trust in lenders.)

The king held frequent councils on how to gather more support. Some of the Catholics at court feared that he would abandon them as he was already abandoning the struggle for repeal of the penal laws and the tests. He had no choice. On October 9, he began demanding reports of the lords lieutenants on abuses committed by "regulators" of corporations. As the regulators had acted with James's instructions and approval, the reversal of the situation might result in very unfair treatment of them. On October 17, he issued the proclamation restoring the charters of most municipal corporations and promising to restore the others when he had taken the necessary legal steps. The same day, he put out of office magistrates, mayors, and aldermen put in by royal order since 1679, except for those towns whose deeds of surrender were already enrolled or against which judgments in quo-warranto proceedings were recorded. The earl of Middleton optimistically remarked that the restoration of the charters had "in my opinion, defeated their [the Dutch] project." But the exceptions weakened the effect. On October 19, the king also authorized a grant under the great seal for the restoration of charters to London's city companies.[51]

The restoration of municipal charters did cause some satisfaction as it became known, and elections were held in many places under the old familiar rules. Cambridge was restored on October 23, Bristol the next day, Dover on October 25. Winchester, Chester, Exeter, and York were among those that did not at first get their old charters back, but James remedied that lack before William landed in the West.[52] No doubt some Protestants regarded removal of Catholic lords lieutenants in the same month as a solid gain. Yet some former magistrates still felt ill used. Sir John Bramston told the new Protestant lord lieutenant of Essex, in expressive phrase, "[S]ome would think one kick of the breech enough for a gentleman." Bramston was one of several gentlemen of Essex who refused to serve at this juncture. There were others elsewhere.[53]

The king could not help knowing of the talk about the birth of the Prince of Wales. About October 21, someone suggested (or he imagined for himself) that he could vindicate the birth by taking, recording, and publishing the testimony of the many persons who had been present in the confinement chamber at the time. The notion had several weaknesses: Much of the testimony would be about matters too intimate and unseemly to be readily talked about; some present had actually seen little or nothing of the birth because of the crowd or their position in the room; some were Catholics whom Protestants would discredit as untrustworthy. Persons who had not been present but were already convinced by prejudice or personal motives that the Prince of Wales was supposititious were hardly likely to change their minds, and a crew of ingenious and unscrupulous writers stood ready to answer any truth with a plausible lie. Queen Maria Beatrice only consented to the taking and publishing of the testimony because of the skepticism of her stepdaughter, Princess Anne.

A messenger delivered to the earl of Clarendon on October 21 a summons to the meeting of the king's council the following day, remarking that all other peers and privy councillors were also summoned. (Such a summons took Bishop Mew away from Oxford before he had restored Magdalen College.) Neither Princess Anne nor the marquis of Halifax could say what the reason was for such a meeting, though the princess thought it had something to do with the Prince of Wales.

On the morning of October 22, Clarendon consulted Halifax and Lords Burlington, Weymouth, and Nottingham at Halifax's house; no one present knew the cause of the summons. Clarendon and Nottingham agreed not to sit as councillors with Father Petre, who as a Catholic was not qualified.

They went together to Whitehall before the meeting, early enough to see the king in private. Clarendon said he would not sit in council with Petre but would be present as a peer. Nottingham "spoke more largely to the same effect." (Nottingham was persuasive but long-winded.) The king had hinted to Petre not to come to the council, but he had not put him out of it. Nottingham urged exclusion of unqualified persons from the council board. They were presumably Lords Melfort, Castlemaine, Dover, Belasyse, Peterborough, and perhaps Moray. Clarendon, Nottingham, and Sancroft chose to sit among the lords, presumably those who were not also privy councillors.[54] Queen Dowager Catherine was present; also the judges, several of the counsel learned in the law, and the lord mayor and aldermen of London. Princess Anne was not there, the king said, because of fear that she would miscarry. (She was not pregnant; her absence was deliberate.)

The depositions on the birth of the Prince of Wales were not effective with those for whom they were intended. There is no point in attempting to prove the birth genuine from them; many who saw the child when he was mature remarked on his resemblance to James II and (even closer) to his uncle Charles. There is no need, either, to refute the attacks made on the depositions by James's enemies.

There is one misrepresentation used against them which should be answered—that the deponents were almost all Catholics or people of no standing. The first witness, Queen Dowager Catherine, who testified that she was with Maria Beatrice during the delivery, was a Catholic, but of very great standing indeed, and an unusually estimable person for the Restoration court. The countess of Arran, wife of the duke of Hamilton's heir, was a Protestant. The countess of Sunderland was the wife of a man of little faith but herself a firm Protestant. Mrs. Elizabeth Bromley was a Protestant. The earls of Craven, Mulgrave, Feversham, and Middleton were all Protestants. Lord Godolphin and Sir Stephen Fox were Protestants. At least two of the physicians present, Sir Charles Scarburgh and Dr. Robert Brady, were apparently Protestants as William III later employed them. (An accoucheur summoned, Dr. Hugh Chamberlain, was actually a Whig. He did not arrive in time.) Not one of these witnesses can be called mean or low, but the pamphleteers were safe because most readers would not know how to answer their statements. Their writings were also bold, and plausible among people who distrusted Catholics and did not know any of them.

Barrillon observed to Louis XIV that the taking of the depositions caused much talk and correctly attributed Anne's failure to testify to her support of the prince of Orange. She did not say a word about the threatened invasion to her father or stepmother, though they often spoke of it before her.[55]

Bishop Lloyd of St. Asaph tried to wreck the plan to publish the testimony. He wrote on October 26 to Sancroft to say that he had heard that the king wished every lord present at the examination of witnesses to sign the attestations as an indication that they were recorded as given. (Secretaries of state regularly signed the written ver-

sion of testimony taken before them.) He suggested that the archbishop excuse himself on some ground such as failure to hear much of
what was said or because the Prince of Wales's birth might come
before Sancroft as a judge (Lloyd presumably meant as a member of
the House of Lords sitting as a court): "[I]f the Judges are called to
set their hands to an Examination of Witnesses *ex parte* before the
cause comes to be heard, it is a strange kinde of preoccupation, that
will make all the world of the Plaintiff's side, and be rather a prejudice than an advantage to the cause."[56] Though Lloyd would not say
so to Sancroft, he apparently wished to deny the depositions any
marks of authenticity and help ruin the Prince of Wales's place in the
royal succession.

Lloyd had heard only a rumor, but the depositions still stand in
the Privy Council Register, and James ordered them enrolled at the
Petty-Bag Office and the Office of Enrolments of the Chancery. This
last, which was said to have been the place in which Charles II had
recorded his declaration that the duke of Monmouth was illegitimate,
took place on October 27. All the deponents "affirm'd" their testimony to be true, under oath.[57]

James's Protestant subjects had come to detest the earl of
Sunderland, his senior secretary of state, both for conversion to
Rome, which they considered self-interested, and for completely slav-
ish service to the king. Catholics doubted Sunderland's sincerity.
Father Petre and the earl of Melfort had attacked him as not strong
enough for the king's religious policy, although he had ruined himself
with Protestants by being too strong, and James accepted much of
Petre's and Melfort's advice, even at that late hour.

An informer also accused Sunderland of betrayal. William had
dismissed, from the position of Mary's major domo, a Genevan
gentleman, Bernard de Budé de Verace. Budé, affecting an air of
austere honesty, had unsuccessfully tried to make the prince and
princess suspicious of the loyalty of another courtier. Mary had
thought him a meddler.[58] William appointed Lord Coote to the vacant
place on March 29, and Budé returned to Geneva. Somehow he
learned of the Dutch armament and wrote several letters to Bevil
Skelton, then at Paris, suggesting that he would reveal William's secrets, but only to King James in person. Skelton was unable to interest the king, some have said because Sunderland persuaded his
master to pay no attention, some that the earl never told the king this
news. Sunderland would not answer Skelton, and he was responsible
for Skelton's recall and incarceration in the Tower.[59] (Barrillon took

notice of Sunderland's incomprehensible ridicule of the possibility of invasion.)

In October, Albeville sent over two men to give information on William's correspondents in England. One, named Greenwood, instead began stirring up the army. The other was Hugh Wickstead, supposed to have been formerly a monk, "a Man well Educated, and Accomplished with all the Qualifications becoming a Gentleman," according to Robert Ferguson. Present in Holland in 1688, "he there by his Ingenious and pleasant Conversation had so Insinuated himself into the Secrets of the Court at the *Hague,* that he soon learnt the whole Intrigue of the intended Invasion, and who were the Managers there and in England."[60] Wickstead arrived in England and had an audience on October 22; at first, he would say nothing, but he then accused Sunderland of treason, though cautioned of the consequences of such a charge by the king himself. Sunderland was present; he asked James to have Wickstead arrested. The king said that the informer was a rascal who did not deserve a hearing. A messenger took Wickstead into custody by order, but the same night the prisoner escaped, leaving a scurrilous letter behind him, much to Sunderland's chagrin. How much this incident may have affected James's opinion is not known, but Barrillon found James's confidence in his secretary very much lessened and believed from many indications that Sunderland would choose to retire.[61] The compiler of James's *Life* tells us that "the King was fully convinced that My Lord Sunderland was not the man he took him for, nor any longer to be trusted, so as soon as they were returned from [recording the testimony of the Prince of Wales's birth at] the Court of Chancery, he order'd My Lord Middleton to fetch the Seals from him."[62]

The compiler, however, was a Jacobite (William Dicconson), and his party was so embittered toward Sunderland that any charge less than treachery would not do. At the time (October 24), James told Barrillon that he was displeased with the earl's lack of firmness and courage. He also told the committee for foreign affairs that he was removing Sunderland, but not for any suspicion of disloyalty or of "correspondence prejudicial to his [James's] service."[63] James did nothing more serious to his minister than remove him from his offices on October 26 or 27, lastly from the Privy Council on the twenty-ninth.[64]

It seems that the king removed Sunderland in part because the threat of invasion had so shaken the secretary that his judgment was no longer reliable. And James felt so much pressure against employment of Catholics at every level of government that he was no longer calling Catholic privy councillors to meetings and had put Catholics out of lieutenancies of counties. If he continued to yield, Sunderland would have to go, and go he did. James replaced him with Viscount Preston, a former envoy in France, joint leader of the House of Commons in 1685, and a Protestant.

When Lord Clarendon called on Princess Anne on the morning after the giving of testimony, she "made herself very merry with that whole affair" and allowed her waiting women to joke about it. When he saw her (in private, this time) on October 31, she professed to think the management of the birth strange and paid no heed to her father's word or to the depositions, of which she must have had accounts.[65] The next day, however, the Privy Council waited on her with the depositions for her consideration, and she had to speak respectfully: "My Lords This was not necessary to be brought to me, for I have so much Duty for the King, that His word must be more to me than these depositions."[66] She did not allow either duty or depositions to influence her belief or her actions. Thus the testimony failed to convince the person whose skepticism had caused its collection, and it failed to convince Protestants in general. Princess Anne did not believe because she did not wish to believe, and many others did not wish to believe, that the Prince of Wales was her legitimate half brother. Some disbelievers are reported to have said that Maria Beatrice "ought to have been deliver'd at Charing Cross."[67] Anne's motives were only more compelling than those of ordinary Anglicans. The episode shows the malice she felt toward her father and stepmother, and her indiscretion, which was probably matched by that of her advisors, Lord and Lady Churchill. (Ailesbury recalled that at a royal review in Hyde Park, Churchill, "he that was the great general afterwards was seen to laugh and loll out his tongue and this is true.")[68]

James never completed the set of concessions that the bishops asked for on October 3. He did return county government to Protestants (for the most part), annul the Ecclesiastical Commission, cease issuing dispensations to allow Catholics to hold office, and restore Magdalen College and the charters of municipal corporations. He did not fill up the vacant sees in Ireland, but he did fill the see of York. Two Catholics, Lords Arundel and Belasyse, were still included in the council that he left at London during the campaign, and Sir Edward Hales, a Catholic, remained lieutenant of the Tower of London until November 27.[69] He does not appear to have withdrawn schoolteachers' licenses from Catholics, and he did not make a satisfactory offer to settle the question of the dispensing or suspending power. Catholic schools in his capital closed only when the teachers and pupils were in physical danger. As for a free parliament, James proclaimed one only just before he abandoned his position.

The king, then, did not give the policy of concessions a fair and full trial, though he thought he was doing so. He trusted the Protestant Lord Godolphin well enough in the autumn to tell him of Louis XIV's secret subsidy, but, according to Barrillon, he trusted even more the Catholic earl of Melfort, one of the least prudent advisers a king ever had.[70] After Sunderland's dismissal, the two secretaries of state, Middleton and Preston, were both Protestants, but he rejected Middleton's best advice, and Preston succeeded Sunderland very late in the day.

And he frustrated his own policy with threats. On October 8, he forbade coffeehouses in London and Middlesex to keep news, except the official *London Gazette,*[71] and two days later commanded the justices of Middlesex and Westminster to allow no discussion of affairs of state. He issued a new proclamation, just as he was removing Sunderland, to threaten ill-disposed persons who spread false news in writing, print, or speech with rigorous proceedings and exemplary punishment. In reaction to William's declarations of the reasons for invading England, he could not refrain from issuing another denouncing the invasion and publications designed "to Seduce Our People, and (if it were possible) to corrupt our Army" and forbidding his subjects to publish or disperse such papers, or to keep or conceal them, without notifying some magistrate or privy councillor.[72] To simple people these were no doubt terrifying menaces, but thoughtful observers knew that they could not be executed and that offenders against the proclamation had little to fear. Thus a member of Lord Paulet's family wrote on November 3, "Sure you doe not expect newse after his Majesty's proclamation to the contrary. Wee are heare such obedient subjects to his comands that we dare not heare itt," and then went on to report the news.[73]

As usual, James received loyal addresses and ordered them printed in the *London Gazette:* from the authorities of London on the restoration of their charter, from the justices of the peace of Cumberland, from the city fathers of Exeter, Carlisle, and Portsmouth. People coming up to London from the country said that the raising of new troops, the concessions, and the king's firmer bearing had improved the state of affairs. The universities at Oxford and Cambridge were going to raise troops of horse for the king, and the London Trained Bands were on foot.[74]

Yet he had not calmed popular feeling. On Sunday, October 7, Father William Petre, brother of the king's favorite Jesuit, was the subject of a riot at the Catholic chapel in Lime Street because he had preached against the King James Version of the Bible. The king then ordered the chapels in the City closed.[75] Early that month, English and Irish soldiers clashed at Portsmouth, and several were killed; at the end of October there was a greater affray in which as many as a hundred may have died.[76] Even Barrillon (whose judgment was sometimes wrong) thought that what seemed to be tranquillity resulting from the concessions was illusory: Many believed that the king had not changed his intention of establishing the Catholic religion in England, and they therefore regarded the Orange party as that of religion and the laws. When the Frenchman reported on October 25/ November 4 that James's position was improving, the report was mistaken.[77] On the contrary, propaganda had alienated the political classes from the king. Tories were shocked that the king seemed to be disinheriting his daughters by implanting a false son in the royal line; Whigs, by their conviction that he meant to overthrow English liberties by use of the dispensing power; the Anglican clergy, that the governor of their church might try to destroy it; Nonconformists, that he would cast them aside when he had exhausted their usefulness. Few believed that James would have made concessions if invasion had not threatened him or that he meant to stand by them if his power survived the emergency. James had paid for his past at the cost of his credit. There was little left to buy a future.

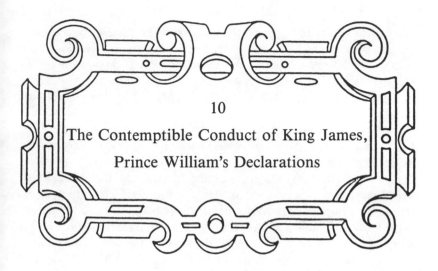

10

The Contemptible Conduct of King James,
Prince William's Declarations

LOOKING BACK on the situation of September 9, 1688, when d'Avaux had given to the States General the memorial on the Dutch armament and had thus added to the revulsion in the Netherlands against King James, the French diplomat reflected, "If that policy had been followed, the plan of the Prince of Orange would have been frustrated, in showing the union existing between the kings of France and England, which would not have allowed the States General to give their troops; but the Marquis of Albeville and the King of England himself spoiled everything by contemptible conduct."[1]

Louis XIV encouraged belief in an existing Anglo-French alliance by means of rumors spread by his ministers abroad. His motive was to divide England from his enemies and especially from the United Provinces, and the rumors contributed to the depth and breadth of the division (though only as an addition to other causes). Yet King Louis intended the memorial presented by d'Avaux on September 8 not so much to worsen Anglo-Dutch relations as to make attack on James II seem more dangerous by showing Louis XIV to be his ally and protector.

It did not in fact worsen those relations, for William had already decided to invade England and had secured the support of the men most necessary to him in doing so. It was only a happy windfall for him that (first) members of the States General and (then) those of the

Council of State, the provincial states, and the governing bodies of the great Dutch cities who did not yet share his confidence (but whose help would be very useful to him) saw laid before them an avowal that James II was allied with the destroyer of Dutch commerce, persecutor of the Protestant religion, breaker of treaties, and general bully of Europe.

Also, in another sense, the story of an alliance was not true. James and Louis had very different views of the world. James wished to preserve the peace and had no conquests in prospect or recent territorial acquisitions to make secure. Louis, on the other hand, would go to war, if necessary, to strengthen himself — for example, by setting up a puppet Archbishop-Elector of Cologne — or to defend his gains made by the Truce of Ratisbon of 1684. James augmented his army in order to be able to repel invasion and repress insurrection; Louis, primarily to impose his will on his neighbors, through aggression if need be. William of Orange was the enemy of both, but for different reasons: of the king of England because the prince refused to lend his help in James's religious policy or in the return of the British troops and was thus a disloyal nephew and son-in-law; of the king of France because William actively opposed Louis's foreign policy, organized and acted as the chief of the other opponents, and (worst) made himself too powerful and independent for a nonsovereign prince and chief commander of a republic. As for Louis's other enemies, James had no enmity for the house of Hapsburg or designs on its possessions. The affairs of German and Italian states concerned him only when they affected British trade, the welfare of British subjects, or the fortunes of his Continental relatives, such as his queen's family. He took a similar line with the Scandinavian kingdoms, Denmark and Sweden, working also to prevent a war between them that might have precipitated a general conflict.

The French army was the largest, most experienced, and best equipped in western Europe. The English one, even late in James's reign, was untried and of only moderate size. James could not permanently enlarge it without parliamentary financial support, which he did not then have. James had equipped it well, but most of its members had not yet seen war, and if William had not invaded the country, it would have had to deal only with uprisings of untrained and ill-armed men.

All this was perfectly well known to the principal figures of the United Provinces; the reader must expect a certain lack of correspondence between fact and assertion in what follows.

Albeville, James's envoy at The Hague, returned to his post early in September (N.S.) after reporting to the king in England on the Dutch situation. Van Citters, he wrote on September 7, was also at The Hague, and people expected Fagel to be there the next day. "Close conferences continue betwixt the pentioner, Dickfelt, Benting, Herbert, Burnet, and others; frequent expresses com and goe." Albeville had asked the Dutch government for an explanation of its warlike preparations. He submitted on September 8 a memorial representing that in view of those preparations the king of England would reinforce his fleet and put himself into a state to maintain the peace of Christendom.[2] The very next day, d'Avaux presented his own memorial, declaring attack on James II to be a breach of peace with Louis XIV.

Albeville's memorial did not receive an immediate reply. He heard Fagel on September 14, expressing his and the States General's "surprise" at the memorial presented by d'Avaux,

> which has opn'd their eyes . . . that they could not believe the King of England was under his [Louis's] tutelage, till now; that they did believe there was som engagement between both Kings, but did not think it, of this nature: That our King was the occasion of their setting a fleet to sea this sumer, for suffering the Algerins (against the treaties) to com into the channell, and lett them have the benefit of his ports; that it would soon appear, how this declaration, of the King of france would be relish'd in England . . . that he would represent it, and their danger to the States.[3]

It is not strange that the king of England recalled Bevil Skelton from France for having suggested the memorial to the marquis de Croissy, the French minister for foreign affairs. Sunderland (whom Skelton suspected of treachery against James) denounced the envoy as affording a justification to the Dutch for arming and to English malcontents for fearing a Catholic alliance against Protestants.[4] Indeed, the opposition did condemn James for being a French satellite. But James was neither more nor less a threat than he had been before.

Albeville continued to press for an explanation of the warlike preparations, even from the deputies of Amsterdam. The latter also told him that the armament was against Algiers, but he thought them ill informed, as they may have been. (It was a peculiarity of Albeville and of his king's methods that he kept asking for answers when the course of events made answers unnecessary. D'Avaux was rapidly gathering pertinent information from agents while Albeville was demanding something official, which would certainly be false, to send home.)[5]

In England, Barrillon wrote on September 8/18, van Citters justified the armament as being made in fear of an Anglo-French attack on the United Provinces. When James replied that there was no plan or proposal for such an attack, the Dutchman insolently asked to have the assurance in writing. However clear James made himself, he did not convince van Citters, who remained a firm believer in the supposed Anglo-French alliance.[6]

James also told van Citters that he was as much surprised by d'Avaux's memorial as the States General had been, and Middleton said that James was too powerful to need foreign protection and too wise to risk prejudicing his foreign and domestic affairs.[7]

King Louis could not understand the English king's reasoning; to him, the Dutch diplomatic demands showed a menacing, rather than reassuring, attitude. He wrote to Barrillon, "The court where you are cannot give a greater sign of weakness than to testify to being annoyed by the declaration that the *sieur* d'Avaux has made according to my order."[8] Though there existed no alliance between England and France, Louis desired one; a clash between James and the States General might help to achieve it. James was averse, knowing that the French alliance would weaken his support at home just when he was arming to resist invasion.[9] Louis regarded care about popularity as a second, hardly less fatal, sign of weakness. Barrillon, in all ways his master's man, wrote with this in mind, on September 20/30, that some important people at the English court hoped for an accommodation with William, but "the King of England will sooner be entirely lost and withdraw from England than submit to anything which might make him dependent on the Prince of Orange . . . he has spoken about it in this sense." James told Barrillon that if William came to England, it was to take the Crown.[10]

The earl of Middleton was one of the king's men who favored accommodation, and as a secretary of state, he seems to have swayed the king's mind. On September 21/October 1, he directed Albeville to talk with the leading men in Holland of James's willingness to secure the Church of England by excluding Catholics from the House of Commons and by giving Anglicans a monopoly of church offices. Middleton wrote, "[T]hough I cannot hope that you can convert them all, so as to make them friends to help Us, yet you must endeavour at least to divide them, so that as Enemys they cannot hurt Us."[11]

James resolved at that time to send Lord Godolphin, a good

Protestant and capable negotiator, to The Hague to compose the differences which had arisen between the king of England on the one
hand, and the States General and the prince of Orange on the other.
Albeville was in the meantime to assure the States General again that
there was no secret treaty binding England to France, and to offer
measures to be taken by James and the Dutch to maintain the Peace
of Nijmegen and the 1684 Truce of Ratisbon. Barrillon remarked that
James intended this offer also to divide the States General from the
prince of Orange. The rigid party at court was too strong, however,
and Godolphin did not go. As to Albeville, nobody at The Hague
paid much heed to anything he said, although he delivered a memorial
to the States General and had it printed.[12]

The Dutch government had committed itself too deeply to go
back; still, some of its members did not have precise knowledge of its
secret plans; it must go on, as though it were right, to achieve a
success that would make questions of right or wrong unimportant.
For the persuasion of the common literate person, someone drew up
an abstract of the supposed treaty of Anglo-French alliance, which
was printed and sold at Amsterdam, Consul Daniel Petit wrote to
Middleton. Observers were apparently expectant but far from over-
confident. Dutch East India and West India shares were down in the
market, as were "obligations upon the Country." Many merchants
were ruined; the famous capitalist Coenraad van Beuningen was said
to lose "already some Tons of Gold."[13] (Van Beuningen also lost his
mind.) "Trade & navigation lye almost dead, Bankrupts are dayly
made." East India shareholders lost especially heavily, Petit wrote on
October 19.[14] (One of the gravest causes of this calamity was the
already-mentioned seizure of Dutch ships in French ports in mid-
September, in express violation of the Peace of Nijmegen, which allowed nine months for withdrawal on each side after a declaration of
war; another was the subsequent interruption of Dutch trade with
France. These actions of Louis XIV, d'Avaux says, silenced the
French party in Holland.)[15]

King James explained his approach to the United Provinces to
the disapproving Barrillon. "Being in such a great peril as he is, and
not seeing Your Majesty [Louis XIV] in condition to succor him, he
had to do everything practicable to save himself, and . . . when he
would be out of such urgent danger he would be able to do what
would agree with his interests and inclination." The French ambassador replied that such reasoning would carry him further, and make
him incapable of resisting the enemies he shared with King Louis. The

demarche would be disagreeable to Louis; perhaps James would not later be able to repair the injury he was doing to the common interest. William would be emboldened, and only the opposition would be pleased. James should rather trust himself and mistrust those who advised such a thing. The king of England took the responsibility upon himself; he had hoped that the approach might begin a negotiation.[16]

Not much later, the king and the ambassador met again. Barrillon told James of Louis's alarm for him and wish to help. James replied, "I no longer know what can be done. The French troops are for the most part at Philippsburg, and the others are going to Italy. What help or diversion can I expect? The king your master's ships could not be ready for a long time, and I believe indeed I would ruin my domestic affairs if the French ships were joined with mine." The ambassador assured him that King Louis regarded his preservation as overwhelmingly important but could not help him against his will. Barrillon wrote to Louis that he hoped thus to open the way to an Anglo-French negotiation and to make James more cautious of treating with the States General. Sunderland promised to keep Barrillon informed but repeated that James could save himself only by the best means he could find.[17]

James vented his opinion of Louis XIV frankly to Bishop Turner on September 26. He "let fall some expressions very remarkable, as if . . . ye French . . . were gone on this expedition [to Philippsburg and the Rhineland] on purpose yt they might expose him to the Dutch, that the French might force him to close intirely with ymselves." Lord Dartmouth told Turner that James had been passionate against Louis XIV "for playing ys trick, as he called it, . . . to force him into a strict League with France if he wd not be sacrificed to Holland." James said that he would not enter such a league and that he would someday be revenged upon the king of France.[18]

Barrillon probably heard only muted expressions from the king of England. He reflected that William might make such use of offers of reconciliation that James would find himself bound to promise whatever was asked of him against France. "The execution," he wrote, however, "cannot be so quick that there are not still means of obstructing it." It seems likely that Barrillon had in mind the objections which some English Catholics lodged against exclusion from Parliament and any proposals made in Holland that might result in penalties for them.[19] These certainly affected King James and may have helped to hinder accommodation, but the principal hindrance was that William did not want a settlement at that time or believe one possible.

The prince of Orange had remarked at a session of the States General on September 20 that the French policy was to make difficulties for Dutch trade and navigation; he suggested strongly the suspected alliance between England and France.[20] On October 8, he met with the States General's deputies for foreign affairs and gave his opinion that the Protestant religion and the independence of the United Provinces were both endangered. The kings of England and France were planning to stamp out Protestantism if they could. It was well known how far King James's ecclesiastical, political, judicial, and military policies displeased his subjects, and from that came the misfortune that James disliked the Dutch government and imagined that it caused all his troubles; he believed that he could not accomplish his work for Catholicism while it had any power. No one could doubt the alliance between the two kings, which d'Avaux's declaration proved, William asserted. James's and Louis's intent was to exterminate "heresy" in England and the Netherlands. If the former ever attained mastery of his country, the joint might of England and France would immediately and without warning confront the United Netherlands. The prince said that he did not mean to depose King James or to possess himself of England but only to arrange that the convening of a free parliament, summoned according to English law and composed of persons legally qualified for membership, should secure the Church of England and free it from danger of oppression.

The deputies for foreign affairs having reported the prince's self-justification and statement of intent, the States General resolved to help him in the execution of his plan, though only as an auxiliary, with troops and ships, by water and by land.[21]

Two days later, Albeville wrote to Middleton of movements of troops to ports and the like. Godolphin's projected mission was still in the air: "When a forrein Minister had represented to Monsr Dickfelt and others, that the fleet should be stopt; till my Lord Godolphins proposalls were known, for it was generally believed his Lordp was coming; he was answer'd by them; what should he com for, all proposalls are now too late."[22]

Moreau, the minister of Poland at The Hague, wrote on October 12, "[T]hese same people, who can only turn their commerce and navigation to account in peace, hope furiously for war"—a paradox indeed. The Dutch, even as Louis XIV had predicted, took James's changes of measures as signs of involvement and weakness. "The

Bantam affair, that of Dr. Burnet, and the recall of the English troops [on which James and the States General disagreed] . . . are very different things from those contained in the memorial by which His Britannic Majesty suddenly proposes to the States to enter with him into the means and expedients most proper to conserve the Treaty of Nijmegen and the truce [of Ratisbon] for twenty years." The States believed, from this and other indications, that William's undertaking could not fail and that it was the only way to preserve the religion and independence, and to reestablish the trade, of the United Provinces.[23]

In England, van Citters used James's new conciliatory policy to save a Dutch ship, *The Arms of Amsterdam,* which put into Dover in bad weather. He complained on October 3 that it had then been prevented from leaving, "as if the fleet of Holland was to make a descent on that coast in a little while," and demanded its release without charge. The earl of Middleton answered that very evening that the king already knew of the incident and had sent his orders for release of the ship as van Citters would have wished. It apparently sailed on October 5. Again, ten Dutch seamen captured by a French privateer and set ashore in England in October were permitted to go to Flanders by packet boat, as they desired, by an order of October 29.[24]

The kings of France and England continued to disagree about joint action. James II had thought the French army could have diverted the Dutch from the invasion by besieging Cologne, which was then in the hands of the allies against France. Louis XIV felt rebuffed, and said so in a letter of October 17, by James's reaction to French troop movements. The king of England had never said that a siege of Cologne would help him in his affairs, and it would have put Louis at a disadvantage. The allies, nearer at hand, could put a strong garrison into the city with greater ease than a French army could have crossed the Rhine and laid siege to so great a place. Moreover, only a large garrison could hold it if taken, and Louis XIV said he could not easily have succored it later. However, he was sending the only help he could, one hundred thousand French ecus (three hundred thousand livres) for Barrillon to pay to James if it seemed that it would not be against Louis's interest to do so (for example, if used to pay troops that were likely to join William against France).[25]

James took heart when Barrillon made the offer known, the latter wrote on October 15/25: "He declared to me that Your Majesty [Louis] was preserving his crown for him" and confided that he was under strong pressure to propose reconciliation to the United Provinces. Help from France confirmed him in his resolution to yield no more than necessary and above all not to alter his good understanding with King Louis. Barrillon explained the decision to attack Philippsburg rather than Cologne. James acquiesced but still seemed to believe that a large French force on the lower Rhine could frighten the Dutch. Although nothing could stop the Prince of Orange's expedition now, such a force could cause the prince and the States General to differ and thus make the expedition more difficult. Barrillon remarked to Louis that he did not know what was practicable in the circumstances, but such a march of French troops would answer courtiers who constantly complained to the king of England that France had still done nothing for him. The ambassador also recommended another payment to James to maintain his determination not to act against Louis's interest.[26]

At The Hague, Albeville went on urging the States General to give him an explicit explanation of the continually growing armament. He heard talk of a declaration by the prince but could not at first obtain a copy, he wrote on October 15/25: "The reason the Manifest can not be had for any money that I offerr'd, is because som men are so describ'd, tho not named, that they may be easily discovered, and that his Majtie would have presently their heads of." Albeville said of the king's general pardon, "I am confident . . . They [the English] and the Scots that are here, do but laugh at all the King can do, that he will not be two months a King." They were sure of general support from England, and of William's preparations "the most part, if not all, is don by money from England."[27]

Fagel actually drew up the prince's declaration; Burnet translated and modified it; John Wildman and other leaders suggested "some few" alterations, which the prince accepted. William signed the finished document on October 10 (N.S.).

Its tone is serious but not bitter; it does not directly denounce the king, although it several times uses the words "Evil Councellours." First it relates the many things that had gone wrong: the use of the dispensing power, the alleged breach of the coronation oath, establishment of the Ecclesiastical Commission and the commission's actions against Bishop Compton and Magdalen College, foundation of Catholic chapels and monasteries, the three questions about repeal of the penal laws and test acts, remodeling of municipal governments, appointment of unqualified judges, prosecution of the seven bishops, actions to control the results of elections, and the doubtful birth of the Prince of Wales. "[M]any both doubted of the Queen's Bigness, and of the Birth of the Child, and yet there was not any one thing done to Satisfy them, or put an end to their Doubts." (This was true at the time of the signature, before James had taken depositions on the subject in the Privy Council.) And so William and Mary, who had their own places in the royal succession, could not excuse themselves from doing all they could "for the Maintaining both of the Protestant Religion, and of the Laws and Liberties of those Kingdomes, and for the Securing to them, the Continual Enjoyment of all their just Rights."

Therefore, "wee" (meaning only William) resolved to go to England with a force "sufficient by the blessing of God, to defend us from the Violence of those Evill Councellours." He had "no other Designe, but to have a free and lawfull Parliament assembled, as soon as is possible." For this purpose all the recent charters were to be considered void, and all the magistrates formerly turned out would be restored to office. The charter of London must be in force and writs for elections addressed to the proper officers. Only candidates qualified by law would be eligible, and the two houses must sit freely. They would make such laws as would secure and maintain the Protestant religion, improving the agreement between the Church of England and Protestant Dissenters, and giving safety from religious persecution to all good subjects, "*Papists* themselves not excepted." Parliament should also do other things, "so that there may be no more danger of the Nations falling at any time hereafter, under *Arbitrary Government*. To this Parliament wee will also referre the Enquiry into the birth of the Pretended Prince of Wales, and of all things relating to it and to the Right of Succession."

William promised his concurrence in everything such a parliament should decide, strict discipline of his troops, and the prompt sending away of the foreign forces among them as soon as could be. He called upon all English subjects to help him and stated his resolution also to settle Scotland and Ireland.

When James shortly carried out some of William's proposals, the prince and his advisors thought this declaration no longer adequate. On October 24, William signed a second and shorter one, also at The Hague. He acknowledged in its first paragraph that some of the "subverters of the Religion and Lawes" of England, having heard of his preparations, had "begun to retract some of the Arbitrary and Despotick Powers, that they had assumed and to vacate some of their Injust Judgments and Decrees." He mentioned vaguely the relief of London from "their Great Oppressions."

Much of this second declaration was a defense of the prince against a charge of intending "to Conquer and Enslave the Nation." He denied the imputation and drew attention to the size of his forces, much too small for such an attempt "if wee were capable of Intending it." Also the lords and gentlemen who were to accompany him would not do so if such were his undertaking. As for James's concessions,

> Wee are . . . Confident that all men see how little weight there is to be laid, on all Promises and Engagements that can now be made . . . And . . . that Imperfect redresse that is now offered, is a plain Confession of those Violations of the Government . . . they lay down nothing which they may not take up at Pleasure: and they reserve entire and not so much as mentioned, their claimes and pretences to an Arbitrary and Despotick power; which has been the root of all their Oppression, and of the total subversion of the Government. And it is plain that there can be no redresse or Remedy offered but in Parliament: by a Declaration of the Rights of Subjects that have been invaded; and not by any Pretended Acts of Grace, to which the extremity of their affairs has driven them.

William and his followers truly believed that James was insincere in his concessions and intended to revoke them, and James's remarks to Barrillon tend to support that belief. But these remarks may themselves have been insincere, and Barrillon feared that James might be forced to commit himself so definitely to war against France that he might be unable to turn back.[28]

Johann Philipp Hoffmann, Emperor Leopold's secretary at London, believed by October 15 (N.S.) that James had already joined the allies against Louis XIV. He wrote that day that the king's "metamorphosis" (meaning the concessions) had happened for the public good. James had made such a declaration on the Peace of Nijmegen and the Truce of Ratisbon as no negotiation could have brought him to, one from which he could not recede. The United Provinces had only to make precise proposals to him, and (though thirsty for vengeance) he would accept them and employ for the good of Europe the forces he had on foot. The prince of Orange had already accomplished all that he had set out to do, therefore, unless he aspired to the Crown against the general belief. Hoffmann foresaw that the prince's expedition would ruin the Catholic religion in England, and, as a representative of a Catholic monarch, he did not wish the prince well. He blamed King Louis for attacking Philippsburg rather than the Dutch city of Maastricht. He seems to have relished the rebuff James gave to van Citters on October 17, when the Dutchman made one last pretence that his country's armament was not intended for use against England and met with such scorn that he had to retire in shame and confusion. He naively hoped and believed that James would enter an alliance against France. But, though somewhat sympathetic, Hoffmann reported on November 2/12 that the king of England had not succeeded in recovering the support either of the nobility or of the common people.[29]

Louis XIV did not blame James for making advances to the States General; he would be willing to maintain secret relations with the king of England, he wrote Barrillon on October 28 (N.S.), if the prince of Orange succeeded in his attempt on England. James would wish to avenge himself; Barrillon should strengthen the wish and persuade him that war against the United Provinces was necessary and that an offensive and defensive alliance with France would help him. Barrillon should discover the terms on which James would conclude such an alliance.[30]

Albeville would have agreed with the king of France. He wrote to Middleton on October 30 (N.S.), "Your Lordp. writes of cultivating their [William's court's] friendship, that is never to be expected, but by being in a condition to make warr upon them, and punishing them."[31] James would undoubtedly have liked to punish his enemies, but he was never to have the means.

Even the French king's money was hard to come by. Asked by James in late October whether the money from Louis's bills of exchange was ready, Barrillon had to reply that it was not; the bills would have been honored promptly if all the exchanges (presumably the offices of goldsmith-bankers) had not been closed. Louis hoped to make a second remittance in cash if James could send a yacht to Calais to receive it. He intended these payments to show that he would not abandon James, provided the latter refused to negotiate with the prince of Orange.[32]

Barrillon replied to his master that at the English court only some of the Catholics (Lords Powis and Castlemaine, and Father Petre) were well disposed in the sense of resisting an accommodation with the States General. On October 31 (O.S.), he had found James open to proposals of revenge and agreeing that time was growing short for joint Anglo-French measures. As to an alliance against France, James said, "I well know how to deny it. And I see clearly in what peril I would be if I let myself be forced to it." Barrillon planned to propose at a later interview that James declare war against the prince and the

States General; he asked his own king whether he should expect a French declaration of war.[33]

On the morning of November 2/12, Barrillon proposed to Hoffmann to save the king of England by hastening the conclusion of peace between the Holy Roman emperor and the king of France. Hoffmann did not record that he was astonished, but he must have been; the war was only a few weeks old. He replied coldly that aggression against the Holy Roman Empire was not a good beginning and that there were already enough treaties that the French did not observe. Barrillon said that parties never observed treaties longer than *raison d'État* and their interest required; the French had acted to prevent a German invasion but were ready to convert the Treaty of Ratisbon into a permanent peace settlement and make valuable restitutions. A short colloquy followed, in which Barrillon urged Hoffmann to write to the emperor's court that France was willing to yield Philippsburg razed and Freiburg in its existing condition. Hoffmann said that Strasbourg (a recent French acquisition, not recognized as French by the emperor) would be the stumbling block, but Barrillon quickly said, "No, no," and left him. Hoffmann concluded from this that the French court was worrying about the situation.[34] Indeed, if Louis XIV would give up any important conquest to help James II, Hoffmann must have been right.

All this was too late. Early in November (N.S.), the States General distributed to members of the provincial states and to ministers of foreign powers copies of a declaration that the States General was constrained to support the prince of Orange against the king of England and for a free Parliament and the Protestant religion.[35] A few days later, copies of William's declarations first came to the king's hands. Others were passed among his subjects in defiance of his proclamations. Barrillon suggested that James declare war. Without disagreeing, James answered that he would reply to the declarations in a fitting manner. Curiously, it seemed that if he declared war first, many Englishmen would look on him as an aggressor. He also thought that to force war (which meant loss of ships and of customs revenue) was likewise to his disadvantage. If the States General declared war first, he might use the fact in his internal affairs. Barrillon argued as usual that caution would encourage his enemies and that the prince of Orange would attribute cautious actions to fear. James was certainly cautious enough: He found it inconvenient to send a yacht to Calais for King Louis's cash, fearing that his subjects would learn of the transaction, and asked instead for bills of exchange, even though they were less handy than cash. He assured Barrillon that he had no resource and support but King Louis, and he would not give him up.[36]

The next day, Louis XIV decided to declare war against the States General, but he deferred publication, he wrote on November 18 (N.S.), to fulfill the threat in d'Avaux's memorial of September 9 that he would treat the first hostile act against James as a rupture. He would defer publication still further if James thought it would help English affairs, but not otherwise. He was firmly resolved on war.[37]

James issued a declaration, not of war but in answer to William's declaration of motives in undertaking the expedition against England, on the same day as Louis's declaration *in petto:* James regarded the invasion as horrid, unnatural, and unchristian in a relation; also, he was troubled that the army of foreigners and rebels would cause "many Mischiefs and Calamities." The prince's real aim was to usurp James's crown, as he showed by assuming the regal style, summoning peers and others to help him (a royal prerogative). William himself was obstructing a free Parliament, which James was nonetheless determined to convoke. Therefore, "we can no ways doubt, but that all Our Faithfull and Loving Subjects, will readily and heartily concur and joyn with Us, in the Entire Suppression and Repelling of those our Enemies and Rebellious Subjects, who have so Injuriously and Disloyally Invaded and Disturbed the Peace and Tranquillity of these Our Kingdoms."[38]

Why did William, the States General, or both, not accept James's offer of alliance against France, coupled with his internal concessions on religion and government? One reason, as William had observed to the Dutch deputies for foreign affairs, was that James had come to regard the Dutch republic as the cause of all his troubles. Whether James was right or wrong on that point, whether he seemed to yield or not, the prince and the United Provinces could expect no good from James. Louis XIV thought it feasible (and desirable) to maintain secret relations with the king of England, even if the latter was forced to an apparent breach; William, who was well acquainted with hypocrisy and double-dealing in public life, would have expected it of James. Also, the prince, the provincial states, and the States General did believe Protestantism to be endangered in England, and Englishmen going to the Netherlands carried news of Protestant discontent and distrust, even during the period (say, October 1 to 15) when James held out most hope of reconciliation. Moreover, the opportunity was unique: Louis was meditating naval assistance to James for the new year, and other factors might have changed, so that postponement of the expedition might have amounted to its abandonment. If James's concessions were only attempts to buy time, the Dutch were firmly decided not to sell it to him.

For this, and for other troubles of James II, Louis XIV was largely to blame. His history of treaty violations and religious persecution, taken together with his injuries to Dutch trade and his known dislike of the prince of Orange and the Dutch state, made him feared and hated, and rendered his allies suspect, even the one who was only suspected to be an ally.

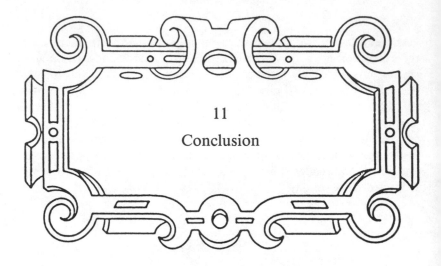

11
Conclusion

JAMES II'S ATTEMPTS to conciliate or divide his enemies, at home and abroad, had failed, and he would have to fight to defend himself, but he had little confidence in his ministers or his army, to which he had given great attention and large sums of money. His religious and foreign policies had isolated him beyond hope of remedy. He would try to fight, rather, and he would lose, for many of his officers would desert him in the crisis and many civilians would appear openly for William or to assert their support for their religion and what they conceived to be the laws of England. His nerve would break when he saw his position so undermined that a token expedition would suffice to topple it. The crumbling of his personality under the pressures of suspicion and treachery reached a climax in flight, which stunned the loyal with dismay and his opponents with incredulous delight.

Freed from his presence and power, fearful of the vengeance he might take if he returned, the representatives of the political classes built the best defense they could by establishing William and Mary on the throne. That action, as some pointed out at the time, would lead to international and civil wars in the future, but Whigs and most Tories preferred that prospect to James's version of peace. Yet some of those who had resisted, despite vivid memories of the king's arrogance and harshness, regretted that he had gone, and some would not accept the government that replaced him. The new world they seemed to inhabit was one in which they were never easy. For Tories, at least, the prerevolutionary regime had had the advantage that obedience to the royal will was a simple guide to action. It was hard for them to accept that an English king had been so wrong as to bar this simplicity for all time and forfeit his kingdom for his posterity. Those things, they had always believed, were impossible.

Whigs, on the other hand, had neglected other possibilities and concentrated their politics on the exclusion of James from the throne; later, they had nursed their hatred of him in secret. When he was gone, there must be other aims and plans, unless they were to have outlived themselves. Or would their blood feud with the Tories supply a raison d'être? Was feud to be the substance of political life? They and Tories alike were helpless to foresee answers to such questions, but common grievances against an unpopular and unreasonable king may have seemed to lay a groundwork for something better.

Whatever happened, politics would soon be very confusing, and therefore disturbing, but the Protestant political classes would never unite, as in 1660, to ask the king to return.

Notes

Abbreviations

A.E.	Archives of the former Ministère des Affaires Étrangerès, Paris
A.R.	Algemeen Rijksarchief, The Hague
A.S.M.	Archivio di Stato, Modena
B.L.	British Library, London
Bodl.	Bodleian Library
C.C.L.	Christ Church Library, Oxford
C.S.P.D.	*Calendar of State Papers, Domestic*
C.T.B.	*Calendar of Treasury Books*
D.N.B.	*Dictionary of National Biography*
H.M.C.	Historical MSS. Commission
J.H.C.	*Journals of the House of Commons*
J.H.L.	*Journals of the House of Lords*
O.A.I.	Oratori e Ambasciatori, Inghilterra (A.S.M.)
P.C.	Privy Council Register
P.R.O.	Public Record Office, London
S.P.	State Papers (P.R.O.)
U.L.C.	University Library, Cambridge
V.C.H.	*Victoria County History*
W.O.	War Office, Secretary's Out Letters (P.R.O.)

INTRODUCTION

1. John P. Spielman, *Leopold of Austria* (New Brunswick, N.J., 1977).

2. For Anglo-Dutch relations before 1688, see my *Charles Middleton: The Life and Times of a Restoration Politician* (Chicago, 1968), pp. 131–37, 177–86, 196–205.

3. K. D. H. Haley, *The First Earl of Shaftesbury* (Oxford, 1968), p. 530.

CHAPTER 1

1. MS. CCL, fol. 25, Christ Church Library, Oxford.

2. G. Ronchi to the Duke of Modena, March 1, 1688, Ambasciatori e Oratori, Busta IV, Archivio di Stato, Modena (A.S.M.).

3. Sancroft and Compton selected ministers to make London more Tory. Robert Beddard, "The Commission for Ecclesiastical Promotions, 1681–1684; An Instrument of Tory Reaction," *Historical Journal* 10 (1967):33.

4. W. Maziere Brady, *Annals of the Catholic Hierarchy in England and Scotland, A.D. 1585–1876* (Rome and London, 1877), pp. 147–51, 243, 281–83; *Journals of the House of Commons (J.H.C.)* 9:252, 256–57. For discussion of the suspending power, see Lois Schwoerer, *The Declaration of Rights, 1689* (Baltimore and London, 1981), pp. 59–64, and W. A. Speck, *The Reluctant Revolutionaries* (Oxford, 1988), pp. 149–51.

5. J. S. Clarke, ed., *The Life of King James the Second, King of England . . .* , vol. 2 (London, 1816), pp. 103–4.

6. G. V. Bennet, "Conflict in the Church," in *Britain after the Glorious Revolution,* ed. Geoffrey Holmes (New York, 1969), p. 159.

7. Thomas Bruce, Earl of Ailesbury, *Memoirs,* vol. 1 (London: Roxburghe Club, 1890), p. 161.

8. Van Citters to Prince William and Fagel, Feb. 6 [N.S.], 1688, Collectie van Citters, 16:27, Algemeen Rijksarchief, The Hague (A.R.).

9. Privy Council Register (P.C.) 2/72:657–58, Public Record Office, London (P.R.O.).

10. *London Gazette,* May 3–7, 1688.

11. Charles Hornby, *The Second Part of a Caveat Against the Whiggs, &c.,* 3d. ed. (London, 1713), p. 46.

12. A. Tindal Hart, *William Lloyd, 1627–1717* (London: Society for Promoting Christian Knowledge, 1952), p. 94; Symon Patrick, *Autobiography* (Oxford, 1839), p. 131; Roger Thomas, "The Seven Bishops and Their Petition, 18 May 1688," *Journal of Ecclesiastical History* 12 (1961):60.

13. John Lowther, Viscount Lonsdale, *Memoir of the Reign of James II* (York: privately printed, 1808), pp. 26–27.

14. Patrick, *Autobiography,* 131.

15. Lonsdale, *Memoir,* 27.

16. Hornby, *Second Part of a Caveat,* 47. I disagree with Roger Thomas's belief that the bishops were thrust into the lead because of fear and indecision ("Seven Bishops," 60).

17. Hart, *William Lloyd,* 95; Thomas, "Seven Bishops," 60.

18. Tillotson was dean of Canterbury, Stillingfleet (St. Paul's), John Sharpe (Norwich), Gregory Haskard (Windsor), Patrick (Peterborough), and Nicholas Stratford (St. Asaph). William Beveridge was archdeacon of Colchester. For the talks, see Thomas, "Seven Bishops," 61.

19. Morrice Entring Book (Morrice MS. Q), pp. 255–60, Dr. Williams's Library, London.

20. Thomas, "Seven Bishops," 61–62.

21. Jonas Proast, "The Case of reading the Declaration for Liberty of conscience," Tanner MS. 28, fol. 32, Bodleian Library (Bodl.).

22. Patrick, *Autobiography,* 132–33.

23. Hart, *William Lloyd,* 96; Patrick, *Autobiography,* 133–34. Speck (*Reluctant Revolutionaries,* 223) thinks the bishops petitioned to force the issue of the suspending power. I disagree.

24. For the "Comprehensive Sense," see Thomas, "Seven Bishops," 64–65; for Sancroft's "Reasons," E. H. Plumptre, *The Life of Thomas Ken, Bishop of Bath and*

Wells, vol. 1 (London, 1888), pp. 288–89. The petition is taken from Plumptre, *Life of Ken,* 1:302–3. Gutch's text differs only in small matters of punctuation and capitalization. John Gutch, ed., *Collectanea Curiosa,* vol. 1 (Oxford, 1781), pp. 336–37.

25. Clarke, *James II,* 2:155–56.

26. Account evidently taken from the bishops, Gutch, *Collectanea Curiosa,* 1:338.

27. *Dictionary of National Biography (D.N.B.),* s.v. "Cartwright, Thomas (1634–1689)."

28. The three foregoing paragraphs draw on Gutch, *Collectanea Curiosa,* 1:338–40. The same account appears in the Appendix to S. W. Singer, ed., *The Correspondence of Henry Hyde, Earl of Clarendon and of His Brother Laurence Hyde, Earl of Rochester; with the Diary of Lord Clarendon* . . . , vol. 2 (London, 1828), pp. 479–80. The biblical allusion is to 1 Kings (Douay, 3 Kings) 19:18.

29. J. R. Western, *Monarchy and Revolution, The English State in the 1680s* (London, 1972), Illustration 2. Thomas's view that some accepted the "Comprehensive Sense" as the bishops' petition is supported by a letter to Roger Kenyon of May 24, 1688; Historical MSS Commission (H.M.C.) *Report XIV,* app. IV, p. 190.

30. Citters made a list of places where reading was performed. Additional MS. 17,677 UUU, fols. 557r, v, British Library, London (B.L.). See also George D'Oyly, *The Life of William Sancroft, Archbishop of Canterbury,* 2d ed. (London, 1840), p. 163. Sir James Mackintosh gives the men's surnames, *History of the Revolution in England in 1688* (London, 1834), p. 252. They are identified with the assistance of George Hennessy, comp., *Novum Repertorium Ecclesiasticum Parochiale Londinense* (London, 1898), p. 119; the *Dictionary of National Biography;* and Venn, *Alumni Cantabrigienses.*

31. Stowe MS. 770, fol. 45r, B.L.; H.M.C. *Buccleuch MSS,* vol. 2, part 1, p. 32; Patrick, *Autobiography,* 135; H.M.C. *Report XII,* app. VII, p. 210.

32. *London Gazette,* May 17–21, 28–31, and May 31–June 4, 1688; David Hatch Hosford, *Nobles, Nottingham and the North: Aspects of the Revolution of 1688,* vol. 4, *Studies in British History and Culture* (Hamden, Conn., 1976), pp. 61–62; Sir John Reresby, *Memoirs,* ed. Andrew Browning (Glasgow, 1936), pp. 494–95.

33. Stowe MS. 770, fol. 44r, B.L.

34. Gutch, *Collectanea Curiosa,* 1:337; T. S. Evans, ed., *Life of Robert Frampton, Bishop of Gloucester* (London, 1875), p. 152.

35. *A Letter from a Clergy-man in the City, to his Friend in the Country, Containing his Reasons for not Reading the Declaration,* May 22, 1688.

36. [T. Birch?], *The Life of the Reverend Humphrey Prideaux, D.D., Dean of Norwich, with Several Tracts and Letters of His* . . . (London, 1748), pp. 41–44.

37. See, e.g., the bishop's letters to Sancroft. Gutch, *Collectanea Curiosa,* 1:342, 358; William Whiston, *Memoirs,* 2d ed. (London, 1753), p. 20.

38. C. E. Whiting, *Nathaniel Lord Crewe, Bishop of Durham (1674–1721), and His Diocese* (London, 1970), p. 172. For a list of those Durham churches, see Denis Granville, *Remains,* ed. G. Ornsby, Surtees Soc. Publications, vol. 7 (Durham, 1865), p. 147. For Cheshire, see P.R.O. 30/53/8, fol. 111r, P.R.O.

39. Anthony Wood, *Life and Times,* ed. A. Clark, Publications, 19, 21, 26, 30, and 40 (Oxford: Oxford Historical Soc., 1891–1895), 26:267.

40. H.M.C. *Hastings MSS.,* 2:184.

41. Gutch, *Collectanea Curiosa,* 1:332–33.

42. Wood, *Life and Times,* 3:267.

43. F. C. Turner, *James II* (New York: Macmillan, 1948), p. 402.

178

Notes

44. Barrillon enclosed a French translation of the bishops' petition in his dispatch of June 3 [N.S.], 1688, Correspondance politique, Angleterre, vol. 165, fol. 337, Archives of the former Ministère des Affaires Étrangères (A.E.), Paris; Van Citters gave a partly erroneous account of these affairs, June 1 [N.S.], 1688, Add. MS. 17,677 UUU, fol. 554r, B.L. I sought but did not find the original of this dispatch in the Algemeen Rijksarchief, The Hague.

45. Corr. pol., Ang., vol. 165, fols. 329v–332v, A.E.

46. Ibid., fol. 351r.

47. Turner, *James II*, 401; Add. MS. 36,707, fol. 29r, B.L.; Corr. pol., Ang., vol. 165, fol. 365, 376v–377r, A.E.

48. Turner, *James II*, 401; J. P. Kenyon, *Robert Spencer, Earl of Sunderland* (London, 1958), p. 195.

49. H.M.C. *Buccleuch MSS*, vol. 2, part 1, p. 32; H.M.C. *Report XII*, app. VII, p. 210.

50. Thomas, "Seven Bishops," 69.

51. Tanner MS. 28, fol. 45, Bodl.; Gutch, *Collectanea Curiosa*, 1:341.

52. Rawlinson MS. Letters 94, fols. 164r–165v, Bodl.

53. Gutch, *Collectanea Curiosa*, 1:342, 344–46.

54. Add. MS. 29,578, fol. 171r, B.L.

55. Account by a clerk of council [Blathwayt?], Egerton MS. 2,543, fol. 270r, B.L.

56. Add. MS. 36,707, fol. 31r, B.L. But see Corr. pol., Ang. 165, fol. 375r, A.E., and PwV 53, Nottingham University, Nottingham.

57. The preceding account rests chiefly on Gutch, *Collectanea Curiosa*, 1:348–51, 351–53; Egerton MS. 2,543, fol. 271r, B.L.; Privy Council Register (P.C.) 2/72, 682–83, P.R.O.

58. Barrillon's dispatch of June 21 [N.S.], 1688, Corr. pol., Ang. 165, fols. 373r–375v, A.E.

59. Ibid.; John Evelyn, *Diary*. ed. E. S. de Beer, vol. 4 (London, 1959), p. 586.

60. Stowe MS. 770, fol. 53r, B.L.

61. Reresby, *Memoirs*, 500; Sir F. W. Hamilton, *The Origin and History of the First or Grenadier Guards*, vol. 1 (London, 1874), p. 295.

62. Edward Carpenter, *The Protestant Bishop, Being the Life of Henry Compton, 1632–1713* (London, 1956), pp. 119–20.

63. Gutch, *Collectanea Curiosa*, 1:358–59.

64. George Ellis, Lord Dover, ed., *Ellis Correspondence, Letters Written during the Years 1686, 1687, 1688, and Addressed to John Ellis . . .* , vol. 1 (London, 1829), pp. 354–55.

65. Add. MS. 29,563, fol. 192r, B.L.; Tanner MS. 28, fol. 69, Bodl.

66. Hart, *William Lloyd*, 109.

67. Reresby, *Memoirs*, 499; Kenyon, *Sunderland*, 195–96; Hart, *William Lloyd*, 108; Clarke, *James II*, 2:165.

68. Edmund Calamy, *Memoirs of the Life of the Late Reverend Mr. John Howe* (London, 1724), p. 140.

CHAPTER 2

1. *The Proceedings and Tryal in the Case of the Most Reverend Father in God, William Lord Archbishop of Canterbury* [and the six other bishops] (London, 1689), p. 1; Add. MS. 29,563, fol. 193r, B.L. *The Proceedings and Tryal,* based on notes taken by a Mr. Blaney at the behest of John Ince, an attorney of the bishops, was approved as accurate by Justice Sir John Powell. The cost of the report was £42 17s. 6d. Gutch, *Collectanea Curiosa,* 2:371.

2. On the Whig barristers and the politico-legal battles of the time, see Michael Landon, *The Triumph of the Lawyers: Their Role in English Politics, 1678–1689* (University, Ala., 1970). For Somers's career to this time, see William L. Sachse, *Lord Somers, a Political Portrait* (Manchester and Madison, Wis., 1975), pp. 1–21.

3. For royal policy and the selection of these judges, see Western, *Monarchy and Revolution,* 54–59.

4. *Proceedings and Tryal,* 13–14.

5. Ibid., 26–28.

6. Ibid., 36.

7. Ibid., 37–43.

8. Ibid., 43–44.

9. Add. MS. 29,563, fols. 192r, 193r, B.L.; Barrillon's dispatch of June 28 [N.S.], 1688, Corr. pol., Ang., vol. 165, fols. 393r, v, A.E.

10. Rawlinson MS. Letters 94, fol. 169, Bodl.

11. Calamy, *Life of John Howe,* 140–41; Morrice MS. Q, p. 269, Dr. Williams's Library, London.

12. Add. MS. 34,515, fol. 38v, B.L.

13. Add. MS. 29,584, fol. 68r, B.L.

14. Herbert Croft, *A Short Discourse Concerning the Reading of His Majesties Late Declaration in the Churches* (London, 1688).

15. Examples are *A Dialogue between the Arch-B. of C. and the Bishop of Heref:; The Clergy's Late Carriage to the King Considered;* and S. T., *Seasonable Advice Humbly Offer'd to the Consideration of the Bishops Against Their Day of Trial.*

16. Barrillon's dispatch of July 3 [N.S.], 1688, Corr. pol., Ang., vol. 166, fol. 24r, A.E.

17. Clarke, *James II,* 2:157.

18. Dover, *Ellis Correspondence,* 1:380.

19. Ibid., 2:3.

20. Morrice MS. Q, p. 276, Dr. Williams's Library, London; Add. MS. 34,515, fol. 83v, B.L.

21. G. E. C., ed., *Complete Baronetage,* vol. 2 (Exeter, 1900–1909), p. 88; *Calendar of Treasury Books (C.T.B.),* 9:649.

22. Burke, *Landed Gentry,* 1882 ed., part 1, p. 869.

23. Dover, *Ellis Correspondence,* 2:56; for Harriott, see W. J. Hardy, ed., *Middlesex County Records, Calendar of the Sessions Books, 1689–1709* (London, 1905), pp. 3, 63.

24. *Calendar of State Papers, Domestic (C.S.P.D.), Feb.–Dec., 1685,* p. 56; W. A. Shaw, *Knights of England,* vol. 2 (London, 1906), p. 271; Narcissus Luttrell, *Brief Historical Relation of State Affairs from September, 1678 to April, 1714,* vols. 5, 6 (Oxford, 1857), p. 65, p. 217, respectively.

25. *C.T.B.*, 8:205, 9:1736. He is confused by G. L. Cherry, *The Convention Parliament* (New York: Bookman Associates, [1968], p. 10), with John Arnold. *C.S.P.D.*, *1687–1689*, p. 139.

26. Foster, *Alumni Oxonienses*, 2:607; Hardy, *Sessions Books*, 29, 84, 125.

27. *C.S.P.D., Feb.–Dec., 1685*, p. 154; *C.T.B.*, 4, passim; Luttrell, *Brief Relation*, 5:258.

28. Edward Chamberlayne, *Angliae Notitia*, 1687 ed., part 1, p. 156.

29. *C.S.P.D., 1686–1687*, p. 7; ibid., *1689–1690*, p. 448.

30. Add. MS. 34,515, fol. 88v, B.L.; Joseph Foster, ed., *The Visitation of Middlesex Begun in the Year 1663* (privately printed, 1887), p. 48.

31. Dover, *Ellis Correspondence*, 2:2.

32. *Proceedings and Tryal*, page facing p. 1; White Kennett, *A Complete History of England*, vol. 3 (London, 1706), p. 485; Dover, *Ellis Correspondence*, 2:5; Add. MS. 34,515, fol. 83v, B. L. Evelyn (*Diary*, 4:588) alone reports nearly sixty present.

33. Kennett, *Complete History*, 3:485.

34. Gutch, *Collectanea Curiosa*, 1:382.

35. Add. MS. 34,515, fol. 83v, B.L.

36. It fills 126 sides of paper. Lansdowne MS. 1,189, B.L.

37. Ibid., fol. 2r.

38. Venn, *Alumni Cantabrigienses*, 2:113, 3:367; *C.S.P.D., Feb.–Dec., 1685*, p. 18. Clavell, the bookseller, had earned money earlier in the year by selling copies of a publication presented at court. PwA 2160, Nottingham University Library, Nottingham.

39. Lansdowne MS. 1,189, fols. 6r–11v, B.L.

40. Ibid., fols. 11v–16r.

41. Ibid., fols. 16r–17v.

42. Ibid., fols. 17v–19v.

43. Ibid., fols. 19v–36v.

44. Ibid., fols. 37r–38r. The words "which the Court rebuked" are omitted from *Proceedings and Tryal*.

45. Ibid., fols. 38r–41r.

46. See, e.g., letter to Viscountess Hatton, June 30, [16]88, Add. MS. 29,563, fol. 207r, B.L.

47. Add. MS. 34,515, fol. 85v, B.L.

48. Ibid., fol. 85r, B.L.; Morrice MS. Q, p. 280, Dr. Williams's Library, London.

49. Lansdowne MS. 1,189, fols. 37r–45r, B.L.

50. Ibid., fols. 45r, v.

51. This colloquy occurs in *Proceedings and Tryal*, 99–100, but not in the MS. account.

52. Lansdowne MS. 1,189, fols. 46r–49v, B.L.

53. Ibid., fols. 53v–54r. The words "All at mercy" occur in *Proceedings and Tryal*, 106, but not in the MS. account.

54. For this proposal, see *Journals of the House of Lords (J.H.L.)*, 11:486–90, 492.

55. Lansdowne MS. 1,189, fols. 55r–66r, B.L.

56. Ibid., fols. 66r–69v.

57. Ibid., fols. 69v–72r.

58. *Proceedings and Tryal*, 128, 130.

59. Lansdowne MS. 1,189, fols. 72r–77v, B.L.

60. Ibid., fols. 80r–81v.
61. Ibid.
62. Ibid., fol. 81v.
63. Ibid., fols. 81v–82r.
64. A year later, the same doctrine was applied on the opposite side. See *A Letter from a Clergy-man in the Country to a Minister in the City Concerning Ministers Intermeddling with State Affairs* . . . (London, 1689).
65. Lansdowne MS. 1,189, fols. 82v–83r, B.L.; *Proceedings and Tryal,* 138–39. Speck (*Reluctant Revolutionaries,* 151–52) supports Allibone's argument.
66. Gutch, *Collectanea Curiosa,* 1:381.
67. Add. MS. 34,515, fol. 88v, B.L.; Sir John Bramston, *Autobiography,* ed. Lord Braybrooke (London, Camden Soc., 1845), 32:310.
68. Jo. Ince to Sancroft, 6:00 A.M., June 30, [16]88, Gutch, *Collectanea Curiosa,* 1:374–75; Lansdowne MS. 1,189, fol. 83v, B.L.
69. H. M. Luckock, *The Bishops in the Tower* (London, 1887), p. 161; Add. MS. 34,515, fol. 88r, B.L.; Dover, *Ellis Correspondence,* 2:5.
70. *Proceedings and Tryal,* 140; Bramston, *Autobiography,* 310–11.
71. Add. MS. 29,563, fol. 206v, B.L.; Van Citters to William and Pensionary Fagel, July 3/13, 1688, Collectie van Citters, 16:160, A.R.
72. Collectie van Citters, 16:160, A.R.
73. H.M.C. *Report VI,* p. 473.
74. Add. MS. 34,515, fol. 88v, B.L.; Loan MS. 29/184, fol. 82v, B.L.; *Public Occurrences Truly Stated,* July 3, 1688.
75. Add. MS. 25,376, fol. 176r, B.L.
76. Newsletter misdated June 30 [for July 1 or 2], 1688, Dover, *Ellis Correspondence,* 2:12.
77. Add. MS. 25,376, fols. 169v, 177r, B.L.
78. Add. MS. 4,251, fol. 239r, University Library, Cambridge (U.L.C.).
79. Patrick, *Autobiography,* 136–37; newsletter of July 9, 1688, P.R.O. 30/25/22, P.R.O.
80. See, e.g., Ivon Gregory, ed., *Hartland [Devon] Church Accounts* (Frome and London, 1950), p. 333.
81. Add. MS. 25,376, fol. 207r, B.L.
82. Gutch, *Collectanea Curiosa,* 1:375; Morrice MS. Q, p. 279, Dr. Williams's Library, London. For an explanation of this customary offer, which was usually accepted, see Henry Maddock, *An Account of the Life and Writings of Lord Chancellor Somers* (London, 1812), p. 162n.
83. Gutch, *Collectanea Curiosa,* 2:368–80.
84. Add. MS. 29,563, fol. 206v, B.L.; Morrice MS. Q, p. 283, Dr. Williams's Library, London; Add. MS. 34,487, fol. 15r, B.L.; Reresby, *Memoirs,* 502.
85. Dover, *Ellis Correspondence,* 2:56.

CHAPTER 3

1. Add. MS. 34,515, fol. 88v, B.L.; Dover, *Ellis Correspondence,* 2:31, 47–48.
2. Kennett, *A Complete History,* 3:486. Dover, *Ellis Correspondence,* 2:62–63. A slightly later writer computed that if the proportion of suspension throughout the kingdom had been as high as in the diocese of Durham, five thousand clergymen would

have been suspended. *The Present Settlement Vindicated, and the Late Mis-Government Proved: In Answer to a Seditious Letter* . . . (London, 1690), p. 21.

3. The original of this document is MS. CCXC, pp. 704–12, C.C.L. It is printed in Gutch, *Collectanea Curiosa,* 1:387–90.

4. Gutch, *Collectanea Curiosa,* 1:391–93.

5. P.R.O. 30/53/8, fol. 121v, P.R.O.

6. Add. MS. 25,376, fol. 225r, B.L.; Collectie van Citters, 16:177; A.R.; Dover, *Ellis Correspondence,* 2:117.

7. Kennett, *Complete History,* 3:485; Add. MS. 29,573, fol. 190r, B.L.

8. Add. MS. 34,487, fol. 21r, B.L.; Add. MS. 25,376, fols. 244v–245r, B.L.; H.M.C. *Report XIII,* app. II (Portland MSS.), p. 159.

9. Dover, *Ellis Correspondence,* 2:130.

10. Add. MS. 36,707, fol. 20r, B.L.

11. H.M.C. *Hastings MSS.,* 2:186; Venn, *Alumni Cantabrigienses,* 2:203; Add. MS. 29,573, fol. 190r, B.L.; Hosford, *Nobles, Nottingham,* p. 139.

12. Hornby, *Second Part of a Caveat,* 51; Wood, *Life and Times,* 3:265 and n; Venn, *Alumni Cantabrigienses,* 2:335.

13. Dover, *Ellis Correspondence,* 2:130.

14. Tanner MS. 28, fol. 158, Bodl.

15. Add. MS. 28,876, fol. 146r, B.L.

16. Add. MS. 34,487, fol. 21r, B.L.; Add. MS. 29,573, fol. 190r, B.L.; Dover, *Ellis Correspondence,* 2:137; Kennett, *Complete History,* 3:486; Luttrell, *Brief Relation,* 1:457; Collectie van Citters, 16:189, A.R.

17. The charge, unfortunately undated, is published in Gutch, *Collectanea Curiosa,* 1:393–97.

18. Dover, *Ellis Correspondence,* 1:137–38.

19. Add. MS. 36,707, fol. 38r, B.L.

20. Dover, *Ellis Correspondence,* 2:100–102; Add. MS. 36,707, fol. 20r, B.L.

21. Dover, *Ellis Correspondence,* 2:108–9.

22. Loan MS. 29/184, fol. 93v, B.L.

23. Luttrell, *Brief Relation,* 1:457.

24. Dover, *Ellis Correspondence,* 2:132; Gutch, *Collectanea Curiosa,* 1:404; Venn, *Alumni Cantabrigienses,* 1:303; *C.S.P.D., 1687–1689,* p. 255.

25. J. Bloxam, ed., *Magdalen College and King James II, 1686–88,* vol. 6 (Oxford: Oxford Historical Soc., 1886), p. 249.

26. Ibid., 221–22.

27. Ibid., 222n; Edward Hasted, *The History and Topographical Survey of Kent,* vol. 1 (Canterbury, 1778–1799), 1:117, 138; *Topographer and Genealogist,* 2 (1853): 532.

28. Bloxam, *Magdalen College,* 250n, 251n; Evans, *Robert Frampton,* 254–58.

29. Evans, *Robert Frampton,* 158.

30. J. R. Bloxam, comp., *A Register of the Presidents, Fellows, Demies . . . of Saint Mary Magdalen College in the University of Oxford,* vol. 5 (Oxford and London, 1853–1885), 5:270.

31. Anthony Wood, *Fasti Oxonienses,* part II, column 403; Wood, *Life and Times,* 3:272–73; Dover, *Ellis Correspondence,* 2:76–77.

32. Add. MS. 41,823, fol. 125r, B.L.; Add. MS. 41,805, fol. 34r, B.L.

33. Add. MS. 22,578, fol. 26r, B.L.

34. Carte MS. 217, fols. 277–78, Bodl.; Wood, *Fasti,* vol. 2, column 403; Wood, *Life and Times,* 3:275 and n.; Collectie van Citters, 16:188, A.R.

CHAPTER 4

1. P.C. 2/72, p. 560, P.R.O.

2. Wood, *Life and Times,* 3:254–55. An even earlier attack on the reality of the pregnancy is in PwA 2119, Nottingham University Library, Nottingham.

3. Collectie van Citters, 16:29, A.R. On propaganda of the period, see Lois Schwoerer, "Propaganda in the Revolution of 1688," *American Historical Review* 132 (1977):843–74.

4. Stowe MS. 770, fol. 8r, B.L.

5. Add. MS. 32,095, fol. 261v, B.L.

6. Add. MS. 25,375, fols. 263v–264r, B.L.

7. J. P. Kenyon, *Robert Spencer, Earl of Sunderland, 1641–1702* (London and New York, [1958]), p. 196 and n.

8. Add. MS. 25,376, fol. 75v, B.L.; Emilia, Marquise Campana de Cavelli, ed., *Les Derniers Stuarts à St.-Germain-en-Laye,* vol. 2 (Paris, 1871), pp. 191–92; P.R.O. 30/25/22, P.R.O.

9. Mary II, *Lettres et mémoires,* ed. Mechtild, Countess Bentinck (The Hague, 1880), pp. 36–41; Add. MS. 17,677 UUU, fol. 549r, B.L.

10. Clarke, *James II,* 2:159; Ailesbury, *Memoirs,* 174.

11. Add. MS. 17,677 HH, fol. 424r, B.L.; Add. MS. 25,376, fol. 116v, B.L.; Corr. pol. Ang., vol. 165, fols. 351–52, A.E.

12. Add. MS. 15,397, fol. 106v, B.L.; Add. MS. 17,677 HH, fol. 433r, B.L.; Sloane MS. 3,929, fol. 62r, B.L.

13. P.C. 2/72, p. 685, P.R.O.; Wood, *Life and Times,* 3:268. Wood had his information from an official messenger passing through Oxford.

14. Corr. pol., Ang., vol. 165, fol. 370v, A.E.; P.C. 2/72, pp. 685–86, P.R.O. A letter addressed to the Earls of Pembroke and Yarmouth as Lords Lieutenants of Wiltshire is Add. MS. 27,448, fol. 342, B.L.

15. Add. MS. 9,341, fol. 51r, B.L.

16. James Macpherson, *The History of Great Britain, from the Restoration, to the Accession of the House of Hannover,* vol. 1 (London, 1775), p. 499. For addresses see *London Gazette,* June 21–25, 25–28; July 2–5, 5–9, 9–12, 16–19, 19–23, and 26–30, 1688.

17. Wood, *Life and Times,* 3:268; H.M.C. *Report XII,* app. II, p. 411; Sir George F. Duckett, comp., *Penal Laws and Test Act,* vol. 1 (London, 1882–1883), p. 268.

18. *Public Occurrences Truly Stated,* June 26, 1688.

19. R. R. Sharpe, *London and the Kingdom: A History Derived Mainly From the Archives at Guildhall,* vol. 2 (London, 1894–1895), pp. 528–29.

20. Wood, *Life and Times,* 3:272.

21. H.M.C. *Report XII,* app. II, p. 411.

22. Wood, *Life and Times,* 3:270–72.

23. *London Gazette,* July 12–16, 1688. The U.L.C. copy is Sel. 3. 235, item 59.

24. Add. MS. 25,376, p. 169v, B.L.

25. S.P. 78 (State Papers, Foreign, France)/151, fols. 182r, v, P.R.O.

26. Session of the States General, June 26 [N.S.], 1688, Staten Generaal 1,803, A.R.; Staten Generaal 11,976, fol. 90r and v, A.R.; Add. MS. 41,816, fols. 8r, v, 83r, B.L.

27. Add. MS. 17,677 HH, fol. 456v, B.L.; S.P. 8 (King William's Chest)/4, item 74, P.R.O.

28. Add. MS. 41,808, fols. 289–90, B.L.; Add. MS. 41,807, fols. 26–27, 134–35, 244–45, 254–55, B.L.

29. S.P. 94 (State Papers, Foreign, Spain)/72, fols. 243r, v, P.R.O.

30. Add. MS. 41,823, fol. 69, B.L.; Add. MS. 17,677 HH fol. 433r, B.L. See also Corr. pol., Ang., vol. 165, fols. 368r, v, A.E.

31. Giacomo Ronchi to the Duke of Modena, June 28 [N.S.], 1688, Oratori e Ambasciatori, Inghilterra, Busta IV, A.S.M. (O.A.I., A.S.M.); PwV 61, Nottingham University Library, Nottingham.

32. Ronchi's dispatch of July 19 [N.S.], 1688, O.A.I., Busta IV, A.S.M.

33. Campana de Cavelli, *Derniers Stuarts,* 2:249–50.

34. Add. MS. 29,573, fol. 180r, B.L.; newsletter, Aug. 10, 1688, P.R.O. 30/25/22, P.R.O.; Venetian newsletter, July 30, 1688, P.R.O. 31/14/151, P.R.O.

35. *Mrs. Frances Shaftoe's Narrative Containing an Account of Her Being in Sir Theophilus Oglethorpe's Family . . .* (London, 1708).

36. Ronchi's dispatches of August 16 and 30 [N.S.], O.A.I., Busta IV, A.S.M.; H.M.C. *Report XIII,* app. 2 (Portland MSS.), p. 159; Campana de Cavelli, *Derniers Stuarts,* 2:249–50; Dover, *Ellis Correspondence,* 2:114–15; Bramston, *Autobiography,* 312. See *Tom Tyler: or The Nurse,* probably published late in 1688.

CHAPTER 5

1. Duckett, *Penal Laws,* 1:74. For the questions, see David Ogg, *England in the Reigns of James II and William III* (Oxford, 1955), p. 188.

2. Western, *Monarchy and Revolution,* 221–22; J. R. Jones, *The Revolution of 1688 in England* (London, 1972), pp. 132, 135–37; PwV 61, Nottingham University Library, Nottingham. For deliberation in Cumberland, see W. A. Speck, "The Orangist Conspiracy against James II," *Historical Journal* 30, no. 2 (1987): 454.

3. Dispatch of December 30 [N.S.], 1687, Staten Generaal, Engeland 5,915, fol. 5, A.R.

4. Lansdowne MS. 1153A, fol. 87v, B.L.

5. Duckett, *Penal Laws.*

6. John Carswell, *The Descent on England* (London, 1969), pp. 240–41.

7. Jones, *Revolution,* 132–33; Lionel Glassey, *Politics and the Appointment of Justices of the Peace, 1675–1720* (Oxford, 1979), pp. 82–89.

8. Western, *Monarchy and Revolution,* 215–16.

9. Speck, *Reluctant Revolutionaries,* 194–95; Carswell, *Descent,* 240.

10. Jones, *Revolution,* 137.

11. Western, *Monarchy and Revolution,* 222–23. For Butler, see Luttrell, *Brief Narration,* 1:400, 415, 421, 481; Kenyon, *Sunderland,* 104, 165. For Brent, see Luttrell, *Brief Narration,* 1:388; C. E. Lart, *Jacobite Extracts . . . ,* vol. 1 (London, 1910–1912), p. 17; E. E. Estcourt and J. O. Payne, *English Catholic Non-Jurors of 1715* (reprinted London, 1969), p. 67 and n. According to Duckett, 1:241n, Brent was a kinsman of the second Lord Carrington. Brent's avarice is referred to by John Miller, *James II, A Study in Kingship* (Hove, 1978), p. 180.

12. Jones, *Revolution*, 145.

13. Duckett, *Penal Laws*, 1:101n, 222; 2:xiii, 218 and n.; *C.S.P.D., Feb.–Dec., 1685*, p. 311; *C.S.P.D., 1686–1687*, pp. 143, 335; Hosford, *Nobles, Nottingham*, 48; Charles Deering, *Nottinghamia Vetus et Nova* (Nottingham, 1751), p. 255.

14. Duckett, *Penal Laws*, 2:15 and n; *C.S.P.D., 1687–1689*, pp. 191–92, 199–200; Charles Dalton, ed., *English Army Lists and Commission Registers, 1661–1714*, vol. 1 (London, 1892–1904): p. 182.

15. Jones, *Revolution*, 128–75.

16. Rawlinson MS. A. 139 B, fol. 186r, Bodl.

17. Jones, *Revolution*, 149, 170–71. Jones's attack on the earlier view is based on one statement by one (admittedly well-informed) observer, William Blathwayt. One could wish for more.

18. Western, *Monarchy and Revolution*, 225.

19. H.M.C. *Hastings MSS.*, 2:182. For Sanders, see *C.S.P.D., Feb.–Dec., 1685*, p. 287; ibid., *1687–1689*, p. 273; *C.T.B.*, vol. 8, part 3, p. 1806; Duckett, *Penal Laws*, 2:245.

20. Add. MS. 34,515, fol. 39r, B.L.

21. Sir Walter Kirkham Blount, Bart., John Hill of Gloucester, and William Pugh of Penryn, Caernarvonshire, are examples. Blount was sheriff of Worcestershire in 1687–1688. Duckett, *Penal Laws*, 1:268, 276; 2:180; *C.S.P.D., 1687–1689*, p. 54.

22. Add. MS. 36,988, fols. 258r, v, B.L. For Hiliard (or Hylyard), see Western, *Monarchy and Revolution*, 50; Venn, *Alumni Cantabrigienses*, 2:369; Duckett, *Penal Laws*, 1:310.

23. Bramston, *Autobiography*, 306–7. Petre was appointed February 4, 1687/1688. *C.S.P.D., 1687–1689*, p. 142; van Citters' dispatch of February 7/17, 1687/1688, Staten Generaal, Engeland 5,915, fols. 51r, v, A.R.

24. Add. MS. 25,375, fols. 193v–194r, 225v, B.L.

25. Corr. pol. Ang., vol. 165, fols. 130v–131r, A.E.

26. P.C. 2/72, p. 611, P.R.O.; *C.S.P.D., 1687–1689*, p. 144.

27. Van Citters' dispatch of February 7/17, 1687/1688, Staten Generaal, Engeland 5,915, fols. 51r, v, A.R.

28. *C.S.P.D., 1687–1689*, pp. 141, 144, 146, 148, 152–53, 156, 158, 168, 172, 179.

29. Dispatch of January 23/February 2, 1687/1688, Add. MS. 25,375, fol. 150v, B.L.

30. Douglas Lacey, *Dissent and Parliamentary Politics in England, 1661–1689; A Study in the Perpetuation and Tempering of Parliamentarism* (New Brunswick, N.J., [1969]), pp. 204–5.

31. P.C. 2/72, pp. 657–81, P.R.O.

32. For James's attitude toward Huguenot refugees in England, see George Hilton Jones, "The Problem of French Protestantism in the Foreign Policy of England," *Bulletin of the Institute of Historical Research* 42(1969):145–57.

33. Van Citters to the States General, April 20 [N.S.], 1688, Staten Generaal, Engeland, 5,915, fols. 99v–100r, A.R.

34. Add. MS. 29,563, fol. 130r, B.L.; Jones, *Revolution*, 229, states that the second Declaration of Indulgence was issued on May 3; this document shows clearly that it was available to the public on April 27 or 28. See also Kenyon, *Sunderland*, 194, where this error seems to originate.

35. H.M.C. *Hastings MSS.*, 2:184; Hosford, *Nobles, Nottingham*, 56; Samuel Newton, *Diary, 1662–1717*, (Cambridge: Cambridge Antiquarian Soc., 1890), octavo series, vol. 23, pp. 92–94.

36. Rawlinson MS. A 139 B, fol. 178v, Bodl.; Staten Generaal, Engeland 5,915, fol. 1194, A.R.

37. R. L. Kenyon and Sir O. Wakeman, eds., *Orders of the Shropshire Quarter Sessions, 1638–1708,* vol. 1 of *Shropshire County Records,* vol. 1 (Shrewsbury, 1902): p. 120; Add. MS. 34,487, fol. 19r, B.L.

38. Hosford, *Nobles, Nottingham,* 74.

39. Jones, *Revolution,* 158; Dover, *Ellis Correspondence,* 2:82. See also John Childs, *The Army, James II, and the Glorious Revolution* (London: St. Martin's Press, 1980), p. 111.

40. Duckett, *Penal Laws,* 2:231–32; for Plymouth, see also Romney Sedgwick, ed., *The House of Commons, 1715–1754,* vol. 1 (New York: Oxford University Press for the History of Parliament Trust, 1970), p. 228.

41. This is an exception to Professor J. H. Plumb's statement on the policy of Charles II and James II in *The Growth of Political Stability in England, 1675–1725* (Baltimore, 1969), p. 29.

42. Duckett, *Penal Laws,* 2:61. For Eston, see *Victoria County History, (V.C.H.) Bedfordshire,* 2:59, 3:8.

43. Paper endorsed "Free Elections" [1688?], Rawlinson MS. D 850, fol. 75r, Bodl. Brackets in original.

44. Hosford, *Nobles, Nottingham,* 48–52.

45. Deering, *Nottinghamia Vetus et Nova.* For Wright, who had been a junior counsel for the prosecution of the seven bishops, see Venn, *Alumni Cantabrigienses,* 4:475; *D.N.B.,* s.v. "Wright, Nathan."

46. Hosford, *Nobles, Nottingham,* 51–53.

47. Kenyon, *Sunderland,* 189.

48. Duckett, *Penal Laws,* 2:227; Jones, *Revolution,* 162–63.

49. Duckett, *Penal Laws,* 1:373; 2:232–33, 264.

50. Barrillon's dispatch of June 3, 1688, Corr. pol. Ang., vol. 165, fols. 329–333r, A.E.

51. G. H. Martin, ed., *The Royal Charters of Grantham, 1463–1688* (Leicester, 1963), pp. 22–23.

52. *C.S.P.D., 1687–1689,* p. 276; Duckett, *Penal Laws,* 1:147, 152. In 1685, Harrington had raised an independent troop of horse at Grantham for James II. Dalton, *English Army Lists,* 2:16n. He had also been Sheriff of Lincolnshire in 1677. *Lincolnshire Notes and Queries,* 24(1936):19.

53. Reresby, *Memoirs,* 502–3, 505.

54. "Ten Seasonable Queries, proposed by a Protestant, that is for Liberty of Conscience to all perswasions," printed by Duckett, *Penal Laws,* 1:199–201.

55. Add. MS. 25,375, fol. 231v, B.L.

56. War Office, Secretary's Out Letters (W.O.) 4/1, pp. 70–71; Entry Books (S.P.) 44/56, p. 409. P.R.O. I find Childs's interpolated remarks on this incident (*Army, James II,* 101) curiously prejudicial.

57. Duckett, *Penal Laws,* 1:78–80.

58. Ibid., 1:83–86.

59. Ibid., 1:86–87.

60. Duckett, *Penal Laws,* 1:87–89; H.M.C. *Report XIII,* app. 7, p. 96. The fourteen were Viscount Downe* (an Irish peer), Sir Henry Goodrick,* Sir Henry Cooke, Bart., Sir Thomas Yarburgh,* Sir Michael Wentworth,* William Lowther, Francis White (recorder of Leeds), Thomas Yarburgh (uncle of Sir Thomas and also of Sir John

Reresby), Thomas Horton, Thomas Vincent, John Ramsden,* Welbury Norton, William Ellis, and Sir John Kaye, Bart.* Names starred are those of members of the Parliaments of 1685 and 1688/1689. Downe, Goodrick, Wentworth, and Kaye all sat in at least two other parliaments as well. See also Reresby, *Memoirs,* 494.

61. Duckett, *Penal Laws,* 1:90–91.

62. Ibid., 1:71–75.

63. Add. MS. 34,487, fols. 19v, 25r, B.L.; John Latimer, *The Annals of Bristol in the 17th Century* (Bristol, 1900), pp. 446–49.

64. Duckett, *Penal Laws,* 1:380–81; Carswell, *Descent,* 241.

65. Reresby, *Memoirs,* 5; newsletter, September 1, 1688, H.M.C. *Downshire MSS.,* vol. 1, part 1, p. 298.

66. S.P. 44/56, p. 426, P.R.O.

67. P.C. 2/72, p. 727, P.R.O.; Duckett, *Penal Laws,* 1:103.

68. The list is printed in Andrew Browning, *Thomas Osborne, Earl of Danby and Duke of Leeds, 1632–1712,* vol. 2 (Glasgow, 1944–1951), pp. 157–63. I count as the irreducible minimum of mistakes Sir Thomas Lee, William Garroway, William Sacheverell, William Leveson Gower, Henry Powle, Sir Gervase Elwes, Sir Samuel Barnardiston, Sir John Fagg, Major John Braman, Henry Herbert, and Richard Hampden. Sir William Williams appears on both lists, as is appropriate to a man with a strong Whig record working for James II as solicitor general. The oddity of endorsement of Somers has also been pointed out by Sachse, *Lord Somers,* 24.

69. Andrew Browning, ed., *English Historical Documents, 1660–1714* (London, 1953), p. 121.

70. S.P. 44/56, pp. 317, 429, 433, 441, P.R.O.

71. Military ranks given here are from Dalton's *English Army Lists;* court posts from Edward Chamberlayne's *Angliae Notitia,* 1687 ed.

72. Childs (*Army, James II,* 107–8) finds thirty-eight. I am more cautious in identifying officers than he.

73. Jones, *Revolution,* 156.

74. Duckett, *Penal Laws,* 1:379.

75. Ibid., 2:235n, 236n; *Members of Parliament. Return to Two Orders of the . . . House of Commons . . . ,* Part I (London, 1878), pp. 548, 550; R. and S. Izacke, *Remarkable Antiquities of the City of Exeter* (London, 1723), p. 186; *C.S.P.D., 1686–1687,* p. 356; *C.S.P.D., 1682,* p. 437; *Gray's Inn Admission Register, 1521–1889* (privately printed, London, 1889), p. 276.

76. Thomas Bailey, *Annals of Nottinghamshire,* vol. 3 (London and Nottingham, 1852–1855), p. 1036; J. W. F. Hill, *Tudor and Stuart Lincoln* (Cambridge, 1956), pp. 188–89, 214.

77. *C.S.P.D., 1686–1687,* p. 46; ibid., *1687–1689,* p. 229.

78. Forty-shilling Freeholder Act of 1429 (8 Henry VI, c. 7).

79. Add. MS. 36,707, fol. 20r, B.L.

80. Reresby, *Memoirs,* 507–8, 510–11.

81. P.C. 2/72, p. 736, P.R.O.

82. Corr. pol., Ang., vol. 166, fol. 203r, A.E.; see also Speck, *Reluctant Revolutionaries,* 129.

83. Lord Dartmouth recorded Newport's (later Lord Bradford's) account of the occasion as a note on Burnet's *History.* Macaulay used it in Chapter 8 of his *History of England.*

84. Add. MS. 41,823, fol. 73v, B.L.

85. See Sunderland to Duke of Berwick (Lord Lieutenant of Hampshire), September 22, 1688, *C.S.P.D., 1687–1689,* p. 280. It is not certain that all lords lieutenant received such an order. Add. MS. 29,563, fol. 268r, B.L.
86. *C.S.P.D., 1687–1689,* pp. 286–87; S.P. 8/2, part 2, fols. 46r, v, P.R.O.
87. Add. MS. 34,487, fols. 29r, v, B.L. For Norton, see Duckett, *Penal Laws,* 1:425; Foster, *Alumni Oxonienses,* 3:1079; Dalton, *English Army Lists,* 1:84; Rawlinson MS. A. 139 B. fols. 192v, 193r, Bodl.
88. Entry for September 16 in transcription of Knatchbull's diary, Add. MS. 52,924, B.L. (folios not numbered). See also Add. MS. 33,923, fol. 435, B.L.
89. Wood, *Life and Times,* 3:277. For Bertie, see *V.C.H., Oxfordshire,* 6:349; Duckett, *Penal Laws,* 1:339; *Members of Parliament,* 1:531, 549, 554.
90. Bramston, *Autobiography,* 316–17; Tanner MS. 28, fol. 183, Bodl. For Astley and Cooke, see G. E. C[ockayne], *Complete Baronetage,* vol. 3 (Exeter, 1900–1909), pp. 56–57, 278.
91. Ralph Thoresby, *Diary,* ed. Joseph Hunter, vol. 1 (London, 1830), p. 188.
92. P.C. 2/72, pp. 738–40, P.R.O.
93. Speck, *Reluctant Revolutionaries,* 132.

CHAPTER 6

1. Gilbert Burnet, *A History of His Own Times,* vol. 3 (Oxford, 1833), p. 220.
2. Several papers relating to this episode are printed in Sir James Ferguson, ed., *Papers Illustrating the History of the Scots Brigade in the Service of the United Netherlands, 1572–1782,* vol. 1 (Edinburgh: Scottish History Soc., vol. 32, 1899), pp. 536–41. Childs (*Army, James II,* 126, 129) gives more details on this episode in the history of these regiments.
3. For treatment of several of these sources of disagreement, see George Hilton Jones, *Charles Middleton: The Life and Times of a Restoration Politician* (Chicago: University of Chicago Press, 1967), pp. 131–37, 177–86, 192–210.
4. This is apparently what Johann Philipp Hoffmann, Imperial secretary in England, referred to in his dispatch of February 3, 1688, telling of troubles the Dutch authorities had had with the British regiments in the past. Campana de Cavelli, *Derniers Stuarts,* 2:171–72. For the prince's policy, particularly on Catholic officers, see Burnet, *History,* 3:220–21.
5. Corr. pol. Ang., vol. 165, fols. 59v, 65v–66r, A.E.
6. Ferguson, *Scots Brigade,* 1:542; S.P. 8/4, fol. 118r, P.R.O.
7. Ferguson, *Scots Brigade,* 1:xxxiv; Campana de Cavelli, *Derniers Stuarts,* 2:168.
8. Add. MS. 41,823, fols. 58v–59v, B.L.
9. Ibid., fol. 60r.
10. Add. MS. 29,578, fol. 154r, B.L.; Add. MS. 25,375, fol. 147r, B.L. Staten Generaal, Engeland, 5,915, fol. 31v, A.R. (transcript, Add. 17,677 HH, fols. 313r, v, B.L.).
11. Ferguson, *Scots Brigade,* 1:543.
12. Jean Antoine de Mesmes, Count d'Avaux, *Négociations . . . en Hollande,* new ed., vol. 6 (Paris, 1754), p. 67. The passage seems to show that William was not at all happy with the recall.
13. Resolution and letter of February 19, 1688, printed in Ferguson, *Scots Bri-*

gade, 1:543–46. The original letter is Add. MS. 41,822, fols. 202–3, B.L. Professor Stephen Baxter misunderstands the permission as given to all "individuals who wanted to return to England and Scotland." Baxter, *William III and the Defence of European Liberty* (New York, 1966), p. 221. Only officers were in fact permitted to go. Childs (*Army, James II,* 132) regards the decision as intended to purge the regiments of officers William could not rely on.

14. Session of the States General, February 8, 1688, Staten Generaal, I, 1,799, A.R.

15. Add. MS. 41,815, fol. 139r, B.L.

16. Onno Klopp, *Der Fall des Hauses Stuart und die Succession des Hauses Hannover in Gross Britannien und Irland,* vol. 3 (Vienna, 1875–1888), p. 418.

17. Add. MS. 41,815, fol. 136r, B.L.

18. Barrillon to Louis XIV, Feb. 12, 1688, Corr. pol., Ang., vol. 165, fol. 91v, A.E.; Ferguson, *Scots Brigade,* 1:546.

19. Add. MS. 41,815, fols. 129r, v, B.L. Cf. Childs, *Army, James II,* 132.

20. Add. MS. 41,815, fol. 137v, B.L.; *An Historical Account of the British Regiments Employed since the Reign of Queen Elizabeth and King James I in the Formation and Defence of the Dutch Republic . . .* (London, 1794), p. 63; Add. MS. 41,815, fol. 137r, B.L.

21. Add. MS. 25,375, fol. 178v, B.L.; Corr. pol., Ang., vol. 165, fol. 92r, A.E.

22. Add. MS. 41,815, fol. 152r, B.L.; d'Avaux, *Négociations,* 6:67.

23. Terriesi's dispatch of February 17/27, 1688, Add. MS. 25,375, fol. 199r, B.L.; Ferguson, *Scots Brigade,* 1:547.

24. Collectie van Citters, vol. 16, pp. 50–51, A.R.

25. George Hilton Jones, *Charles Middleton,* 73, 121–22. Terriesi confirmed the cause of de Paz's dismissal. Add. MS. 25,375, fol. 221r, B.L.

26. A. Moreau to the King of Poland, February 24, 1688, Add. MS. 38,494, fol. 35v, B.L. One cannot always rely on Moreau, who says that only one officer asked permission to leave and one asked for time to consider.

27. Add. MS. 41,823, fols. 62r, v; Add. MS. 41,821, fol. 32r; Add. MS. 41,815, fol. 172r, B.L.

28. Dalton, *English Army Lists,* 2:89.

29. *Historical Account of the British Regiments,* 63.

30. Add. MS. 41,815, fols. 147r–148r, B.L.

31. Add. MS. 41,821, fols. 36r, 43r; Add. MS. 41,815, fol. 173r, B.L.; Dalton, *English Army Lists,* 2:232.

32. Laurence Eachard, *The History of the Revolution* (London, 1725), p. 93.

33. Add. MS. 41,815, fol. 182v; Add. MS. 41,821, fol. 43r, B.L.; S.P. 78/151, fols. 146v, 160r, P.R.O.

34. Add. MS. 41,815, fol. 173v, B.L.

35. Burnet, *History,* 3:220; Campana de Cavelli, *Derniers Stuarts,* 2:179; *Historical Account of the British Regiments,* 63; Eachard, *History of the Revolution,* 93; Add. MS. 25,375, fol. 254r, B.L.

36. Dalton, *English Army Lists,* vol. 2; Ferguson, *Scots Brigade,* vol. 1.

37. *C.T.B.,* VIII, *1685–1689,* pp. 1789–90, 1814; Add. MS. 32,095, fols. 251r–252r; Add. MS. 41,821, fols. 32r, 36r, 38r–39r, 43r, B.L. Childs (*Army, James II,* 133) seems sure that there were 104.

38. Add. MS. 41,815, fol. 162; Add. MS. 41,823, fol. 61r, B.L.

39. S.P. 8/4, fol. 126r, P.R.O.

40. Corr. pol., Ang., vol. 165, fols. 91v–92r, A.E.
41. Louis XIV to Barrillon, March 9 [N.S.], 1688, ibid., fols. 143r–144r, A.E.
42. Add. MS. 41,823, fol. 66v, B.L.
43. Klopp, *Der Fall,* 4:3.
44. Add. MS. 25,375, fols. 163v–165v, 169r, v, B.L.; Staten Generaal, Engeland, 5,915, fols. 29r–30v, A.R.; Add. MS. 38,494, fols. 52v–53r, B.L.
45. See, e.g., Sunderland to Sir Richard Bulstrode, February 24, 1687/1688, S.P. 104 (Secretary's Letter Books)/187, p. 275, P.R.O.; also Barrillon to Louis XIV, April 5 [N.S.] 1688, Corr. pol., Ang., vol. 165, fols. 215r–216r, A.E.; George Hilton Jones, *Charles Middleton,* 189.
46. Ronchi to Duke of Modena, March 16 [N.S.], 1688, O.A.I., Busta IV, A.S.M.
47. Dalton, *English Army Lists,* 2:151–56, 158, 160, 162.
48. Add. MS. 17,677 HH, fols. 338r–340r, B.L.; Staten Generaal, I, 1,800, A.R.
49. "Extrait du Registre des Resolutions des . . . Estats Generaux," March 3/13, 1688, Collectie van Citters, vol. 30, A.R.
50. Add. MS. 41,823, fols. 63r–66r, B.L.; session of the States General, April 5, 1688, Staten Generaal, I, 1801, A.R. Most of Albeville's memorial and the whole capitulation appear in Ferguson's *Scots Brigade,* 1:556–60.
51. Dalton, *English Army Lists,* 2:231.
52. Add. MS. 32,095, fols. 255r–256r, B.L.
53. *Complete Peerage,* s.v. "Cutts of Gowran"; *Transactions of the Essex Archaeological Society,* vol. 4 (1869), pp. 37–38.
54. Add. MS. 41,805, fols. 23r, v, B.L.
55. Add. MS. 41,821, fol. 79r, B.L. For Ferguson, see Dalton, *English Army Lists,* 2:238; for Cutts's commission, see Raad van State, vol. 109, fol. 195v, A.R.
56. Ferguson, *Scots Brigade,* 1:561–65.
57. Ibid., 565.
58. Corr. pol., Ang., vol. 165, fol. 216r, A.E.
59. Add. MS. 41,815, fol. 251r, B.L.
60. Add. MS. 25,375, fol. 254r, B.L.
61. Add. MS. 41,815, fols. 250r, 251v–252r, B.L.
62. Corr. pol., Ang., vol. 165, fols. 215v, 274v–275r, A.E.
63. S.P. 77 (State Papers, Flanders)/55, fol. 425r, P.R.O.; George Hilton Jones, *Charles Middleton,* 190–91.
64. Add. MS. 41,821, fols. 167r, v, B.L.
65. Add. MS. 41,821, fols. 225r, 238v, B.L.
66. W.O. 4/1, pp. 79–80, P.R.O.
67. PwA 2160, Nottingham University Library, Nottingham; R. H. George, "The Financial Relations of Louis XIV and James II," *Journal of Modern History* 3 (1931):406.
68. S.P. 44/165, pp. 29–30; W.O. 4/1, pp. 81–82, P.R.O. For transfers from the Irish army, see Childs, *Army, James II,* 134.
69. Add. MS. 34,515, fol. 89r, B.L.
70. Shakerley to Blathwayt, July 1, 1688, Add. MS. 38,695, fol. 19r, B.L. For Shakerley, see Foster, *Alumni Oxonienses,* 4:1338.
71. Newsletter of June 9 [1688], H.M.C. *Report XIV,* app. II, p. 409.
72. Add. MS. 41,821, fol. 58r, B.L.
73. Ibid., fols. 93r, v.
74. Add. MS. 41,815, fol. 250r, B.L.

75. Ferguson, *Scots Brigade,* 1:505, 506n; Dalton, *English Army Lists,* 2:9; S.P. 8/2, fols. 37v–38r, P.R.O.
76. Add. MS. 41,816, fol. 104r, B.L.
77. Dalton, *English Army Lists,* 2:123, 160; Ferguson, *Scots Brigade,* 1:513.
78. Besides those already cited, see Add. MS. 34,487, fol. 17r; Add. MS. 41,816, fol. 86v, B.L.
79. Add. MS. 25,376, fol. 190r, B.L. I point out that Terriesi was at a distance and admitted to no Dutch secrets.
80. Add. MS. 41,816, fol. 72v, B.L.
81. Add. MS. 41,815, fol. 249v, B.L.
82. Add. MS. 41,821, fol. 167v, B.L.; *C.S.P.D., 1687–1689,* p. 401.
83. *C.S.P.D., 1687–1689,* p. 189.

CHAPTER 7

1. Robert Fruin, et al., *Geschiedenis der staatsintellingen in Nederland tot den val der republiek* (The Hague, 1922), pp. 292–94; G. N. Clark, *The Dutch Alliance and the War against French Trade, 1688–1697* (Manchester, 1923), p. 15.
2. Jacques Basnage, *Annales des provinces unies depuis . . . la paix de Münster jusqu'à* [celle de Nimègue] (The Hague, 1719–1726). For the government of the city, see G. W. Kernkamp, vol. 1, part 2 of A. Bredius, et al., *Amsterdam in de seventiende eeuw* (The Hague, 1901–1904).
3. J. E. Elias, *De Vroedschap van Amsterdam,* vol. 1 (Haarlem, 1903–1908), p. xxxvi.
4. D. J. Roorda, "The Ruling Classes in Holland in the Seventeenth Century," in *Britain and the Netherlands,* vol. 2 of *Historische studies uitgegeven vanwege het Instituut voor Geschiedenis der Rijksuniversiteit te Utrecht,* vol. 20, ed. J. S. Bromley and E. H. Kossmann (Groningen, 1964), p. 132.
5. Fruin, *Geschiedenis der staatsintellingen,* 297.
6. C. F. Sirtema van Grovestins, *Guillaume III et Louis XIV: Histoire des luttes et rivalités politiques entre les puissances maritimes et la France,* new ed., vol. 5 (Paris, 1855), p. 423.
7. Ibid., 5:422. Two lists of these officers, dated June 19 and August 23, 1687, are items 190 and 195 in Raad van State, bundle 1932, A.R. The later is the fuller, totaling 295 of all commissioned ranks.
8. D'Avaux, *Négociations,* 6:2, 4–5.
9. Ibid., 6:43–44.
10. Egidius Rats to the States General, January 7, 1688, Staten Generaal 11,187, A.R. Folios in this register of letters, from England, France, Spain, Italy, and Turkey are not numbered.
11. D'Avaux, *Négociations,* 6:49–50. The French pretended that foreign salt was not good enough. Baxter, *William III,* 211.
12. Jones, *Revolution,* 195.
13. D'Avaux, *Négociations,* 6:54–57.
14. Ibid., 6:58.
15. Ibid., 6:65–66, 77.
16. Ibid., 6:88.
17. Add. MS. 25,376, fol. 186r, B.L.

18. D'Avaux, *Négociations,* 6:99.

19. Ibid., 6:98, 105.

20. Ibid., 6:105–6.

21. Lists dated as received (at The Hague) on October 9, 1688, Staten Generaal 11,187, A.R.; Baxter, *William III,* p. 211; Jones, *Revolution,* 195.

22. P. J. Blok, ed., *Relazioni Veneziane, Venetiaansche berichten over de Vereenigde Nederlanden van 1600–1795,* vol. 7 (The Hague: Rijks geschiedkundige publicatiën, 1909), p. 314.

23. Andrew Lossky, " 'Maxims of State' in Louis XIV's Foreign Policy," in *William III and Louis XIV, 1680–1720, Essays for Mark Thomson,* ed. R. M. Hatton and J. S. Bromley (Liverpool, 1967), p. 8.

24. See, e.g., Hendrik van Bilderbeeck, Dutch resident at Cologne, to the States General, May 25, 1688, Staten Generaal 6,171 (Duitsland), A.R.

25. P. J. W. Malssen, *Louis XIV d'après les pamphlets répandus en Hollande* (Paris and Amsterdam, [1937]), pp. 43–63.

26. D'Avaux, *Négociations,* 6:7–8.

27. Baxter, *William III,* 210–11. For his treatment of Protestants interceded for by the English government, see George Hilton Jones, "The Problem of French Protestantism," 146–50, 152–55.

28. D'Avaux, *Négociations,* 6:26–27.

29. Staten Generaal 11,976, fols. 2v–3r, A.R.

30. Staten Generaal, Engeland, 5,915, fol. 31v, A.R. (A transcript is Add. MS. 17,677 HH, fols. 313r, v, B.L.). Working with other materials, Professor Jean Orcibal (*Louis XIV et les Protestants* [Paris, 1951], pp. 150–52) has come to similar conclusions as to the effect of Louis's actions on James's reputation.

31. D'Avaux, *Négociations,* 6:95.

32. George Hilton Jones, *Charles Middleton,* 142–46, 149–150; Corr. pol., Ang., vol. 166, fols. 95r, v, A.E.

33. Bilderbeeck to the States General, June 8, 1688, Staten Generaal 6171 (Duitsland), A.R.

34. Fruin, *Geschiedenis der staatsintellingen,* 299; Geoffrey Holmes, "Post-Revolution Britain and the Historian," in *Britain after the Glorious Revolution,* ed. Geoffrey Holmes (London and New York, 1969), p. 19. In my opinion, Holmes does not see European responsibilities as an English contemporary of William's would have done. Most Englishmen then thought "Europe" was "abroad."

35. J. F. Gebhard, *Het Leven van Mr. Nicolaas Cornelisz. Witsen,* vol. 1 (Utrecht, 1881–1882), pp. 310, 316.

36. Ibid., 317–18; N. Japikse, *Prins Willem III, de stadhouder koning,* vol. 2 (Amsterdam, 1930–1933), p. 234.

37. Gebhard, *Witsen,* 1:321–22; Jan Wagenaar, *Vaderlandse Historie,* vol. 15 (Amsterdam, 1770–1789), pp. 427–28.

38. The foregoing three paragraphs are based on Wagenaar, *Vaderlandse Historie,* 15:428–431.

39. As this declaration was soon printed, copies are to be found in many places besides the entry of the States General's session of September 9, Staten Generaal, vol. 1,806, A.R. See, e.g., Collectie van Citters, vol. 43, under the same date, A.R.

40. D'Avaux, *Négociations,* 6:110–11.

41. Jones, *Revolution,* 273.

42. Gebhard, *Witsen,* 1:329–31; N. Japikse, ed., *Correspondentie van Willem III*

en van Hans Willem Bentinck, kleine serie, vols. 23, 24, 26, 27, 28 (The Hague: Rijksgeschiedkundige publicatiën, 1927–1937), part 1, 1:57.
43. Sirtema van Grovestins, *Guillaume III et Louis XIV,* 5:427.
44. Collectie van Citters, vol. 16, p. 165, A.R.; Wagenaar, *Vaderlandse Historie,* 15:440.
45. Add. MS. 41,816, fol. 170v, B.L.

CHAPTER 8

1. Laurence Eachard, *The History of the Revolution and the Establishment of England in the Year 1688* (London, 1725), p. 115.
2. See K. H. D. Haley, *William of Orange and the English Opposition* (Oxford, 1953).
3. Carstares to Bentinck, Aug. 2 [O.S.], 1687, Japikse, *Correspondentie,* part 2, vol. 2, p. 759; R. H. Story, *William Carstares: A Character and Career of the Revolutionary Epoch (1649–1715)* (London, 1874), pp. 152–53.
4. *A Letter Writ by Mijn Heer Fagel, Pensioner of Holland, to Mr. James Stewart, Advocate, Giving an Account of the Prince and Princess of Orange's Thoughts concerning the Repeal of the Test, and the Penal Laws* (London, 1688).
5. Story, *William Carstares,* 155.
6. John Northleigh, *Parliamentum Pacificum,* 2d ed. (London, 1688), pp. 59–60.
7. Ibid., 64–66, 70, 74.
8. Session of the States General, April 9, 1688, Staten Generaal, I, vol. 1,801, A.R.; van Citters to James II, April 16/26, 1688, Staten Generaal, Engeland, 5,915, fol. 107r, A.R.
9. *A Letter Writ by Mijn Heer Fagel . . . the 9th of April, N. Stile 1688* (1688), reprinted in *Their Highness the Prince and Princess of Orange's Opinion about a General Liberty of Conscience, &c.* (London, 1689).
10. [Gilbert Burnet], *Reflections on a Late Pamphlet Entitled Parliamentum Pacificum* (Amsterdam, 1688), pp. 1–2, 4, 6.
11. Ibid., 7–8.
12. D'Avaux, *Négociations,* 6:70.
13. Add. MS. 17,677 HH, fol. 394v, B.L.
14. Add. MS. 41,821, fol. 35v, B.L.
15. Muller, *Wilhelm . . . und . . . Waldeck,* 17, 19.
16. Hornby, *Second Part of a Caveat,* 55, 57.
17. Albeville to Middleton, June 22, 1688, Add. MS. 41, 816, fol. 68v, B.L.
18. Add. MS. 34,515, fols. 46r, v, B.L.; see also [Abel Boyer], *The History of King William the Third,* part 2 (London, 1702), p. 146; Add. MS. 28,053, fol. 345r; and Lansdowne MS. 937, fol. 96r, B.L. In every case, January 27 is the date mentioned.
19. Add. MS. 25,375, fols. 177v, 178r, B.L.
20. Add. MS. 41,816, fol. 47r, B.L. The publication *A Discourse to the King* reflected severely on James's popery and absolutism. A copy that Albeville enclosed is bound in the same volume, as fols. 49–50.
21. Add. MS. 41,815, fol. 253r, B.L.
22. Ibid., fol. 249v; Add. MS. 41,821, fol. 96r, B.L.
23. Add. MS. 41,816, fol. 24v, B.L.

24. Add. MS. 25,376, fols. 35r–36r, B.L.; session of the States General, April 5, 1688, Staten Generaal, I, 1,801, A.R.; Add. MS. 41,815, fol. 194r, B.L. This is the only suggestion I have seen that Thompson's murder was political. *C.T.B.*, *1676–1679*, p. 1206; *C.S.P.D.*, *1678*, p. 223. For the Peyton affair, see my *Charles Middleton*, 183–85.

25. S.P. 77/55, fol. 427r, P.R.O.

26. Add. MS. 41,821, fol. 167v, B.L.

27. A.16 XI.a., 177a, Koninklijk Huisarchief, The Hague; d'Avaux, *Négociations*, 6:80.

28. Kenneth Ellis, *The Post Office in the Eighteenth Century: A Study in Administrative History* (London, 1958), pp. 62, 65.

29. Dalrymple, *Memoirs of Great Britain and Ireland*, vol. 2, app., part 1, pp. 214–15, 218.

30. Japikse, *Correspondentie*, part 2, vol. 3, pp. 12, 32–33.

31. Foxcroft, *Halifax*, 1:494.

32. Corr. pol., Ang., vol. 165, fols. 345v–346v, A.E.

33. Add. MS. 41,816, fols. 72r, v, B.L.

34. Add. MS. 41,821, fols. 176r, v, B.L.

35. Add. MS. 41,823, fol. 69r, B.L.

36. Barrillon to Louis XIV, July 5 [N.S.], 1688, Corr. pol., Ang., vol. 166, fol. 17r, A.E. Princess Mary points out of Zuilesteyn's missions that her husband "could not do less without doing more than he was ready for." Mary II, *Lettres et Mémoires*, ed. Mechtild, Countess Bentinck (The Hague, 1880), pp. 74–75.

37. Staten Generaal, Engeland, 5,915, fol. 158r, A.R.; Add. MS. 17,677 HH fol. 456v, B.L.

38. D'Avaux, *Négociations*, 6:94.

39. E.g., Jones, *Revolution*, 239–40.

40. The letter is printed by Dalrymple, *Memoirs*, vol. 2, app., part 1, pp. 228–31.

41. Hornby, *Second Part of a Caveat*, 58.

42. Dalrymple, *Memoirs*, vol. 2, app., part 1, pp. 231–32; Horwitz, *Revolution Politicks*, 52–53.

43. Add. MS. 25,376, fols. 215r, v, B.L.; Dalrymple, *Memoirs*, vol. 2, app., part 2, pp. 235–39.

44. Add. MS. 34,515, fols. 67v–68r, B.L.; Ranke, *History of England*, 4:400. Among recent writers, Baxter (*William III*, 231) and Jones (*Revolution*, 252) take this republican possibility more seriously than I can.

45. Mary II, *Lettres et Mémoires*, 75–76.

46. See George Hilton Jones, "William III's Diplomatic Preparations for his Expedition to England," *Durham University Journal* 79, no. 2 (June 1987):233–45.

CHAPTER 9

1. Dover, *Ellis Correspondence*, 2:201.

2. Ibid., 201–2; Add. MS. 29,563, fol. 268r, B.L.; Add. MS. 32,096, fol. 331r, B.L.

3. Plumptre, *Thomas Ken*, 2:15.

4. Probably John Duff, rector of Rayleigh, or John Bromley, rector of Hadley ad Castrum. See *C.S.P.D.*, *1686–1687*, p. 374; and *1687–1689*, p. 84, for names of several

former Anglicans, released from their canonical duties and allowed to keep schools, who retained their titles and incomes.

5. Turner's MS. "Memoirs Civil and Eccles, from the time in wch the landing of ye Pr. of Orange was apprehended . . . ," Add. MS. 32,096, fols. 331r–332v, B.L.

6. Among other offices, Thynne held the secretaryship for the presentation to spiritual benefices in the Chancery. Chamberlayne, *Angliae Notitia,* 1687 ed., part 2, p. 130; *C.S.P.D., 1686–1687,* pp. 57, 287.

7. Gutch, *Collectanea Curiosa,* 1:420–21.

8. Copies of both proclamations are bound in the British Library volume 816.m.3.

9. Plumptre, *Thomas Ken,* 2:14–16; Thomas Sprat, *The Bishop of Rochester's Second Letter . . . to the Earl of Dorset and Middlesex* (London, 1689), pp. 26–27; Add. MS. 41,823, fol. 76v, B.L. The heads of September 24, 1688, signed by Sancroft, Compton, Mew, Turner, Lake, Sprat, Ken, and White, are preserved in Tanner MS. 28, fols. 187–88, Bodl.

10. Add. MS. 29,563, fol. 275r, B.L. A copy of the proclamation of September 28 is bound in the British Library volume 816.m.3 (24).

11. Gutch, *Collectanea Curiosa,* 1:41–43; Plumptre, *Thomas Ken,* 2:16–17; Stowe MS. 770, fols. 85r–88r, B.L.

12. Add. MS. 38,175, fol. 138v, B.L.

13. Add. MS. 22,578, fols. 31r, v, B.L.

14. Edmund Bohun, *The History of the Desertion,* reprinted in *A Collection of State Tracts, Publish'd on Occasion of the Revolution in 1688 . . . ,* vol. 1 (London, 1705): 48; Add. MS. 45,731, fol. 26r, B.L.; S.P. 44/338, p. 119, P.R.O.; Corr. pol., Ang., vol. 166, fols. 333r, v, A.E.; Russel J. Kerr and I. C. Duncan, eds., *The Portledge Papers* (London, 1928), pp. 47–48.

15. P.C. 2/72, p. 745, P.R.O.; Plumptre, *Thomas Ken,* 2:18. The form is printed in Gutch, *Collectanea Curiosa,* 2:416–18.

16. Tanner MS. 28, fol. 202, Bodl.; Gutch, *Collectanea Curiosa,* 1:423–24; P.C. 2/72, pp. 749–51, P.R.O.; Bohun, *History of the Desertion,* 48–50.

17. Corr. pol., Ang., vol. 166, fols. 300r, 310v–311r, A.E.

18. Singer, *Correspondence . . . of Clarendon,* 2:193–94.

19. D'Oyly, *Sancroft,* 210–12.

20. H.M.C. *Report XII,* app. VII (Le Fleming MSS.), p. 216; dispatch of October 12/22, 1688, O.A.I., Busta IV, A.S.M.

21. Egerton MS. 2,618, fol. 150r, B.L.; James Macpherson, ed., *Original Papers: Containing the Secret History of Great Britain, from the Restoration, to the Accession of the House of Hannover,* vol. 1 (London, 1775), pp. 272–74.

22. J. N. Magrath, ed., *The Flemings in Oxford,* vol. 2 (Oxford: Oxford Historical Soc. Publications 62, 1913), p. 234; Add. MS. 29,563, fol. 210r, B.L.

23. Joseph Gillow, *A Literary and Biographical History . . . of the English Catholics,* vol. 3 (London and New York, 1885–1902), pp. 169–70; Bloxam, *Magdalen College and James II,* 247, 265; Add. MS. 38,175, fol. 138, B.L.

24. Stowe MS. 770, fol. 98r; Add. MS. 29,563, fol. 308r, B.L.; Corr. pol., Ang., vol. 167, fols. 52v–53r, A.E.

25. Gutch, *Collectanea Curiosa,* 1:425–26.

26. Ibid., 1:427–29.

27. Ibid., 1:429–30; Stowe MS. 770, fol. 104r, B.L.

28. Tanner MS. 28, fol. 218, Bodl.

29. Gutch, *Collectanea Curiosa,* 1:430–32.

30. Ibid., 1:438.

31. Ibid., 1:433.

32. Ibid., 1:433–36.

33. Gutch, *Collectanea Curiosa,* 1:436–40.

34. D'Oyly, *Sancroft,* 227; Ronchi's dispatch of October 11 (N.S.), 1688, O.A.I., Busta IV, A.S.M.

35. Gutch, *Collectanea Curiosa,* 1:417–18.

36. Hart, *William Lloyd,* 114; John Stevens, MS. fragment of an autobiography, Lansdowne MS. 828, fols. 10r, v, B.L.

37. H.M.C. *Report I,* app. (Sir John Salusbury Trelawny MSS.), p. 52; Sprat, *Bishop of Rochester's Second Letter,* 49.

38. Dover, *Ellis Correspondence,* 2:285 and n.

39. Magrath, *Flemings in Oxford,* 2:238–39; John Nichols, *The History and Antiquities of the County of Leicester* (London, 1795–1815), vol. 4, part 2, p. 838n.

40. Add. MS. 27,979, fol. 29r; Add. MS. 29,563, fol. 268r, B.L.

41. Add. MS. 25,377, fols. 30r, v, B.L.; Corr. pol., Ang., vol. 166, fols. 235v–236r, 243r, A.E.

42. Add. MS. 29,563, fol. 277r, B.L.; Dover, *Ellis Correspondence,* 2:235; A. F. Havighurst, "James II and the Twelve Men in Scarlet," *Law Quarterly Review* 69 (1953):543.

43. Add. MS. 29,563, fol. 268r, B.L.

44. Dispatch of October 2 (N.S.), 1688, O.A.I., Busta IV, A.S.M.

45. Corr. pol., Ang., vol. 166, fols. 273r, 298r, A.E.

46. Add. MS. 17,677 UUU, fol. 621r; Add. MS. 45,731, fol. 26v, B.L.; John Lowther, Viscount Lonsdale, *Memoir of the Reign of James II* (York, privately printed, 1808). Besides Braddon, the excepted persons were Samuel Johnson (author of *Julian*), Thomas Tipping, and Sir Rowland Gwynne.

47. Add. MS. 25,377, fol. 33r, B.L.

48. S.P. 31/4, part 1, fols. 104r, 105r, 106r–107v, P.R.O.

49. Corr. pol., Ang., vol. 166, fol. 321r, A.E.; Beaven, *Aldermen of London,* 1:98, 2:115; Sharpe, *London and the Kingdom,* 2:531; H.M.C. *Report XII,* app. VII, p. 213.

50. H.M.C. *Report XII,* app. VII, p. 213; Corr. pol., Ang., vol. 166, fols. 331v–332r, A.E.; Add. MS. 17,677 UUU, fol. 649r, B.L.

51. Corr. pol., Ang., vol. 166, fol. 308v, A.E.; *C.S.P.D., 1687–1689,* p. 306; *London Gazette,* October 8–11, 15–18, 1688; Add. MS. 41,823, fol. 78v, B.L.; S.P. 44/338, p. 119, P.R.O.

52. Newton, *Diary,* 96; John Latimer, *The Annals of Bristol* (Bristol, 1900), p. 450; Add. MS. 28,037, fol. 49r, B.L.; P.C. 2/72, pp. 752, 785–86, P.R.O.

53. Bramston, *Autobiography,* 325–26; Glassey, *Justices of the Peace,* 97–98.

54. Singer, *Correspondence . . . of Clarendon,* 2:195–96.

55. Corr. pol., Ang., vol. 167, fol. 22v, A.E.

56. Gutch, *Collectanea Curiosa,* 2:363–64.

57. Dover, *Ellis Correspondence,* 2:258; *C.S.P.D., 1687–1689,* p. 327. James's later recollection was in error. See Clarke, *James the Second,* 2:203.

58. Japikse, *Correspondentie,* part 1, vol. 2:10n; Mary II, *Lettres et mémoires,* 66; J. H. Hora Siccama, *Aanteekeningen en verbeteringen,* 721.

59. Kennett, *Complete History,* 3:488; [Abel Boyer], *The History of King William the Third* (London, 1702), part 2, pp. 193, 219; Campana de Cavelli, *Derniers Stuarts,* 2:307–8; Rapin-Thoyras, *Histoire d'Angleterre,* 10:107–8.

60. [Robert Ferguson], *The History of the Revolution* (London, 1706), p. 18; [Boyer], *History of King William,* part 2, p. 219.

61. Barrillon to Louis XIV, Nov. 4 [N.S.], 1688, Corr. pol., Ang., vol. 167, fols. 25r–26v, A.E.; S.P. 44/54, pp. 396–97, P.R.O.; H.M.C. *Report XII,* app. VII (Le Fleming MSS.), p. 217; *London Gazette,* October 22–25, 1688.

62. Clarke, *James II,* 2:203.

63. Corr. pol., Ang., vol. 166, fols. 341v–342v, A.E.; P.C. 2/72, pp. 782–83, P.R.O.; *C.S.P.D., 1687–1689,* pp. 336–37.

64. Literal reading of James's *Life* (Clarke 2:203) would date Sunderland's dismissal October 23. But the secretary was still signing official letters on the twenty-fifth. Lord Clarendon would have Sunderland dismissed on October 26, which agrees approximately with Barrillon, who reported the event in a dispatch of November 6 [N.S.] or October 27 [O.S.], 1688. *C.S.P.D., 1687–1689,* p. 330; Singer, *Correspondence of . . . Clarendon,* 2:197; Corr. pol., Ang., vol. 167, fols. 33v–34r, A.E. James's memory, or the documents available to the author of the *Life,* must have failed at this point.

65. Singer, *Correspondence of . . . Clarendon,* 2:196–98.

66. P.C. 2/72, p. 785, P.R.O.; Clarke, *James II,* 2:202.

67. Eachard, *History of the Revolution,* 148.

68. Ailesbury, *Memoirs,* 1:184–85.

69. *C.S.P.D., 1687–1689,* p. 364; Clarke, *James II,* 2:221; P.C. 2/72, p. 796, P.R.O.

70. Clarke, *James II,* 2:190; Barrillon to Louis XIV, October 25 and November 8 [N.S.], 1688, Corr. pol., Ang., vol. 166, fol. 346r; vol. 167, fols. 43v–44r, 53v, A.E.

71. H.M.C. *Report XII,* app. VII (Le Fleming MSS.), p. 214; Dover, *Ellis Correspondence,* 2:243.

72. James II, proclamations dated at Whitehall, October 26 and November 2, 1688, published in *London Gazette,* October 25–29 and November 1, 1688, respectively.

73. H.M.C. *Report XII,* app. V (Rutland MSS., vol. 2), p. 122.

74. *London Gazette,* October 4–8, 8–11, 11–15, and November 8–11, 1688; Corr. pol., Ang., vol. 167, fols. 24r, v, A.E.; Dover, *Ellis Correspondence,* 2:245, 247.

75. H.M.C. *Report XII,* app. VII, pp. 214–15; Add. MS. 17,677 UUU, fol. 627v, B.L.; Campana de Cavelli, *Derniers Stuarts,* 2:290.

76. H.M.C. *Report XII,* app. VII, pp. 214, 218; Add. MS. 41,805, fols. 89r, v, B.L.; Staten Generaal, Engeland, 5,915, fol. 186v, A.R. (For a transcript, see Add. MS. 17,677 HH, fol. 490r, B.L.) Cf. Childs, *Army, James II,* 99.

77. Corr. pol., Ang., vol. 166, fols. 346v–347r; vol. 167, fols. 23r, v, A.E.

CHAPTER 10

1. D'Avaux, *Négociations,* 6:111.

2. Add. MS. 41,816, fols. 171r, v; Add. MS. 41,821, fols. 249r, v, B.L.

3. Add. MS. 41,816, fols. 175r, v, B.L.

4. Clarke, *James II,* 2:179–80.

5. Add. MS. 41,816, fols. 183r, v, B.L. See d'Avaux's dispatch of September 16,

1688 (*Négociations,* 6:120–22) for a sketch of William's actual plan.
6. Corr. pol., Ang., vol. 166, fols. 197r–198v, A.E.; Klopp, *Der Fall,* 4:65.
7. Add. MS. 41,823, fols. 71v–72r; Add. MS. 17,677 UUU, fols. 592v–594r, B.L.
8. Corr. pol., Ang., vol. 166, fol. 212v, A.E.
9. Ibid., fol. 231v.
10. Ibid., fols. 245v–246r.
11. Add. MS. 41,823, fol. 73v, B.L.
12. Corr. pol., Ang., vol. 166, fols. 256r, v, 259r–260v, A.E.; Add. MS. 25,377, fol. 10v, B.L.; session of the States General, October 6, 1688, Staten Generaal 1,807, A.R.; *London Gazette,* September 27–October 1, 1688.
13. Add. MS. 41,816, fols. 199r, v, 214v–215v; Add. MS. 45,731, fol. 24v, B.L.
14. Add. MS. 41,816, fol. 245v, B.L.
15. D'Avaux, *Négociations,* 6:135, 142, 160–61.
16. Dispatch of October 7 [N.S.], Corr. pol., Ang., vol. 166, fols. 278v–280r, A.E.
17. Corr. pol., Ang., vol. 166, fols. 280r–283r, A.E.
18. Add. MS. 32,096, fol. 332v, B.L.
19. Corr. pol., Ang., vol. 166, fols. 285v–287r, A.E.
20. [Secret notes], session of the States General, September 20, 1688, Staten Generaal 4,029, A.R.
21. [Secret notes], session of the States General, October 8, 1688, Staten Generaal 4,030, A.R.
22. Add. MS. 41,816, fol. 228v, B.L.
23. Add. MS. 38,495, fol. 29r, B.L.
24. Add. MS. 41,806, fols. 207r, v, 214r; Add. MS. 17,677 UUU, fol. 629, B.L.; S.P. 44/97, p. 6, P.R.O.
25. Corr. pol., Ang., vol. 166, fols. 302r–304r, A.E.
26. Corr. pol., Ang., vol. 166, fols. 339r–341r, 349r, v, A.E.
27. Add. MS. 41,816, fols. 251r–252r, B.L.
28. See, e.g., his dispatch of October 7, 1688, Corr. pol., Ang., vol. 166, fols. 279r, v, A.E.
29. Campana de Cavelli, *Derniers Stuarts,* 2:283, 286–87, 299, 306–7.
30. Corr. pol., Ang., vol. 166, fols. 336r–337r, A.E.
31. Add. MS. 41,816, fol. 266r, B.L.
32. Corr. pol., Ang., vol. 167, fols. 31r, v, 35v–36r, A.E.
33. Ibid., fols. 49r–52r, 54v–55r.
34. Campana de Cavelli, *Derniers Stuarts,* 2:309–10. Cf. Morrice MS. Q, p. 400, Dr. Williams's Library, London.
35. Reports from Brussels, November 9, 1688, and from The Hague, P.R.O. 30/25/22, P.R.O.
36. Corr. pol., Ang., vol. 167, fols. 62r–63v, 69r, A.E.
37. Ibid., vol. 167, fol. 57v.
38. James II, Declaration, Whitehall, November 6, 1688. The Houghton Library (Harvard University) and the British Library both possess copies of this declaration.

Select Bibliography

MANUSCRIPT SOURCES

British Library, London:
Add. MSS. 15,397, 17,677 HH and UUU, 25,375–77, 27,979, 28,037, 28,053, 29,563, 29,573, 29,578, 29,584, 32,095–96, 33,923, 34,487, 34,515, 36,707, 38,175, 38,494, 41,805–8, 41,815–16, 41,821, 41,823, 45,731
Egerton MSS. 2,543, 2,618
Lansdowne MSS. 828, 937, 1,189
Loan MS. 29/184
Sloane MS. 3,929
Stowe MS. 770
Public Record Office, London:
P.C. 2 (Privy Council Register)/72
P.R.O. 30/53 (Powis Papers)/8; 25(Venetian MSS.)/22
S.P. 8 (King William's Chest)/2, 4
S.P. 31 (Letters and Papers, James II)/4
S.P. 44 (Entry Books)/ 54, 56, 97, 165, 338–39
S.P. 77 (State Papers, Foreign, Flanders)/55
S.P. 78 (State Papers, Foreign, France)/151
S.P. 94 (State Papers, Foreign, Spain)/72
W.O. 4 (War Office, Secretary's Out Letters)/1
Dr. Williams's Library, London:
Morrice MS. Q (Morrice Entring Book)
Bodleian Library, Oxford:
Rawlinson MSS.A.139 B; Letters 94
Tanner MS. 28
Christ Church Library, Oxford:
MSS. CCL, CCXC
Algemeen Rijksarchief, The Hague:
Collectie van Citters, 16, 30, 43
Staten Generaal, 1,799–1,801, 1,803, 1,806, 4,029–30, 5,915–16, 6,171, 11,187, 11,976

Koninklijk Huisarchief, The Hague:
  A.16.IX, a.15, 177a
Ministère des Affaires Étrangerès (Relations Extérieures):
  Correspondence politique, Angleterre, 165–67
Archivio di Stato, Modena:
  Ambasciatori e Oratori, Inghilterra, Busta IV
Nottingham University Library:
  Portland Papers, PwA, PwV

NEWSPAPERS

London Gazette
Public Occurrences Truly Stated

PRINTED SOURCES AND CONTEMPORARY ACCOUNTS

Ailesbury, Thomas Bruce, Earl. *Memoirs.* 2 vols. London: Roxburghe Club, 1890.
Blok, P. J., ed. *Relazioni Veneziani, Venetiaansche Berichten over de Vereenigde Nederlanden van 1600–1795.* Rijks Geschiedkundige Publicatiën. Vol. 7. The Hague, 1909.
Bloxam, J. R., ed. *Magdalen College and King James II, 1686–1688.* Oxford Historical Soc. Publications. Vol. 6. Oxford, 1886.
Bohun, Edmund. *The History of the Desertion.* Reprinted in *A Collection of State Tracts, Publish'd on Occasion of the Revolution in 1688.* . . . Vol. 1. London, 1705.
[Boyer, Abel.] *The History of King William the Third.* London, 1702.
Bramston, Sir John. *Autobiography.* Edited by Richard Neville, Lord Braybrooke. Camden Soc. Publications. Vol. 32. London, 1845.
[Burnet, Gilbert.] *Reflections on a Late Pamphlet Entitled Parliamentum Pacificum.* Amsterdam, 1688.
Burnet, Gilbert. *A History of My Own Time.* 6 vols. Oxford, 1833.
Calendar of State Papers, Domestic.
Calendar of Treasury Books.
Calender of Treasury Papers.
Campana de Cavelli, Emilia, Marquise. *Les Derniers Stuarts à St.-Germain-en-Laye.* 2 vols. Paris, 1871.
Chamberlayne, Edward, comp. *Angliae Notitia.* London, 1687.
Clarke, Sir J. S., ed. *The Life of James the Second, King of England.* . . . 2 vols. London, 1816.
Dalton, Charles, ed. *English Army Lists and Commission Registers, 1661–1714.* 6 vols. London, 1892–1904.

d'Avaux, Jean-Antoine de Mesmes, Count. *Les Négociations . . . en Hollande.* New ed. 6 vols. Paris, 1754.

Dover, George Agar-Ellis, Lord, ed. *Ellis Correspondence, Letters written during the Years 1686, 1687, and 1688, and Addressed to John Ellis.* . . . 2 vols. London, 1829.

Duckett, Sir George F., comp. *Penal Laws and Test Act.* 2 vols. London, 1882–1883.

Evans, T. S., ed. *The Life of Robert Frampton, Bishop of Gloucester.* London, 1876.

Evelyn, John. *Diary.* Edited by E. S. de Beer. 6 vols. London: Oxford University Press, 1955.

Fagel, Gaspar. *Letter . . . to Mr. James Stewart, Advocate, Giving an Account of the Prince and Princess of Orange's Thoughts Concerning the Repeal of the Test, and the Penal Laws, A.* London, 1688.

Ferguson, Sir James, ed. *Papers Illustrating the History of the Scots Brigade in the Service of the United Netherlands, 1574–1782.* 3 vols. Edinburgh: Scottish History Soc., 1899–1901.

Gutch, John, ed. *Collectanea Curiosa.* 2 vols. Oxford, 1781.

Heim, H. J. van der, ed. *Het Archief van de Raadpensionaris Antonie Heinsius.* 3 vols. The Hague, 1867–1880.

Historical Manuscripts Commission's Publications:
Report XII, appendix, part 2. Cowper MSS. London, 1888.
Report XII, appendix, part 7. Le Fleming MSS. London, 1890.
Report XIII, appendix, part 2. Portland MSS. London, 1893.
Report XIV, appendix, part 4. Kenyon MSS. London, 1894.
Buccleuch MSS., vol. 2, part 1. London, 1903.
Hastings MSS., vol. 2. London, 1930.

Hornby, Charles. *The Second Part of a Caveat against the Whiggs &c.* 3d ed. London, 1713.

Japikse, Nicolaas, ed. *Correspondentie van Willem III en Hans Willem Bentinck.* 5 vols. Rijks Geschiedkundige Publicatiën, kleine serie. Vols. 23–24, 26–28. The Hague, 1927–1937.

Journals of the House of Commons, vol. 10, 1688–1693. [London], 1803.

Journals of the House of Lords, vol. 14, 1685–1691, n.p., n.d.

Kennett, White, et al. *A Complete History of England.* 3 vols. London, 1706.

Kerr, Russel J., and Duncan, I. C., eds. *The Portledge Papers.* London, 1928.

Letter from a Clergy-man in the City to His Friend in the Country, Containing His Reasons for Not Reading the Declaration, A. May 22, 1688. [London? 1688.]

Lonsdale, John Lowther, Viscount. *Memoir of the Reign of James II.* York: privately printed, 1808.

Luttrell, Narcissus. *Brief Historical Relation of State Affairs from September, 1678 to April, 1714, A.* 6 vols. Oxford, 1857.

Macpherson, James, ed. *Original Papers; Containing the Secret History of Great Britain, from the Restoration, to the Accession of the House of Hannover.* 2 vols. London, 1775.

Magrath, J. R., ed. *The Flemings in Oxford.* Vol. 2. Oxford Historical Soc. Publications. Vol. 62. Oxford, 1913.

Mary II. *Lettres et mémoires.* Edited by Mechtild, Countess Bentinck. The Hague, 1880.

Newton, Samuel. *Diary, 1662–1717.* Cambridge Antiquarian Soc. Publications, octavo series. Vol. 23. Cambridge, 1890.

Northleigh, John. *Parliamentum Pacificum.* 2d ed. London, 1688.

Patrick, Symon. *Autobiography.* Oxford, 1839.

Proceedings and Tryal in the Case of the Most Reverend Father in God, William, Lord Archbishop of Canterbury [and the six other bishops], *The.* London, 1689.

Rapin-Thoyras, Paul de. *L'Histoire d'Angleterre.* Rev. ed. 3 vols. Basle, 1740.

Reresby, Sir John. *Memoirs.* Edited by Andrew Browning. Glasgow, 1936.

Singer, S. W., ed. *The Correspondence of Henry Hyde, Earl of Clarendon and of His Brother Laurence Hyde, Earl of Rochester; with the Diary of Lord Clarendon. . . .* 2 vols. London, 1828.

Sirtema van Grovestins, C. F. *Guillaume III et Louis XIV: Histoire des luttes et rivalités entre les puissances maritimes et la France.* Rev. ed. 8 vols. Paris, 1855.

Sprat, Thomas. *The Bishop of Rochester's Second Letter . . . to the Earl of Dorset and Middlesex.* London, 1689.

State Tracts: Being a Farther Collection of Several Choice Treatises Relating to the Government. . . . London, 1692. Reprinted London, 1973.

Thoresby, Ralph. *Diary.* Edited by Joseph Hunter. 2 vols. London, 1830.

Wood, Anthony. *Life and Times.* Edited by A. Clark. 5 vols. Oxford Historical Soc. Publications. Vols. 19, 21, 26, 30, 40. Oxford, 1891–1895.

SECONDARY WORKS

Bailey, Thomas. *Annals of Nottinghamshire.* 4 vols. London and Nottingham, 1852–1855.

Basnage, Jacques. *Annales des provinces unies depuis la paix de Münster, jusqu'à* [celle de Nimègue]. 2 vols. The Hague, 1719–1726.

Baxter, Stephen. *William III and the Defence of European Liberty.* New York, 1966.

Beddard, Robert. "The Commission for Ecclesiastical Promotions, 1681–84: An Instrument of Tory Reaction." *Historical Journal* 10 (1967): 11–40.

Bredius, A., et al. *Amsterdam in de seventiende Eeuw.* 3 vols. The Hague, 1901–1904.

Browning, Andrew. *Thomas Osborne, Earl of Danby and Duke of Leeds, 1632–1712.* 3 vols. Glasgow, 1944–1951.

Calamy, Edward. *Memoirs of the Life of the Late Reverend Mr. John Howe.* London, 1724.

Carpenter, Edward. *The Protestant Bishop, Being the Life of Henry Compton, 1632–1713.* London, 1956.

Carswell, John. *The Descent on England.* London: Cresset Press. 1969.

Childs, John. *The Army, James II, and the Glorious Revolution.* New York, 1980.

Deering, Charles. *Nottinghamia Vetus et Nova.* Nottingham, 1751.

D'Oyly, George. *The Life of William Sancroft, Archbishop of Canterbury.* 2d rev. ed. London, 1840.

Eachard, Laurence. *The History of the Revolution and the Establishment of England in the Year 1688.* London, 1725.

Elias, J. E. *De Vroedschap van Amsterdam.* 2 vols. Haarlem, 1903–1908.

Ennen, Leonard. *Frankreich und der Niederrhein, oder Geschichte von Stadt und Kurstaat Köln seit dem 30 jährigen Kriege bis zur französischen Occupation.* 2 vols. Cologne and Neuss, 1855–1856.

Foster, Joseph, comp. *Alumni Oxonienses . . . 1500–1714.* 4 vols. Oxford, 1891–1892.

Foxcroft, H. C. *The Life and Letters of Sir George Savile, Bart., First Marquis of Halifax.* 2 vols. London, 1898.

Fruin, Robert, et al. *Geschiedenis der staatsintellingen in Nederland tot den val der republiek.* The Hague, 1922.

Garland, J. L. "The Regiment of MacElligott, 1688–1689." *Irish Sword* 1 (1949–1953): 121–27.

Gebhard, J. F. *Het Leven van Mr. Nicolaas Cornelisz. Witsen.* 2 vols. Utrecht, 1881–1888.

George, R. H. "The Financial Relations of Louis XIV and James II." *Journal of Modern History* 3 (1931): 392–413.

Glassey, Lionel. *Politics and the Appointment of Justices of the Peace, 1675–1720.* Oxford, 1979.

Hamilton, Sir Frederick W. *The Origin and History of the First or Grenadier Guards.* 3 vols. London, 1874.

Hart, A. Tindal. *William Lloyd, 1627–1717.* London, 1952.

Hennessy, George, comp. *Novum Repertorium Ecclesiasticum Parochiale Londinense.* London, 1898.

Historical Account of the British Regiments Employed since the Reigns of Queen Elizabeth and King James I in the Formation and Defence of the Dutch Republic . . . , An. London, 1794.

Hora Siccama, J. H. *Aanteekeningen en verbeteringen op het . . . register op de journalen van Constantijn Huygens den Zoon.* Werken uitgegeven door het Historische Genootschap gevestigd te Utrecht. Series no. 3./ Vol. 35. Amsterdam, 1915.

Horwitz, Henry. *Revolution Politicks: The Career of Daniel Finch, Second Earl of Nottingham, 1647–1730.* Cambridge, 1968.

Hosford, David Hatch. *Nobles, Nottingham, and the North: Aspects of the*

Revolution of 1688. Studies in British History and Culture. Vol. 4. Hamden, Conn., 1976.

Immich, Max. Papst Innocenz XI. Berlin, 1900.

Izacke, R. and S. Remarkable Antiquities of the City of Exeter. London, 1723.

Japikse, Nicolaas. Prins Willem III, de Stadhouder koning. 2 vols. Amsterdam, 1930–1933.

Jones, George Hilton. Charles Middleton, The Life and Times of a Restoration Politician. Chicago, 1967.

————. "The Problem of French Protestantism in the Foreign Policy of England." Bulletin of the Institute of Historical Research 42 (1969): 145–57.

Jones, J. R. The Revolution of 1688 in England. London, 1972.

Kenyon, J. P. Robert Spencer, Earl of Sunderland. London, 1958.

Klopp, Onno. Der Fall des Hauses Stuart und die Succession des Hauses Hannover in Gross Britannien und Irland. 14 vols. Vienna, 1875–1888.

Lacey, Douglas. Dissent and Parliamentary Politics in England, 1661–1689. . . . New Brunswick, N.J., 1969.

Miller, John. Popery and Politics in England, 1660–88. Cambridge, 1973.

————. James II, A Study in Kingship. Hove, 1978.

Muller, P. L. Wilhelm von Oranien und Georg Friedrich von Waldeck: Ein Beitrag zur Geschichte des Kampfes um das Europäische Gleichgewicht. 2 vols. The Hague, 1873–1880.

Plumptre, E. H. The Life of Thomas Ken, Bishop of Bath and Wells. 2 vols. London, 1888.

Ranke, Leopold von. A History of England, Principally in the Seventeenth Century. Translated by G. W. Kitchin et al. 6 vols. Oxford, 1875.

Roorda, D. J. "The Ruling Classes in Holland in the Seventeenth Century." In Britain and the Netherlands. Vol. 2. Edited by J. S. Bromley and E. H. Kossmann, pp. 109–32. Historische studies uitgegeven vanwege het Instituut voor Geschiedenis der Rijksuniversiteit te Utrecht. Vol. 20. Groningen, 1964.

Rousset, Camille. Histoire de Louvois. 2d ed. 4 vols. Paris, 1861–1863.

Sachse, W. L. Lord Somers, A Political Portrait. Manchester and Madison, Wis., 1975.

Schwoerer, Lois. "Propaganda in the Revolution of 1688." American Historical Review 132 (1977): 843–74.

————. The Declaration of Rights, 1689. Baltimore, 1981.

Sharpe, R. R. London and the Kingdom: A History Derived Mainly from the Archives at Guildhall. 3 vols. London, 1894–1895.

Speck, W. A. Reluctant Revolutionaries, Englishmen and the Revolution of 1688. Oxford, 1988.

Story, R. H. William Carstares: A Character and Career of the Revolutionary Epoch (1649–1715). London, 1874.

Thomas, Roger. "The Seven Bishops and Their Petition, 18 May 1688."
   Journal of Ecclesiastical History 12 (1961): 56–70.
Turner, F. C. *James II.* New York, 1948.
Venn, J., and J. A., comps. *Alumni Cantabrigienses . . . Part I [to 1751].* 4
   vols. Cambridge, 1922–1927.
Victoria County Histories:
   Bedfordshire.
   Oxfordshire.
Wagenaar, Jan. *Vaderlandse Historie.* 21 vols. Amsterdam, 1770–1789.
Western, J. R. *Monarchy and Revolution, The English State in the 1680s.*
   London, 1972.
Wiebe, Renate. *Untersuchungen über die Hilfeleistung der deutschen Staaten
   für Wilhelm III van Oranien im Jahre 1688.* Göttingen, 1939.

Index